INTRODUCTION TO COMMUNICATION STUDIES

Second Edition

edited by

Enid S. Waldhart
James L. Applegate

with special editorial assistance of
Stephanie Zimmerman

Contributors

John R. Baseheart
Robert N. Bostrom
Patsy Cook
R. Lewis Donohew
Murali Nair
Philip C. Palmgreen
Eileen Berlin Ray
Ramona R. Rush
Beverly Davenport Sypher
Howard E. Sypher
Norm Van Tubergen

University of Kentucky

Kendall/Hunt
Publishing Company
Dubuque, Iowa

Chapter Opening Photo Credits
  Pages iv, 16, 38, 58, 72, 94, 110, 130, 148, 184: University of Kentucky Photographic Services.
  Page 168: Myria Allen.

Illustrations
  Mark Daniel Vantreese

This edition has been printed directly from the authors' manuscript copy.

Copyright © 1985, 1987 by Kendall/Hunt Publishing Company

Library of Congress Catalog Card Number: 87–82122

ISBN 0–8403–4469–4

Printed in the United States of America
10 9 8 7 6 5 4 3 2 1

TABLE OF CONTENTS

CHAPTER

CHAPTER 1

INTRODUCTION

"To continue," continued the minister impatiently. "Once a week by Royal Proclamation the word market is held here in the great square and people come from everywhere to buy the words they need or trade in the words they haven't used."

"Our job," said the count, "is to see that all the words sold are the proper ones, for it wouldn't do to sell someone a word that had no meaning or didn't exist at all. For instance, if you bought a word like ghlbtsk, where would you use it?"

"It would be difficult," thought Milo—but there were so many words that were difficult, and he knew hardly any of them.

"But we never choose which ones to use," explained the earl as they walked toward the market stalls, "for as long as they mean what they mean to mean we don't care if they make sense or nonsense."

"Innocence or magnificence," added the count.

"Reticence or common sense," said the undersecretary.

"That seems simple enough," said Milo, trying to be polite.

"Easy as falling off a log," cried the earl; falling off a log with a loud thump.

"Must you be so clumsy?" shouted the duke.

"All I said was—" began the earl, rubbing his head.

"We heard you," said the minister angrily, "and you'll have to find an expression that's less dangerous."

The earl dusted himself off as the others snickered audibly.

"You see," cautioned the count, "you must pick your words very carefully and be sure to say just what you intend to say. And now we must leave to make preparations for the Royal Banquet."

"You'll be there of course," said the minister.

But before Milo had a chance to say anything, they were rushing off across the square as fast as they had come.

"Enjoy yourself in the market," shouted back the undersecretary.

"Market," recited the duke: "an open space or covered building in which—"

And that was the last Milo heard as they disappeared into the crowd.

"I never knew words could be so confusing," Milo said to Tock as he bent down to scratch the dog's ear.

"Only when you use a lot to say a little," answered Tock.

Juster, 1961, pp. 42–44*

*Excerpt from <u>The Phantom Tollbooth</u>, by Norton Juster. Copyright, Random House, Inc. Reprinted by permission.

Milo's adventures in The Lands Beyond take him to Dictionopolis at the Foothills of Confusion, through the Forest of Sight to Point of View, transport him to the Island of Conclusions in the Sea of Knowledge, and finally to the Mountains of Ignorance where he conquers the evil demons and saves the inhabitants of the Kingdom of Wisdom. During his travels, Milo learns that reality depends on one's point of view, jumping to conclusions is easy, but getting back is difficult, and most importantly for our present concerns, Milo discovers that communication is central to everyday life.

Those in the field of communication, of course, would have explained the importance of communication in human existence to Milo had he asked, possibly saving the boy from his sometimes harrowing journey. But would Milo have thought to ask? Communication is so much a part of our daily activities that most of us take our ability to communicate for granted. Yet, as Milo realized, communication is a complex process, at times rather confusing and not as easy or simple as one might imagine. In this chapter we will examine what the communication process involves and why it is important to learn more about communication.

WHAT IS COMMUNICATION?

DEFINING COMMUNICATION

More than likely, if you asked the other students in this class to define communication, you would likely get many different responses. Of course, there may be some similarities among the definitions, including terms such as "sender," "receiver," "transmitting," "words," and "meaning," but there would also be differences. For example, one student might include "understanding" as a necessary component of the comunciation process, while another might stress effective listening.

In fact, those in the field of communication disagree about what is meant by the term "communication". For Watzlawick, Beavin, and Jackson (1967) communication is "all behavior in an interactional setting" (p. 48). Those authors stress that all our actions involve communication and therefore "one cannot not communicate" (p. 49). Miller (1962) provides another definition, arguing that "communication has as its central interest those behavioral situations in which a source transmits a message to (a) receiver(s) with conscious intent to affect the latter's behaviors" (p. 92). Miller's definition agrees with that of Watzlawick, Beavin, and Jackson in focusing on behaviors. But for Miller, those behaviors must be intentional and must be an attempt to influence another person or persons if the behaviors are to be considered comunciation.

A more recent definition of communication is proposed by Buerkel-Rothfuss (1985): "We define communication as a reciprocal process through which individuals create and share meaning" (p. 7). Buerkel-Rothfuss suggests that the communication process involves communicators making sense of their experiences and sharing their interpretations with others. Like Miller, Buerkel-Rothfuss stresses that individuals influence others when they communicate. However, for

Buerkel-Rothfuss, the reciprocal nature of the communication process involves mutual influence of those interacting: so her definition uses the term "communicator" rather than sender and receiver.

These different definitions indicate the importance of clearly stating what we mean when we use the term "communication." Just as the count told Milo, "You must pick your words very carefully and be sure to say just what you intend to say," it is important for us to select a definition of communication that is clear and meaningful. So, in this chapter we will first present a definition we believe is useful in studying communciation and then examine more closely the components in it. Studying this definition will provide a framework for understanding your own and others' communicative behaviors.

We define communication in this text in the following manner:

**Communication is the process of purposeful
interaction between at least two people
through the use of verbal and/or nonverbal messages
which occur in a particular context.**

Given this definition you can see that there are a great many activities that qualify as communication. When you write to your Aunt Minnie or when you listen to the traffic reports, you are involved in communication. Other activities that meet this definition are what you will be studying in this course. Now we will focus on specific aspects of this definition.

PROCESS

Central to our definition of communication is the notion of process. Often when we think of a "process" we think of something which has a set of orderly, defined steps which we take to arrive at some predetermined end point, such as the process of registering for classes or the process of solving a mathematical problem. For example, students registering for classes must first obtain a schedule of courses, fill out the required forms, and submit their requests to the appropriate academic office. Often, students must also have their proposed schedules approved by a faculty advisor as a part of the registration process. Not following the steps defined by the university or college can result in the student not reaching the end point of actual class registration. This meaning for process implies that for something to be a process, there must be an orderly sequence of steps or procedures through which one must proceed to reach some end point at which the process has been completed.

However, when we study communication, we take a somewhat different approach to the notion of process. The importance of this concept was suggested over two thousand years ago by the Greek philosopher Heraclitus who contended that no person could ever step in the same river twice. Not only is the person different on the second occasion of dipping a foot in the water, but so is the water itself as well as the entire situation. Continual change is the basis of this notion of process. This notion denies the possibility that any two things, people, events,

4

experiences, or whatever are ever identical, repeatable, and/or alike. As such, **process is a view of events and relationships as dynamic, ongoing, changing, and continuous** (Berlo, 1960).

Considering communication as a process means that we make three important assumptions: 1) we look at differences as well as similarities among stimuli (objects, events, or people); 2) we assume that people, objects, and events all change over time; and 3) we avoid a two-valued orientation.

First, we accept that premise of the uniqueness of people, events, and objects, and we become aware of and sensitive to these differences. We assume that no two people, events, or objects are <u>exactly</u> the same in all aspects; there are always some differences between them, although sometimes these differences may seem almost imperceptible. We learn to "index" people, objects, and events, to label each as a unique, one-of-a-kind phenomenon. That is, we take the familiar labels or stereotypes we've learned which emphasize similarities among characteristics and we add a way to distinguish each individual unit. So, instead of just having a label for a group of people, such as "secretaries," "journalists," or "golfers," we identify individuals within each group and recognize their unique characteristics. Thus, while Joe, Martha, and Susan are journalists, we can index Joe as $journalist_1$, Martha as $journalist_2$, and Susan as $journalist_3$. This acknowledges the similarity that Joe, Martha, and Susan are journalists, yet also distinguishes them as unique individuals. These indexes to the differences then help us respond to general statements like "Journalists will do anything for a story" by asking "<u>Which</u> journalist are you talking about?" While the labels and stereotypes are helpful in generalizing information, if we don't also pay attention to differences, we only have a part of the picture, and one that is often inaccurate.

Second, we assume that virtually everything changes and changes constantly over time; nothing remains static. In fact, sometimes it has been claimed that the only thing in our world that is constant is change itself. Even such objects as chairs or desks, skyscrapers, and the like which we generally assume to be static, non-changing entities are actually in a state of constant change. Wind and rain, for example, erode the bricks and mortar of buildings; students sliding in and out of desks and chairs wear off some of the wood particles, and so forth. But beyond that, change is inherent in the physical objects themselves; if one were to have the necessary instrumentation, one could "observe" the molecular activity that is occurring within the wood or metal of the desk and the bricks of the building.

More important to our communication focus, though, is the concept of change in people and events. Each of us changes over time. We change during the course of a day physically (we experience moments of hunger or thirst, we may develop a headache or muscle ache, etc.) as well as psychologically or emotionally (we feel happy, sad, indifferent, angry, frustrated, etc.) depending on what is happening around us and what we are doing at any particular time. We may not "look" different to someone who sees us (although people who know us well may "sense" our feelings based on how we look to them), but we know that the person we were this morning at 7:00 a.m. is not exactly the same person we are right now or will be later on today. These changes will affect how we will interact with another person, for if we feel ill or if we feel angry (or even happy) our feelings may interfere such that we may not be able to concentrate on what the other person says or does. These changes in us also occur from one day to the next and one year to the next, so there is virtually no way we could mean it when we say to someone whom we've not seen in a while, "You haven't changed a bit!"

Events around us also change continually. We can identify some which are very drastic such as an assassination of a national leader or the occurrence of an earthquake. Others may not be so dramatic, such as having a surprise test or having a paper due or expecting to see a friend at a particular time. Circumstances thus change throughout a day as well as from day to day and year to year. And, it is important for us to keep reminding ourselves of this change by indexing by time (as well as what we'd said earlier about indexing people, objects, and events).

A third assumption underlying the notion of process is that communication cannot be understood from a two-valued bipolar orientation. A two-valued orientation refers to an either-or view. For example, from a two-valued orientation communication in any particular situation would be categorized as either right or wrong. In defining communication as a process, we recognize that there is seldom just one "right" way to communicate in a given situation. Rather, various communicative behaviors may be appropriate depending on the individuals involved, the topic, and the situation. Only when these various aspects fit together well, can we describe the communication as appropriate or effective.

Communication, then, is neither right nor wrong, good nor bad; it may vary in degree of appropriateness or effectiveness. We think of communication behaviors as falling along a continuum ranging from very effective to very ineffective, with some behaviors being more effective than others. For example, Neil gave the following instructions to his new neighbor for driving to the town's library: "Turn right from our street onto Broadway. Go about six blocks, past Nelson Park and across two sets of old railroad tracks. The first traffic signal is Washington, a one-way street going north. Stay on Broadway for two more blocks, then turn right on University. A men's clothing store and a bank are on that corner. Drive two blocks and you'll see the library on the left, at the corner of Illinois and University." The neighbor listened carefully to the directions, but became confused when he reached the first traffic signal and found that Washington was a one-way street going south. After asking a pedestrian on the corner where the library was, the neighbor learned that the rest of Neil's instructions were indeed accurate. Neil's communication behaviors, then, were neither very effective nor very ineffective, rather they were only somewhat effective. If, however, the neighbor already knew approximately where the library was, Neil responding that "the library is on the corner of University and Illinois" may have been sufficient and very effective.

This example illustrates the difficulty of putting communicative behaviors in the neatly ordered categories of a two-valued orientation. Communication rarely involves either-or statements because it is such a complex process. Viewing communication as a process, then, can at times be frustrating and difficult because communication "depends on" how the many factors interact.

INTERACTION

Interaction refers to the process of one behavior affecting other behavior. In a tennis match, for example, what you do affects what your opponent does. When you walk on a crowded street, you are affecting the other walkers by your actions. If you sneeze loudly during a minister's sermon, you are affecting the behavior of other church members when they turn to look at you. Almost all of our lives are taken up by interactive behaviors. However, not all of this interaction is communicative, so we will need to restrict what we mean when we use the term "interaction."

PURPOSE

Interaction is not communicative unless the participants wish it to be communicative. That is, the participants have a **purpose** or a reason for communicating. Of the many purposes or reasons which might be cited, here we will consider three of the most often used — to persuade, to inform, and to express emotions or feelings.

To communicate to **persuade** another means that our purpose is to in some way influence the behavior or attitudes of that person — to change the other's beliefs or attitudes, to reinforce beliefs or attitudes which the person already holds, or to form a belief or attitude where none had previously existed. Some communication scholars even argue that <u>all</u> communication behavior has as its overriding purpose this influencing of the behavior of the receiver whether the intended change is small or large, immediate or delayed. Remembering that viewing communication as a process requires the avoidance of a two-valued orientation, we can also discuss communication behaviors as varying in their degree of persuasive intent. Thus, political candidates campaigning during election time communicate for the primary purpose of persuading you to vote for them. Convincing a friend to accompany you to the opera or to see the midnight showing of "Attack of the Killer Tomatoes" is also mainly persuasive in intent. Other times a persuasive purpose may not be so clear. For example, television documentary on the plight of blacks in South Africa may have as its purpose to inform viewers, yet also be persuasive in presenting a particular view of South Africa which influences the attitudes and/or behaviors of the viewers.

When we communicate to **inform**, our purpose is to tell another person something which s/he did not already know. Classroom lectures are communication with the primary purpose of informing or explaining about a procedure or event or subject. In addition, there are many times when we more casually or informally communicate with an informing purpose. Showing a friend how to use a new camera lens, providing directions to a particular location as Neil did with his neighbor, and describing a recent vacation of winter camping in Nova Scotia are examples of communication which is intended to inform. As with persuasion, communication behaviors may vary in the degree to which they are informative. While detailing your experiences winter camping, you might also be trying to persuade your friend to go with you on your next trip. Although your main purpose is to inform about an event, how you inform your friends is influenced by your desire for their company on future winter camping expeditions.

Last, we may communicate to **express emotions** or feelings. Sometimes this expression of emotion is very serious such as saying, "I love you," or expressing anxiety about a particular task you've been given at work. At other times, we may express emotions in a lighter manner ("I enjoy scuba diving" or "I'm glad it's Friday"). It may be very general, such as "I feel good," or something more specific like, "Listening to you read to your nephew makes me realize how much I care about you and your family." Expressions of feeling may reflect our emotions at that particular moment, such as anger about another's behavior, or may be concerned with maintaining our social relationship with the other person.

The purpose or reason why individuals communicate may be singular and straight-forward. For example, we typically view television evening news as informative while the advertisements broadcast by the stations are designed to be persuasive. Writing a letter to the television station's general manager concerning our strong feelings about the station's programming would be an example of expressing emotions. In these cases, the purpose of the communication is clear and easily identified.

More often, however, we interact for multiple reasons or purposes. We may try to convince another to go to a movie and at the same time just want to be with that person. Or, we may explain a political issue to a person and simultaneously try to persuade that person to vote for our candidate. Still other times, we may discover that each of the participants not only has a different purpose for interacting but that those purposes may be contradictory!

When we claim that "communication is the process of **purposeful** interactive behavior" we do not mean that we are always aware of the reason(s) why we communicate. When asked for directions to the town's library, Neil probably did not stop to ponder his purpose in responding to his neighbor. If questioned as to why he provided the directions, Neil might be able to think of several reasons, such as to provide the neighbor with information, to portray himself as a helpful and friendly person, or to demonstrate his knowledge of the town. Neil may even have had reasons he was not aware of, such as helping his neighbor out so he could ask his neighbor for a favor at some other time or convincing the neighbor that he (Neil) was the best person on the block to obtain directions from.

Usually we are able to think back on a particular interaction and identify the purpose or purposes involved. Even when we may claim to interact for "no special reason," as with greeting someone we pass on the sidewalk, we do have some motive or purpose although we may not be aware of it. The key is to realize that we never communicate for "no reason at all."

"Purposeful interactive behavior," then, helps describe communication, but it is clearly not sufficient to define it. What must be added is another element, the participants, in the interaction.

PEOPLE

It may seem obvious that people must be included in any definition of communication. Many individuals, however, believe they "communicate" with their pet dog or canary. Therefore, we must further clarify what we mean by communication.

Our ability to communicate springs from the basic nature of our humanity. Compared to other animals, we are in many ways almost pitiful creatures. We are not as swift as the cheetah, cannot fly as high as the eagle, swim as well as the otter, or hunt as well as the lion. Even with the brain capacity and the prehensile hand, humans would be distinctly second-rate species. However, it is the ability of humans to use symbols to communicate with each other which distinguishes them from the rest of the animal kingdom. Paleontologists have often used this feature — the evidence of the use of symbols and communicative activity — to distinguish between fossils of primitive humans and those of human-like apes.

This does not mean that animals do not "communicate" among themselves. We know that many animals engage in activity that appears to be communicative. An angry dog may snarl to warn others that it is ready for action. Bees use very precise dance rituals to inform each other about the location of new sources of honey. Beavers signal other beavers with their tails when danger is imminent. In all these instances there is some kind of interaction among the animals. But the interaction is very different from what people do when they communicate with each other. We use not only nonverbal signals (comparable to the dog's snarl, bee's ritual, or beaver's tail signal) but we also are able to use word symbols which we can combine in countless ways to communicate with other people. Animals limit their interaction to the immediate situation; they are unable to discuss what happened in the past or to anticipate what may come in the long range future. The ability to express thoughts, then, makes the communication activity of human beings quite different from animals!

It is true, however, that there have been some interesting experiments which attempted to teach symbol-using behavior and "language" to animals such as chimpanzees. Premack and Premack (1983) claimed that they had been able to build a "reading" and "writing" vocabulary of about 130 words for one young chimpanzee named Sarah. Sarah eventually was able to obtain a language level comparable to that of a two-year-old child. This suggests that some animals may have the capacity to communicate as humans do. However, the fact remains that the chimpanzees on their own do not engage in this same kind of symbol-using behavior. In addition, the teaching process took a great deal of time, suggesting distinct differences in capacity and in learning abilities as well as suggesting the complexities involved in human communication.

More important, though, than our capability for communication is a basic fact of human nature — **each of us needs to communicate with others.** This fundamental need may be as important as our needs for food, water, and shelter. In fact, often we are able to fill those needs through our communication with another person or persons. But, we also communicate for our personal well-being,

9

individual feelings of self-worth, and for resolving particular problems we have. Still other times we communicate for enjoyment and socialization, such as when we share stories or when we get together informally for "just talking," passing time, or "bull" sessions.

Our definition of communication, then, is concerned with human communication and the ability of people to use symbols in expressing their thoughts and ideas. The symbols communicators use form the next component of the communication process we will discuss — messages.

MESSAGES

Most communication messages involve both verbal and nonverbal elements. The verbal component of a message is the written or spoken words the communicator uses. Neil's neighbor asks, "How do I get to the library?" and Neil responds, "Let me show you on the map while I explain the directions." Neil and his neighbor have used verbal symbols or language in their interaction. However, the words they used are only one aspect of the message.

The verbal symbols in the message, whether spoken or written, are modified or influenced by nonverbal behaviors. The nonverbal components of messages include behaviors such as tone of voice, facial expression, gestures, and eye contact. For example, when Neil responds to his neighbor, he may smile, look directly at the neighbor, and talk in a friendly tone of voice, indicating his intent to be helpful. Thus, both the words or verbal symbols and the nonverbal cues combine to form a message or messages for the other person.

For those in the field of communication, the message component of the communication process is of central concern. As Buerkel-Rothfuss (1985) states: "Messages represent the 'what' of communication, the observable substance of the interaction" (p. 13). While communication scholars are interested in, for example, people's perceptions, new technology in the mass media, and motivations for choosing a particular occupation, the communication discipline is above all concerned with the process of producing, receiving, and transmitting messages.

CONTEXT

Context refers to the time and place in which a particular communicative interaction occurs. Contexts may differ by physical location, time of day, number of participants, and behaviors considered acceptable there. We would expect communication at a ten-year high school reunion to be quite different from the communication between a salesperson and customer in a department store. Differences in context involve differences in the expectations of each communicator for communication.

We can also recognize similarities across contexts. Although the notion of process in communication stresses that no two communication events are identical, we can and do make generalizations about interaction situations. Contexts such as job interviews, sermons, business memos, committee meetings, and television news are examples of situations which occur with sufficient regularity to allow us to generalize about the communication process that occurs there. Thus, while we cannot predict precisely what the anchor will say in any one news broadcast, we are reasonably sure of the general format and types of topics which will be included. An applicant preparing for a job interview may not know the exact questions the interviewer will ask, but the interviewee does have a general set of expectations as to the communication that typically occurs in an employment interview.

In this text, we will discuss four general contexts of communication: interpersonal, small group, organizational, and mass communication contexts. These contexts will serve as a basic framework for the format of the text (see Figure 1.1).

We have defined communication as: "the process of purposeful interaction between at least two people through the use of verbal and/or nonverbal messages which occur in a particular context." This definition includes a wide-range of activities such as talking on the telephone with your grandmother or watching your favorite soap opera in the student center. In our definition we have also indicated what we do not consider to be communication, such as your basset hound's droopy eyes "telling" you s/he is sad or your behavior in simply walking along the street.

Foundations

Biological	Chapter 2
Psychological	Chapter 2
Symbolic	Chapter 3
Cultural	Chapter 4

Contexts

Interpersonal	Chapters 5 & 6
Small Groups	Chapter 7
Organizational	Chapter 8
Mass	Chapters 9 & 10

Future Directions

New Technology	Chapter 11

Figure 1.1 A Framework for Studying Communication

It should be evident from the definition of communication and discussion of each of the components that communication is a complex process. It should also be apparent that communication is at the center of our everyday life. The complexity and centrality of communication to our very existence serve as the basis for why communication is so important to study.

WHY STUDY COMMUNICATION?

"Dictionopolis will always be grateful, my boy," interrupted the king, throwing one arm around Milo and patting Tock with the other. "You will face many dangers on your journey, but fear not, for I have brought you this for your protection."

He drew from inside his cape a small heavy box about the size of a schoolbook and handed it ceremoniously to Milo.

"In this box are all the words I know," he said. "Most of them you will never need, some you will use constantly, but with them you may ask all the questions which have never been answered and answer all the questions which have never been asked. All the great books of the past and all the ones yet to come are made with these words. With them there is no obstacle you cannot overcome. All you must learn to do is use them well and in the right places."

Juster, 1961, pp. 98–99*

Although Milo was at first skeptical of the power of the king's gift, he soon discovered the wisdom of the king's statements that "all you must learn to do is use them [words] well and in the right places." This is also true for us — the key is learning to communicate well. Although we acquire the skills to communicate symbolically as very young children, our effectiveness as communicators in achieving our goals varies greatly. It is important to realize that a first step in improving your communication skills is to better understand what happens when we communicate. Through this course and the chapters in this text we hope you will obtain such an understanding of the process of communication, the foundations of communication, and the contexts in which it occurs — interpersonal, small group, organizational and mass communication contexts.

Furthermore, studying the communication process is important for us as individuals and also, in a more global sense to our society. Communication is central to our social interactions, (the very image we have of ourselves) our scholastic endeavors, and whatever profession we pursue. Each of these areas in which studying communication can benefit the individual will be discussed below.

Effective communication skills are central to creating and maintaining our social relationships. Communication _is_ our link to others. Even if our communication skills generally seem adequate, we've all experienced communication events which didn't go as well as we had hoped. Sometimes we just can't think of a topic to talk about or we may feel that we don't know the appropriate words to use in expressing our thoughts. Meeting his future father-in-law for the first time, Gregory was so worried about saying something "wrong" that he didn't say anything at all. Other times we may say something without stopping to consider the consequences of our statements. Gregory's fiancee, angry with him for his silence said, "Is our conversation boring you Gregory? Maybe we should talk about something more relevant, like our upcoming wedding. Or aren't you interested in that either?"

*Excerpt from <u>The Phantom Tollbooth</u>, by Norton Juster. Copyright, Random House, Inc. Reprinted by permission.

The results of these less-than-effective communicative activities may range from minimal to very serious. If Gregory responded with "Of course, I'm interested darling. Let's discuss some of our plans with your father. I'd like to hear his opinion," the incident might be quickly forgotten. If, however, Gregory said, "I don't care about the arrangements for the wedding," and promptly left, the effect on his relationship with his fiancee and her parents would probably be severe. Whichever course the conversation took, all the participants can learn from the experience. Understanding how problems have occurred in the past can, at the very least, lead to an awareness of potential communication problems in future social situations.

Our communication abilities are intricately tied to our self-concept. The beliefs about who we are, our self-concept, develop from evaluating our behaviors and others' perceptions of us as we interact with others. Our self-concept serves as a resource from which we create our identity in a given situation. How we communicate with others presents a particular image or identity to them. For example, if you frequently interrupt others while they are speaking you may be seen by them as a rude and domineering person. Also, the way we feel about ourselves influences how we communicate. If you see yourself as a friendly, outgoing person, you will probably talk more easily with others in an unfamiliar setting than if you see yourself as quiet and shy. Finally, how others communicate with us influences how we see ourselves. If, for example, after you give a presentation to your company's department heads you receive several compliments from your audience, you may upgrade your image of yourself as a public speaker.

The ability to pursuing academic goals requires effective communication skills. A recent report by the College Entrance Examination Board (1983) emphasizes the importance of communication in higher education: "The skills of reading, writing, listening, and speaking will be necessary as college students are called on to read a wide variety of materials; to write essays, reports, and term papers; to express themselves aloud; and to listen to and learn from discussions and lectures." Whatever the subject, the learning process involves active student participation. Developing an understanding of the communication process greatly enhances any student's ability to improve those communication skills essential to the classroom setting.

In addition to specific academic goals, one of the underlying reasons you have for attending the university is to get a good education. We sometimes even add the qualifiers of "a good broad liberal" education. The nature of communicative behavior is so closely connected to fundamental truths of human behavior, and in order to understand communication, we of necessity must study the nature of humankind. As such, studying communication can be considered one of the most "liberal" of the liberal arts and certainly something which has an impact on our whole future.

Finally, and perhaps most important, **the ability to communicate effectively is the most valued asset in the corporate world** (DiSalvo, 1980). Although effective communication skills are obviously essential for lawyers, radio announcers, proofreaders, teachers, and newspaper columnists, competent communication is central to accomplishing your objectives in any occupation. A 1979 survey of 170 corporations asked the question: "What are the most common reasons for _not_ offering someone a job?" Sixty-five percent of the respondents answered, "Poor communication skills" (Endicott, 1980). Regardless of the type of business and position, employers consistently stress that the people they hire be competent in communication skills such as speaking, listening, interviewing, small group discussion, as well as writing and presenting formal reports. Roger Smith, Chair of the Board for General Motors, in a 1984 speech at Northwestern University, left no doubt as to the centrality of communication in organizations: "Everything we do depends on the successful transfer of meaning from one person or group to another. In fact, it's not much of an exaggeration to say that communication is really what business is all about!"

While merely understanding the communication process will not guarantee an improvement in your communication effectiveness, we believe that if you are ever to improve your own communication skills, you first must understand what is needed in particular context. Then you need time for practicing your communicative skills, both ridding yourself of habits which have been less than fully effective in the past as well as for developing new, more effective ones. The various projects/activities that you do in this course along with your heightened awareness of the communication process will serve as a beginning for improvement of you own communication skills.

KEY TERMS

process
interaction
purpose
messages
context

CHAPTER 2

CHAPTER 2

BIOLOGICAL AND PSYCHOLOGICAL
FOUNDATIONS FOR COMMUNICATION

We all have times when it seems we are really able to "get through to" another person with our communication. Occasionally we totally "miss the boat," or we fall somewhere in between these two extremes. How well we communicate at any given time depends on many factors, the most fundamental being the way in which we as individuals process information. In communication terms we refer to human information-processing as the intrapersonal dimension, i.e., what occurs within the individual. The importance of intrapersonal communication lies in the proposition that the manner in which we perceive and process information provides the foundation for all of our communication experiences.

We will discuss human information-processing in three chapters. This chapter will focus on our biological and psychological foundations. The next chapter will look at symbolic factors including verbal and nonverbal symbols and Chapter 4 will discuss cultural factors affecting communication. Then, based on all of these general foundations, we can consider some of the factors which influence how we communicate with others in each of four communication contexts — interpersonal, small group, organizational, and mass media.

In a sense what all these chapters do is to identify limits or boundaries on our processing of information which, in turn, constrain our communication and influence our effectiveness as communicators both in our sending and receiving of messages. Once you understand these limits or constraints, some of which are easily observable and others which are not, you can begin to analyze more accurately your own communication behaviors and to work on improving the effectiveness of your communication with others.

BIOLOGICAL FOUNDATIONS

What we know about our world comes to each of us through one or more of our physical senses. We see, hear, taste, touch, and/or smell the stimuli in the environment around us. We know how a caress feels when someone touches us; we know how delicious a thick, juicy T-bone steak smothered in mushrooms is because we have tasted the steak and smelled the aroma; and we know that there are such objects as desks, skyscrapers, and the like because they exist in the form of physical stimuli that we can see. The world around us is full of all kinds of stimuli — people, objects, sounds, smells. Through one or more of our senses we are constantly "taking in" and processing these stimuli; that is, we are perceiving our world or making sense out of it.

Even though we are capable of receiving many stimuli via our sensory organs, we are unable to do anything about a particular stimulus unless our brain allows it. Our brains are composed of a number of different parts. The largest and perhaps most important part is the **cerebral cortex** where we form our ideas about others and the world. This area controls our speech, hearing, vision, and decision-making.

The cerebral cortex has two hemispheres or sides. Each side functions somewhat differently from the other. The right side of the brain seems to control spatial tasks as well as visual and music perception. The left side of the brain appears to control our ability to use language. However, while each side is specialized, the two sides are connected by the **corpus callosum** which allows information to transfer between the hemispheres. In other words, communication occurs even between the cells (neurons) inside the brain.

Within the brain, the transmission of neural messages takes place by means of an electro-chemical process. Nerve cells don't meet; there are narrow gaps between them. When a neuron "fires," an electrical current sweeps through it, stimulating production of certain chemicals known as **neurotransmitters**. The chemicals cross the gap to the receptor site on the surface of the next cell. There another chemical action may take place, causing that cell to fire and, in turn, transmitting the current.

At each given receptor site the activity which occurs can vary considerably. One or a combination of two or three functions can occur. Some chemicals bind, but do not turn on any action; they simply occupy space, preventing other chemicals from binding. Others excite the cell to fire. Still others can occupy the site and have additional effects, such as opening a chemical channel which allows (electrically charged) ions to enter the neurons. Thus the signaling process can either be facilitated or inhibited, depending on the chemical agents which are present at each binding site or receptor (Schemeck, 1982). Through **neural communication** the brain operates as our central information-processing center. However, the cerebral cortex will not actively process information unless another portion of the central nervous system, the reticular formation, gets it ready or activates it.

RETICULAR FORMATION

A subcortical region of the brain, the **reticular formation** is a column of nerve cells located in the central core of the brain stem, which extends through the lower portion of the brain. This "gatekeeper" type of nerve tissues appears to function in two ways: 1) it controls the arousal threshold, e.g., whether an individual is asleep or awake; and 2) it receives and transmits messages to and from the cortex. Impulses can travel either ascending pathways to the cortex or descending ones, to control motor functions (Berlyne, 1960).

The reticular formation is divided into two distinct areas. The lower portion, the **collaterals**, seems to be responsible for general arousal or activation of the entire cortex, a process which is relatively long-lasting in duration. The upper portion, the **thalamus**, is more selective in nature, intensifying electrical discharges in specific cortical areas, while withholding them in others. The latter action is relatively shorter-lived, such as in the transmission of pain impulses. This implies that individuals can react to their environment in one of   two ways—with a general and non-focal awareness (which may be conscious or non-conscious) or with a highly conscious and focused attention to some particular stimulus while being only marginally aware of the rest of the field (Vernon, 1966). All the while, the reticular formation monitors and regulates — facilitating and inhibiting — the messages from the sensory receivers.

The reticular formation has been identified as the crucial physiological determinant of our ability to pay attention to any particular stimulus. When the reticular formation is excited, a portion of it sends impulses to alert the cortex. This activation or arousal pattern can be measured with electroencephalograph (EEG) tracings. The brain wave patterns indicate levels of alertness from deep sleep to intense excitement. If the arousal state of the reticular formation is too high or too low it will not be receptive to incoming stimuli. For example, it is difficult to gain the attention of someone who is deeply engrossed in reading a novel or watching an exciting show on television. On the other hand, if an individual is sleeping soundly, he or she might not be aware of a severe thunderstorm.

Donohew (1981) has suggested that **arousal** is at the heart of the attention process. Arousal is a physiologically heightened state of readiness which provides an organism with energy to act. A person who is aroused would be awake, alert, and possibly excited, as opposed to one who is calm, unaware or even asleep. Arousal can be thought of as a prerequisite for many types of human behavior, especially those which are purposive or goal-seeking in nature (Finn, 1982). Christ (1985) claimed that while arousal operates physiologically, we perceive it psychologically. We will consider later in this chapter how there appear to be differences among individuals in their need for activation or arousal.

PHYSIOLOGICAL LIMITATIONS

The physical apparatus each of us has for perceiving our world is limited; we simply cannot perceive all that is out there. Certainly the perceptual mechanisms of the human organism are built in such a way that we can see, hear, smell, touch, and taste. However, we are not physiologically endowed to perceive all stimuli. For example, the human organism is incapable of hearing sound frequencies below 20 cycles per second and above 20,000 cycles per second. Dogs can experience the sensation of sound at frequencies greater than 20,000 cycles per second (which is why dog whistles work well for training dogs but not for training children!). Another example is the human visual apparatus which is capable of "seeing" only one-seventeenth of the total light spectrum available and clearly unable to see x-rays, infrared, and ultraviolet rays of light.

There is a significant spectrum of our environment, then, which we can never experience due to the limitations of human physiology in its receiving mechanisms. In addition, we recognize limits in our physiological capabilities due to our particular sensory apparatus. Some of us may have hearing losses which further limit the range of sound frequencies available to us. Others may be unable to detect certain differences in color — i.e., be "color blind" — or to see objects beyond certain distances. Still others may be limited in their capabilities to "feel" by touch, to taste, and/or to smell. As a result we clearly are limited in what each of us is able to "take in" via our sensory receivers. And what we cannot physiologically receive, we cannot process and/or use.

PSYCHOLOGICAL FOUNDATIONS

The biological foundations for communication which we discussed in the previous section are concerned with the physiological aspects of human information processing. The **psychological foundations** for communication refer to our **affective** (emotional) and **cognitive** (thinking) responses to stimuli we encounter in our environment. Our processing of information received from the senses involves four psychological components — attention, perception, comprehension, and retention. We will discuss each of these separately.

ATTENTION

Our processing of information begins with attention. We must pay attention to a particular stimulus in our environment if we are to process anything about that stimulus. The process of "paying attention," however, is very complex. To "attend to" anything means that the reticular formation must be activated to focus on a particular stimulus. That is, among the continual incoming stimuli received from the senses, the reticular formation selects what you will attend to at any given moment. However, you need not be consciously aware of these responses for the processing to take place.

The attention process is often facilitated by such external characteristics as color, contrast, intensity, movement, and change (Bakan, 1966). All of these work to increase the chances of a given stimulus gaining a person's attention. Change which provides variety is of special interest to communicators because it is needed not only to attract but also to maintain the attention of a receiver. Thus, for example, during classroom lectures professors are much more likely to keep your attention if they occasionally raise or lower their voices to emphasize a point. Gesturing, writing on the board, or the shift from lecture to group discussion in which you can hear the sounds of different voices, also are important as means of change in order to maintain your attention.

Anything that functions to focus our attention on a stimulus enhances the attention process. Everything else functions as **noise** at that particular time and, as such, interferes with our information-processing. Noise need not refer only to loud physical sounds which we can hear; it refers to anything — internal or external — which can distract us from attending to a particular message or thought process.

The attention process may also be inhibited by external factors. As a particular stimulus is repeated or recurs, habituation occurs. **Habituation** refers to a decrease in neural response due to repetition (or "habitual")

21

recurrence of a stimulus. Thus, as you listen to a person who speaks in a monotone voice, you may find yourself no longer paying attention because that voice has no variation. Your reticular formation has determined that you will not attend to the voice stimulus and it will then turn to other stimuli which your senses are receiving.

Attention to external stimuli may be diminished by internal stimuli such as memories or ideas, which compete with external "messages" for our attention. When our attention shifts to these mental processes, we describe it as **ideational attention,** or what we commonly call "daydreaming." Sometimes we shift to daydreaming because of habituation or sometimes because some element in a message triggers off our associations. But what is most interesting is that some aspect of external stimuli may be responsible for our shift toward ideational attention (Palmgreen, 1971).

Some researchers believe it is quite possible that individuals stumble along through their communication environments without being fully aware of their behavior but instead operating much of the time on "automatic pilot" (Berger, 1979; Bowers & Bradac, 1982; Laberge & Samuels, 1980; Langer, 1980; Roloff, 1980). Finn (1982) referred to this process as **automaticity** and claimed that our brain pays full attention to new stimuli but that over time the processing becomes almost automatic. That is, the human brain can process well-known or familiar stimuli at an unconscious or less-than-fully-conscious level. This allows attention, which is a scarce resource, to focus exclusively on what is new to the brain — novel or less familiar stimuli.

Think, for example, of the number of times you've driven home from classes or work and, as you got out of the car, suddenly realized that you're not quite sure how you got there. That is, during the time you were driving, you were unaware of obeying traffic signals, of starting, stopping, shifting gears, making turns, and all the other sometimes complicated moves required to drive a vehicle from one location to another. Although driving home may be your most easily remembered experience of this nature, the process of acting or behaving while we are not (or only partly) aware of what we are doing actually occurs quite frequently.

The concept of automaticity, which would certainly account for situations like our driving the car even though we were not conscious of doing so, makes it important for us to think of our behavior as not necessarily being either cognitive or affective. Rather, it indicates that perhaps we need to explain our behavior in terms of a continuum ranging from affective to cognitive (Donohew, Nair, & Finn, 1984). As such, we could then clearly identify and explain some of our behaviors (such as your reading this book to understand communication process, or to get enough information to pass the next test) as being primarily cognitive. Other of our behaviors (such as the urge to hug a friend or to get a pizza at 10 p.m.) would be more clearly affective. Most of our processing behaviors probably involve some combination of both affect and cognition.

The key point here is that our attention is not something static but is something dynamic, ever-changing, and is based on the selectivity of the reticular formation.

PERCEPTION

Once the reticular formation identifies which sensory stimuli are to be attended to, what we do in terms of our immediate response is called **perception.** When we encounter any stimulus, such as a person, photograph, television program, or voice recording, we begin the perceptual process. This perceptual experience has five general characteristics:

1. **immediacy** – we are almost instantaneously aware of the stimulus;
2. **structure** – we tend to perceive objects as wholes and not just parts;
3. **stability** – these stimulus objects remain the same regardless of how they might be illuminated;
4. **meaningfulness** – we perceive these objects in terms of our previous experience and in terms of their relationship(s) to other objects; and
5. **selectivity** – we attend to only a limited number of stimulus objects out of an array of many (Tagiuri, 1969).

This classification system seems to make sense for a variety of reasons. First, when we encounter a stimulus object, such as a person, we do not perceive that person in a series of perceptual stages. Instead, we are immediately aware that "someone is there." We also are aware that it is someone (a person) and not some odd collection of shoe laces, flesh, hair, clothing, etc. In addition, regardless of where we encounter this person (in a fog, on the beach, etc.) we can recognize him/her <u>as a person</u> rather than say a chair or some other object. We may further recognize this person as a friend, a stranger, a relative, or a boss. In other words, we assign some kind of meaningful position in our scheme of things to that "someone." Finally, when we encounter this person, we probably focus on some specific aspect. We may notice the color of hair or if s/he has a noticeable accent and then focus on that and thus miss the color of the belt, or the hairstyle, or the style of shoes, and so on.

We find, then, that we must simplify any complex stimulus by focusing our attention on a limited number of stimuli. This is called **selective perception.** We further reduce the complexity of the full stimulus array by categorizing, labeling, or coding the stimulus. After our almost instantaneous categorization, we make any number of snap judgments or inferences about the stimulus object. In addition, if the stimulus object is a person, we may raise questions about the causes of that person's behavior. In making these decisions we reduce complex judgments to relatively simple operations. These virtually automatic simplifying mechanisms allow us to process information very rapidly.

Although these processes may lead to mistakes in judgment, they do allow us to cope with time constraints, vast amounts of information, and information uncertainty. Beyond these initial inferences we may also organize and integrate all the information we have stored to form a composite judgment or impression of that person.

The focus of this text is on communication as a human activity. While a great deal of work on the general perceptual process is applicable to communication, the remainder of this section will concentrate on the perception of persons rather than the perception of objects. Research on person perception (or social perception as it is also known) has two major divisions: the study of personal and social factors that affect our general perceptual processes and the study of how we perceive other persons.

PERSON PERCEPTION

When people are the objects of perception, the perceptual process immediately becomes more complex. We recognize people as having emotions, belonging to particular groups, and/or possessing certain personality traits. We form impressions of others based on our assumptions about people and our expectations about them. In addition, the degree to which we are interpersonally attracted to others influences our perceptions of them. We will examine more closely these aspects of person perception in this section.

Response Sets

Response sets refer to the sets of expectations we have about a particular object, person or situation. The individual who is "set" to respond is prepared, either consciously or unconsciously, to respond to particular stimuli in particular ways, and to make any necessary "adjustments" (or what we would consider distortions) in their processing. For example, you may infer that because your neighbor jogs every morning, s/he is very health conscious. You then fit or adjust other information about your neighbor into the set of expectations you have about him/her and about people who are "health conscious." Or, to put it another way, our **response set** affects not only what we perceive but whether we will perceive it accurately.

Some of the response sets frequently identified in person perception include halo effects, logical errors, and assumed similiarity. **Halo effects** occur when we make a global evaluation of another and then apply it across several areas of expertise. For example, professional ball players are judged as expert in their particular game. Because of the halo effect, the tendency is to presume their expertise extends to such things as automobile tires, shampoo, or nuclear reactors (a claim often reinforced by advertising) about which they probably have little more knowledge or expertise than does the average consumer. Logical errors occur when we attempt to extrapolate from insufficient or faulty information. And, we often assume that because another person comes from the same part of the country or the same background as we do that the person is like us. This assumed similarity can then cause us many problems especially when we discover that our assumptions have been inaccurate.

One common finding in this area has been that we usually are oversensitive to individual differences. Inaccuracy may result for a number of reasons including failure to notice relevant stimuli, coding behavior or context, or drawing

24

incorrect conclusions about the person's intentions. Inaccuracies also result from our necessity to impose order on rich or complex stimuli.

Recognizing emotions

One of the first scholars to undertake a systematic exploration of how people **recognize emotions** was Charles Darwin. In 1897 Darwin wrote a book in which he concluded that people were pretty good at decoding other people's expressions. However, in the early 1900's a number of experimental studies were done with photos to measure just how accurate people were in recognizing emotion shown by other people. This work suggested that people actually were not very good at recognizing emotions; unfortunately, this work had a number of shortcomings.

Later researchers were able to show that respondents could do quite well if adequate category schemes were provided and when emotional expressions were placed in some context. These later results tend to correspond well with our own experiences in that we can easily recognize expressions of grief at a funeral or expressions of joy at a wedding. However, many times the context may not help us to correctly interpret an emotional expression. For example, in an old John Wayne movie in which he has just been addressed in a profanity-laced sentence, our hero himself was confused enough to utter a famous line calling for clarification: "Smile when you say that, mister."

Categorizing People

Recently a number of scholars have started to examine how we **identify specific people and groups.** Psychologists interested in the study of stereotypes and prejudice have found this to be an especially fruitful area of inquiry. In general, these researchers have found that categorizing and stereotyping appear to be a natural reaction in our attempts to simplify a complex social world. Large amounts of information need to be assimilated and this assimilation process appears to involve both categorization and simplification.

When we attempt to categorize what we are perceiving, the very category (or the label or the stereotype) we use simultaneously influences our information-processing. Consider, for example, a well-known study by Kelley (1950) in which students were told by the researcher that their regular instructor would be replaced on that day by another instructor. In order that they might know something about this replacement, a brief written description of the new instructor was given to each student. Half of the students received a description of the instructor as a "rather cold person, industrious, critical, practical, and determined." For the other students, the instructor was described as "warm" instead of "cold."

The substitute teacher then appeared, taught the class, and left. After he left, the students were asked to evaluate the instructor using both open-type descriptions and a check list of traits. During the class the researcher had recorded the number of times each student talked with the instructor as a behavioral indicator of the warm-cold variable.

The results clearly indicated that the students who had received the "warm" description found that instructor "more considerate of others, more informal, more sociable, more popular, better-natured, more humorous, and more humane," than did those who had received the "cold" description. In addition, the individuals who had received the "warm" introduction participated more in class than did those individuals who received the "cold" description. The categories, clustering constructs, or schema that we use influence not only what we perceive and comprehend at the moment but also our subsequent behavior because we attend only to selected aspects.

Forming Impressions

How we **form impressions** of people has been a major area of interest in studying communication. Impression formation is affected by our assumptions about the nature of people in general as well as by our own expectations. If we generally think people are competitive, then we probably will view a particular individual as being competitive. If we generally think of people as cooperative, we probably "see" behaviors as cooperative. This becomes a kind of **self-fulfilling prophecy;** that is, because we expect certain things, we then focus our attention so that we actually "see" only those things (and avoid or discount anything we have not expected).

When we form an impression of another, it is not just their sum of all the information we have about the other. Rather, our impression is a dynamic product of some pieces of information which apparently are more heavily weighted and which modify the picture. For example, our impression can be influenced by the order in which the information is presented. Thus, what we see first or hear first (i.e., primacy) has been consistently shown to have a disproportionate impact on how we view another person. But occasionally, the last thing we recall about another (i.e., recency) may have a greater impact than we might expect on what we remember about that person.

Even though our initial perceptions of people may not be accurate, Newcomb (1960) found that in judging others' personalities we tend to become more accurate as we increase our time of interaction with that person. However, O'Keefe (1984) and others have argued this relationship is not always so. Over time we may start to take our friends' attitudes for granted and whenever we do this, we may actually end up with decreasing accuracy in judging personalities. Generally, though, if we are given broad enough categories and sufficient contextual information, our accuracy increases.

Attraction

Another factor which affects our perception of others is the degree of attraction. What makes people initially attracted to others is a matter of much interest. By attraction we mean **interpersonal attraction:** the desire to interact with another person, to communicate and to share activities. A large number of qualities have been studied for their contribution to interpersonal attraction. Some factors seem more important to attraction early in a relationship while others exert more effect later. We will focus on four factors that heavily influence initial attraction to others although their effect certainly is not limited to those early stages.

Proximity exerts a powerful influence on the decision to begin a relationship with another person. Proximity means simply the physical or geographic closeness of others—their availability. We tend to be more attracted to those people who are naturally a part of our daily activities. Some studies have shown that friendship formation is influenced more by proximity than physical beauty or perceived similarity with others (Festinger, Schacter, & Back, 1950). Because of this proximity we tend to distort our perceptions of those with whom we deal regularly (co-workers, classmates, etc.) so that we see them as more physically attractive, similar to us, or intelligent than they are, while overlooking some possible negative qualities.

Social desirability also affects interpersonal attraction. What makes someone socially desirable is often culturally defined. Physical beauty, status, and monetary wealth all are important to social desirability in American culture. What makes us attracted to another is, in part, what makes that person desirable or valued in our culture. Curiously, not everyone seeks out those who rate the highest on a social desirability scale. People tend to be more attracted to those whom they see as similar to themselves in social desirability. This is known as the "matching hypothesis," since most of us hypothesize that we have a better chance of relational success with those similar to us (i.e., those we "match") in social desirabiltiy.

Perceived similarity is a third important determinant of attraction. The more similarities we see between ourself and another, the more attracted we tend to be to them. At first, similarity in appearance, social status, age, dress, and occupation seem most important in determining whether people are attracted. As they continue in contact with each other, though, these more external qualities become less important than perceived similarity in attitudes and opinions (e.g., you both like sports and politics). Note, however, that what counts here is **perceived** similarity. Two people may be very similar, but if they fail to perceive that similarity, the actual similarity will have no effect on attraction.

A fourth factor affecting attraction is **reciprocity**. When you show interest in others, talk with them about yourself, share time, possessions, etc., you expect them to do the same — to reciprocate. At minimum, the interest and concern they show for you should be equal to what you give to them. If they reciprocate at even higher levels, you are all the more likely to be attracted to them.

Nothing will reduce attention early in a relationship more than the failure to immediately reciprocate the other's behavior. Ask yourself, for example, what your reaction would be if you met someone at a party and enthusiastically said, "Hi, I'm Bill, a freshman communication major from Elmtown. I just got into town," and the other person responded in a low key tone, "I'm Jack." How would you react?   Why? Clearly, the other person has not reciprocated either to the degree of interest suggested by your tone or to the information about yourself which you provided.

It is quite apparent, then, that our information-processing abilities are limited and are affected at almost any point by our needs and values at that particular time.   Furthermore, because this processing is done internally, we often fail to check up on ourselves. We simply "assume" that what we see, hear, or know is the way it is. We need to be cautious not only about the inaccuracies we may make in perceiving but also about potential inaccuracies in the perceptions of others with whom we communicate.

Instructions

Often we are told how we should comprehend what we should perceive; that is, we are given a set of instructions as to what to expect. In communication classes we often present the stimulus figure in Figure 2.1 with a set of instructions about the "person" students see in the picture. The figure can be seen as either an old, ugly woman or as a young, attractive woman. Numerous studies have used figures similar to the one used by Boring (1930).

Figure 2.1 An Old or Young Woman

One half of the class received instructions (usually in written form) that they would see the picture of an ugly old woman and then write a brief description of that person. The other half of the class was told that they would see the picture of a pretty young woman and then write a description of her. It is quite clear from the results of all the studies that those individuals "set" to see the old woman actually see her more often than they see the young woman, and those set to see the young woman, do indeed see the young woman. Furthermore, it is interesting to note that once one's perceptions have been "set" to see either the old or young woman, it is often quite difficult to see the other woman. Some individuals, in fact, find it impossible ever to see the other woman.

Perceptual errors

We don't usually stop to think about the reality of the world that surrounds us. Typically we believe that whatever we see, hear or smell in the world is real. But is it? Of course it is, at least to some extent. However, there is some very persuasive evidence that people often make gross errors and incorrect inferences in viewing their "reality". For example, a number of studies in the psychology of testimony have shown that less than 10% of the information contained in short auto accident films is reported in the immediate testimony of the eyewitnesses (Loftus & Loftus, 1980). When we see an accident occur, we often can identify the vehicles and the direction which they were traveling, but the vast majority of details cannot be recovered even if we were asked immediately to write down everything we saw. Obviously, over time these details further deteriorate and unless we constantly rehearse what we say, we may forget or inaccurately remember even central details.

We are not always completely inaccurate in our views of a situation. Nonetheless, there are social and personal factors that appear to work against accurate perception. First, there are certain **properties of the stimulus** itself that appear to influence our perception. If we place a great value on something, it may lead us to overestimate its presence or our contribution to it. For example, if you played on a championship basketball team, you may later overestimate your contribution to the team's success. If we are **familiar** with a stimulus, we recognize it more quickly and more accurately. And, if the stimulus is especially **intense** or vivid, it will have more of an effect on our judgments. This does not rule out the possibility of subliminal perception, but it does suggest that it is of secondary importance at most.

A number of personality factors and our implicit personality theories also influence our perception as well. We will consider both of these aspects more fully later in the chapter when we discuss individual differences in our information-processing.

COMPREHENSION

As we process information we try to "make sense of" or to comprehend what this stimulus means to us. As such, we become interested in those cognitive (thinking) mechanisms that help us understand and define realities for us.

Most researchers seem to agree that we employ schemas or cognitive frameworks in our understanding and defining of reality. **Schemas** generally are defined as mental organizing frameworks, built up through experience, which are necessary for interpretation, comprehension, and enhanced recall of information. Schemas can be conceptualized as systems of interrelated constructs or thematic clusters of cognitively similar content material. Schemas are referred to by various names including "thematic clusters," "frames," "construct systems," "implicit theories," "scripts," etc., but the concepts are similar. Regardless of the term used, most scholars believe we use schemas both in encoding and decoding stages of information processing.

These schematic structures appear to do more than just help us understand what is going on, they also play a role in helping us predict others' behaviors and influence our behavior and goals as well. This reciprocal relationship is of great interest to many communication researchers. Fiske and Taylor (1984) divide schema into four areas: (1) **person schemata** which are used in understanding others' goals and traits; (2) **self-schemata** which contains information about your own behavior, personality, and appearance; (3) **role schemata** which includes information on broad social categories such as sex, race, occupation, etc., and; (4) **event schemata** which contains knowledge of typical or scripted behavior in episodes like restaurant visits, classes, church meetings, etc. Of course, other types of social schemas may exist.

Schemas can help us understand what another person is like, but they also can hinder our efforts to really understand someone, especially if they invoke a stereotype. How do schemas evoke stereotypes? It's probably a function of how schemas develop.

First, as people develop schemas, they have more schema-relevant information about themselves and others in the groups in which they belong. These groups might include family, people in the neighborhood, male-female relationships, etc. We seem to develop rich, complex schemas about members of our own groups and somewhat impoverished schemas about others. Some researchers have called this a "frequence of interaction" hypothesis.

Presumably, in-group schemas are more complex and differentiated, because perceivers must come up with ways to understand a collection of diverse instances involving persons in their own group. This rich background of experience with the in-group generates a larger number of dimensions along which individual members may be judged. Our knowledge of out-groups, being based on fewer and less varied experiences, generates fewer dimensions.

When we think about either the whole out-group or a member of it, we tend to perceive and evaluate these others in relatively global, approach/avoidance terms. We tend to perceive out-group members as either good or bad. On the other hand, in-group members, cannot be so readily categorized because they can be perceived as good in some respects and bad in others, not simply labeled as either one or the other.

This conceptualization spotlights prejudice and stereotyping in a somewhat different light. We do not want to suggest that some people do not have "knee-jerk" responses to some categories of people; rather we would like to argue that if we have an undifferentiated schema for another, we are more easily polarized when making judgments. That is, we are very likely to evaluate another in either an extreme "good" or an extreme "bad" way if we have relatively simplistic schemas for understanding them. For example, we have a category for "Californians" even though we may never have visited or lived there or even know individuals who live there. So what we have is a superficial image or undifferentiated schema—"Californians have tans and roller skate." This simplistic schema is likely to exist until we acquire more information. As we accumulate information the schema begins to change to take it all into account and our conceptualizations then are described as more elaborate, differentiated, or complex.

Almost any stimulus we experience and attempt to process exists within a particular context or surroundings which affects how we will process it. For example, consider the following series of symbols: E, D, C, 13, A, and 16, 15, 14, 13 , 12. Note the fourth symbol in each series. How did you perceive it? In the series of capital letters, did you perceive the fourth symbol as the letter "B"? In the series of numbers, did you see the fourth symbol as the number "13"? How we perceive the symbol is based on our mental set induced by the context. This is an example of how we can become mentally set to perceive various aspects of reality. We often see, hear, smell, feel, and taste what we "expect" to see, hear, smell, feel, and taste, depending on the environment or context.

RETENTION

Once we comprehend a particular thing which we have perceived, our brains are capable of storing this information. Our storage system consists of two types: **short-term memory,** storage which lasts for up to 60 seconds; and **long-term memory,** storage which lasts beyond one minute and capable of being retained for a lifetime. We store information as we have perceived and comprehended it, whether or not that information is accurate.

Retention of information appears to be affected by many of the same forces influencing other aspects of our information-processing. It is influenced by time, such that we are more likely to remember something which came first (primacy) or something last (recency) than something in the middle. It is influenced by frequency of use, so that you are more likely to retain information for long periods of time if you make use of that information in conversation, in application, on the job, etc. It is also influenced by what is already stored there. "New" information is likely to be retained if it is not too similar to previously stored information. On the other hand, if the new information somehow interferes with the old (i.e., either too similar or else contradictory), it won't be retained. It is important to emphasize here that how the information was stored can affect whether or not you will be able to retrieve a particular piece of information when it is needed.

INDIVIDUAL DIFFERENCES IN HUMAN INFORMATION PROCESSING

The four aspects of human information processing — attention, perception, comprehension, and retention — can be accomplished very quickly and without our awareness. Each aspect is affected by what is selected as a focus at that moment. Selectivity throughout the processing, in turn, will greatly affect how we can communicate with others about a particular piece of information. This selectivity is very complex and is affected not only by the prominence of stimuli in the environment and by conscious forces we exert, but also by powerful unconscious factors based on our physiological and psychological needs and emotions, all of which are stored in the brain. Now we turn to the role that individual need and personality play in the attention process which lies at the base of human information processing.

In our information-processing, what we select or focus on at any particular point will depend on both cognitive and affective factors. Here we will group them under two broad headings—"needs" and "personality." Other factors related to our beliefs, attitudes, experiences, language, and culture will be discussed in later chapters. In the past researchers in both communication and psychology have focused primarily on **cognitive** explanations for our processing behaviors. That is, they assumed that we consciously proceed through our thinking and that we make "rational" decisions based on that processing. **Affective** explanations, on the other hand, which would suggest that we have little conscious control over our behaviors were not considered satisfactory because we would then be only "irrational" or emotional. Some recent research suggests that we need to more carefully examine these explanations.

NEEDS

Physical needs

Our physical needs can certainly influence our selectivity. Consider the situation of two individuals sitting at a lunch counter, each individual scanning the menu for items of food to order. One individual is hungry while the other is only thirsty. Both individuals have available for processing the same physical stimuli (i.e., the words, pictures, and numbers on the menu), but each will probably select different items to attend to initially. The hungry individual will probably first see the hamburgers, fish, and/or steak dinners on the menu, whereas the individual who is thirsty will undoubtedly notice first the list of beverages on the menu.

Or, consider the results of a study by Bruner and Goodman (1947) which illustrates the effect of one's needs on the process of selectivity in perception. These researchers had two groups of children judge the size of various numbers of coins. One group of children was very poor, coming from a settlement house environment in one of Boston's slum areas; the other group of children was from a progressive school in one of the more affluent areas of Boston which served children of professional and business people. The group of poor children consistently overestimated the size of the coins considerably more than did the others which the investigators concluded came from the greater need for money by the poor children than by the rich children. For the poor children the need for money led them to perceive money in a very distorted way.

Need for activation

Arousal or **activation** is a fundamental element in those processes which provide us with the energy to act. More than one third of the volume of the brain involves pleasure centers which seek continuous stimulation. Although we often are not aware of it arousal is a silent motivator of many of our behaviors, especially exposure to new experiences. For each of us there appears to be an optimal level of arousal or activation at which we feel most comfortable (Donohew, Palmgreen, & Duncan, 1980). Some individuals are risk-takers who have a high need for activation and want an almost steady stream of it. Others prefer safer, more predictable kinds of activities. They have a low need for activation and prefer to stay with familiar people in familiar environments. Arousing stimuli which might attract persons with a high need for activation probably would be threatening or frightening for persons with a low need. Conversely, stimuli which appeal to low-need people might be interpreted as boring or dull by high-need individuals.

According to the theory proposed by Donohew, Palmgreen, and Duncan (1980), people enter information-exposure situations with the expectation of achieving or maintaining their optimal state. They then experience either positive or negative affects (feeling or mood) depending on their perceptions of whether or not the optimal state is achieved. If they experience a positive affect, a pleasant feeling, they will continue to expose themselves to an information source. Individuals who experience unpleasant affects, anxiety, or feelings of boredom, however, will ordinarily stop their exposure to an information source. In other words, individuals will attempt to minimize a negative affect (either from under- or over-stimulation). In this way needs and feelings work to either inhibit or facilitate the attention process.

Individuals also try to seek and maintain an optimal level of arousal in order to keep their minds vigilant and alert (Zuckerman, 1979). Because of this tendency to search for novel stimuli, however, our attention may shift rapidly from one sensory stimulus to another. As such, gaining a person's "attention" does not guarantee holding it. Attention will shift, especially as the arousal level changes. Because arousal is a fundamental variable affecting whether a person will attend to certain stimuli, communicators need to be aware of the different factors that influence arousal and consequently attention.

For example, level of arousal may be affected by the style of a message. In one study, the same basic set of facts was used in writing two news stories, one composed in a "traditional" newswriting style which presented facts in descending order of importance and one a "narrative" style which used a time order (Donohew, 1981). The study hypothesized that, regardless of the level of need for activation, readers would show more arousal for and would be more likely to continue to seek those messages written in a narrative style. The "narrative" style generally produced higher levels of change in arousal. Both psychological affect (or mood) and physiological arousal changed in the same direction. Furthermore, the changes that occurred were good predictors of whether the individual wanted either to continue exposure to or to avoid that kind of message.

A similar approach indicates that people like to be entertained so that any message which offers new information (i.e., it is unpredictable), is potentially enjoyable. However, to provide the pleasureable arousal that all of us are assumed to seek, the message must pass three "tests" (Finn, 1982). First, it must be easy to understand. Next, it must be novel (otherwise it would be redundant and boring) based on the arousal that the stimulus generates. Finally, it must generally fit what we believe. If it does all three, a person enjoys a pleasant feeling. If it doesn't, it is perceived as threatening because it produces a feeling of uncertainty and/or anxiety.

PERSONALITY FACTORS

One personality factor affecting the attention process involves whether people can be classified as augmenters or reducers. **Augmenters** are people who react to stimuli intensely, pay more attention to objects and events, and exaggerate their size and importance. Lester (1974) found that when augmenters were blindfolded they estimated the size of a wooden block as larger than it really was. If augmenters experience an increase in their arousal level, due to more stimuli than they can handle, they narrow their perceptual field and subsequently pay attention only to a particular stimulus in their environment while ignoring or "shutting out" the rest. On the other hand, **reducers** decrease the intensity of whatever they sense. They function at lower levels of arousal and have been labeled (by Lester) as stimulus-hungry thrill seekers, continually scanning their perceptual field for excitement or novel stimuli.

Another personality factor which has been shown to affect the attention process is the degree to which a person is dogmatic. **Dogmatic** persons have strong beliefs and opinions and thus will ignore or close their minds to information that is discrepant from what they already know or believe. **Open-minded** persons, on the other hand, are more willing to consider all sides of an argument or issue and seem to pay attention to a variety of information sources. However, this tendency to consider all sides has been shown to create stress among the open-minded, possibly because it requires a restructuring of their cognitions (Donohew & Palmgreen, 1971). Researchers analyzed both the psychological and physiological responses of college students who were exposed to reading material concerning the war in Vietnam. Participants who were open-minded experienced greater stress when exposed to information that was not consistent with their beliefs than did dogmatic subjects. The researchers concluded that open-minded persons might be motivated to expose themselves both to discrepant and supportive material because failure to do so would run counter to their self-concept of being open-minded. Such an action would possibly create even greater stress, especially if open-mindedness were a belief the individual highly valued.

IMPLICIT PERSONALITY THEORY

Implicit personality theories can be considered to be clusters of personal constructs or schema, which are in essence stereotypes we hold about how people behave. A **stereotype** is a set of characteristics that we associate with a category of people. We not only form impressions of others but we also combine certain of these constructs to provide us with our own explanations or "theories" about how people function. We describe these theories as naive or implicit because we carry them in our heads (often without our awareness that they're there) and we seldom talk about them explicitly with others. These theories help speed up our information-processing because once they are in place they provide us with our own way to understand and explain behaviors. Think, for example, about your theory of "nice people" or "smart people" or "politicians" or "athletes." Try to identify explicitly all of the assumptions you have made about how people whom you label as nice or smart or politicians or athletes work. Do you expect that nice things happen to nice people? How do you <u>know</u> this? The information doesn't just come magically from nowhere; it comes from a set of characteristics which you have previously clustered together as your way to deal with people "like that." That is, from your initial labellings of a person whom you now see, you have a surprisingly full-blown explanation about the whole personality of people "like that" and how they think or believe about other aspects/areas in their lives.

For example you may have labeled a person as "smart" because of an answer s/he gave today in class. Once you've categorized that person as smart, your brain (your processing system) has ready to go a whole set of accompanying constructs or shema. This way you don't spend a lot of time thinking about each person from scratch; you already know (or think you thus know) about the whole person. Implicit personality theories help us simplify our information-processing by providing us with our own built-in explanations.

Some communication scholars have suggested further that these implicit theories may also provide insights into how we think we communicate with others (Sypher, 1980). It may be that when we are asked to report on how we communicate, we use these implicit theories to retrieve information. Such situations may lead us mistakenly to retrieve conceptually similar behaviors, qualities or traits that do not accurately reflect the actual behavior. Hence, we may infer behavioral consistency that is more a reflection of our own labels of similarity than an accurate account of how we (or others) really communicate. More recent research by Sypher and Sypher (1984) has also shown that role schemata may also influence the way we see our own as well as others' (supervisors, subordinates, and peers) communication behavior.

These and other studies point out the complexity of human information-processing. They are presented here to familiarize you with some of the factors which underlie and affect the overall process of communication.

SUMMARY

Our processing of information involves attention (to whom and to what we pay attention), perception (how we perceive people, objects, and ideas), comprehension (how we come to make sense of people, objects, and ideas), and retention (what and how accurately we can remember those people, objects, and ideas).

Each of these aspects in information-processing is very much affected by a complex set of biological, affective (feeling) and cognitive (thinking) factors within each individual. The conscious and unconscious ways we select and organize information at each stage of processing is affected by a variety of factors (cognitive and affective processes, personality, needs, etc.). The result is that each of us creates our own, somewhat unique set of "information" about persons, objects, and ideas we encounter, in turn, this influences who each of us will be able to communicate with and about those people, objects, and ideas.

KEY TERMS

activation
arousal
attention
automaticity
comprehension
corpus callosum
habituation
ideational attention
implicit personality theory
long-term memory
neural communication
noise
perception
response set
retention
reticular formation
schema
selective perception
self-fulfilling prophecy
short-term memory
stereotyping

CHAPTER 3

SYMBOLIC FOUNDATIONS
FOR COMMUNICATION

While our biological and psychological foundations influence our information processing, it is our ability to express our ideas and emotions symbolically which allows us to interact with others. We now need to consider the symbolic foundations which include all use of symbols in our message-making. That is, they include both linguistic (or verbal) and non-linguistic (or nonverbal) aspects. While it is difficult to actually separate our verbal/language messages from our nonverbal messages, for the sake of convenience here we will first discuss the verbal factors, language and meaning, and then examine the nonverbal factors which influence our message-making behavior in communication contexts.

VERBAL SYMBOLS: LANGUAGE

What is language? It is quite probable that if a number of individuals were asked this question, the most prominent response would be something like: "Language is all of the words and sentences that individuals use to express their thoughts and ideas." Although this definition may be suitable for an everyday understanding of language, it is not sufficiently helpful here as we try to understand the nature of the language process. We can more fully define language by describing a set of characteristics that define language as an especially important resource for communication. We will consider each of these characteristics separately.

LANGUAGE IS COMPOSED OF A SET OF SOUNDS

All the human languages that we know of first began as a set of sounds. Among the 3500 distinct languages in the world today most are available only in oral form. Only about 500 of these languages also exist in a written form.
Each sound that can be identified is called a **phoneme.** No single language uses all possible sounds or phonemes. English, for example, does not include the gutteral sound of "cht" that German does or the rolling "rr" sound that Spanish does. Many Oriental languages don't include different sounds for the "l" and "r" as English does. The sounds of the language we learn first often make it difficult for us to learn the sounds of a different language. (Note that when a language exists in written form, the number of different phonemes is not necessarily the same as the written symbols.)

LANGUAGE ARBITRARILY CONNECTS SOUNDS AND REFERENTS

In any language the sounds used by individuals and the objects, events, or ideas to which these sounds refer are connected only in an arbitrary way. That is, there is no inherent connection between the particular set of sounds chosen to refer to an object, event, or idea and the object, event, or idea itself. Any sounds could have been chosen to refer to or represent the object. For example, English speakers use the sounds of c-h-a-i-r to refer to or stand for a physical object which generally has four legs, a flat seat and may or may not have a back and/or arms. They could have just as well used the sounds of b-l-i-p this particular class of objects. However, in the development and evolution of our language system, the sounds of c-h-a-i-r came to be used to refer to this class of objects.

This arbitrary connection is also apparent when we see that different languages use different sounds to refer to the same object or event. For example, in Spanish the sound for a four-legged animal with ears and a tail that makes a sound of "woof" is <u>perro</u>, whereas in French this same animal is called a <u>chien</u> and in German it is called a <u>hund</u>. Thus, the connection between the label <u>dog</u> and the object is indeed an arbitrary one.

Furthermore, the connection between sounds and the things to which they refer is unpredictable. That is, typically there is nothing in the nature of the sounds or in the object that would lead one to predict what sound will be used to represent a thing. (One possible exception to this is those sounds which are onomatopoeic in nature; i.e., such sounds as "hiss" or "boom" are more like the actual noises they represent.) As such, an individual unfamiliar with a particular language would be unable to predict accurately particular sounds with the object, idea, or event to which they refer.

LANGUAGE IS STRUCTURED

While the sounds and their referents are not predictable in a language, it is possible to predict some things in any given language because each language consists of recurrent patterns or structure. These patterns are both phonological and grammatical.

The **phonological structure** refers to those combinations of sounds which are used in a language. English consistently puts certain sounds together so that it needs a vowel sound in between consonants. Also, some sounds only appear in certain positions or combinations. For example, the "ng" sound only appears at the end of an English word, never at the beginning and "czw" could not be said without adding some vowel sound.

Each language has its own pattern for phonological sound combinations which are most often learned without formal training for one's native language but through more formal training in the phonology for other languages. As such, if we hear particular sounds we can identify or predict something about the language even if only that it must be "foreign" because it is not our own way of putting sounds together.

The **grammatical structure** in a language refers to the patterns for putting together combinations of words/sounds in sequence. In English most sentences follow a pattern of subject-verb-object. Adjectives can be used to modify or qualify nouns; adverbs do so for verbs. Noun-verb combinations need to be adjusted in particular ways, as with "I say" but "he says" or "I am" but "you are". Changing the noun-verb order makes it different. For example, "This is a sandwich" declares something while "Is this a sandwich" asks a question.

These very patterns help build into a language system what is called **redundancy,** so that if you should happen to miss one or two words (because of static on the phone or muffled sounds of the speaker or even because you were "listening" to something/someone else), you can still generally make sense of the sentence unit. Consider this English sentence, "The boy _____ to the ball _____ ." What could be filled in the blanks to complete the sense of the sentence? In the first blank you might put <u>went</u> or <u>hurried</u> or <u>meandered,</u> whereas in the second blank you use works like <u>park,</u> <u>game,</u> or <u>field.</u> But you would not put <u>strange</u> or <u>handsome</u> in the first blank or words like <u>run,</u> <u>between,</u> or <u>brilliant</u> in the second blank because that is not the way this language is structured. These patterns, then, allow the language user to make predictions about an entire sentence from knowledge of only fragments of sentences.

An additional result of the structure of language is the notion of **substitutability.** For example, in the sentence, "The boy ran to the ball field," we could replace the word <u>ran</u> with any number of other verbs such as <u>hurried,</u> <u>walked,</u> and <u>wandered,</u> or we could replace the word <u>field</u> with other terms such as <u>park,</u> <u>game,</u> and <u>room</u> because these words are from the same type or form (verbs and noun objects respectively). This characteristic of extensive substitutability for the various parts of our language separates human language behavior from various forms of animal "language." Humans are capable of making these substitutions of one word for another. Animals, no matter how diligently they may try, cannot make these symbolic substitutions. A parrot, for example, can be taught to say, "Polly wants a cracker," but on its own, the parrot cannot voluntarily substitute other words to make a new utterance such as "Polly wants an ice cream cone." Thus, the ability of humans to substitute other words of the same type or form class is one of the characteristics of language that makes language usage exclusively a human activity.

LANGUAGE IS CONVENTIONAL

A group of people agree about how to use a language. This does not mean that the group meets as a body and decides how sentences will be formed or what words will be used to refer to what object or idea or event. Rather, it means that over time (in some cases even over centuries) people in a group have come to <u>use</u> language in like ways. These "conventions" thus identify what will be acceptable to that group.

Sometimes these conventions have been declared publicly and officially. Russia has 112 officially recognized languages. Indonesia's 150 million people speak 200 regional dialects and languages. In India, where Hindi is the official language, the constitution recognizes 16 regional languages and there are more than 1,650 additional languages and dialects. Ghana has more than 56 languages or dialects; Mexico's Indians speak more than 200. The nations of Europe have 28 official national languages. Latin Americans speak Spanish and Portuguese plus hundreds of Indian languages and dialects. Currently English serves as the common language of the educated and scientific world.

Other times what is to be the language of the group is difficult to determine. The Separatist movement in Canada which is urging Quebec to pull out of the nation developed because it has French as its language while the rest of Canada use English. The United States once was referred to as a "melting pot" in which diverse cultures and languages blended rapidly. However, in 1975 Congress amended the Voting Rights Act to require governments in some areas of the country to print ballots in languages ranging from Spanish to Aleut. Former Senator and semanticist S. I. Hayakawa in 1984 headed a group trying to require that all ballots be printed only in English which would be declared the sole official language of the United States. He explained his stand this way, "We can speak any language we want at the dinner table, but English is the language of public discourse, of the market place and the voting booth." Senator Walter D. Huddleston of Kentucky has proposed a constitutional amendment making English the only official language of the U.S. Supporters of this movement complain that separate languages would end the nation's cultural identity and lead to a situation paralleling Canada's problems with Quebec.

Once a given language is accepted by a group or culture, it becomes a very significant way to define that group or any member of the group. Furthermore, the language of the group or culture is perpetuated by its very social system so that each generation hands down that language to succeeding generations.

Of course, as with most conventions, language can change as long as the changes are accepted by the group. Words in a language can be changed relatively quickly. Certain words are "in," i.e., accepted and currently used; others become archaic, obsolete and not used. Grammatical structure may also change, but it happens much more slowly—for example, think of the changes in the English language from Elizabethan times to our contemporary usage.

LANGUAGE IS COMPLETE

When we say that a language is complete, we mean that it not only has a structure but that the users of a particular language are capable of making appropriate linguistic responses to any situation, even on the first occurrence of that situation. This does not mean that no new words will ever be needed or that we must keep all the words we have. In fact, we would expect that upon the occurrence of some unique event or experience, language is complete to the extent the individual language user would be perfectly capable of coining terminology to talk about the event. For example, as contemporary space and computer technology developed, new words were coined to refer to these new objects which hadn't previously existed.

LANGUAGE IS MEANINGFUL

Each set of verbal symbols (letters or sounds combined into various units) constituting a language has meaning associated with it. This set of verbal symbols and the various ways we use them to "mean" (to make sense of) things make human language different from all other animal "communication." Because this concept of meaning is so complex and also so important to our communication behavior, we will treat it more thoroughly in the next section.

MEANING

We will look now at two important aspects of meaning, the locus of meaning and types of meaning, in order to demonstrate the importance of meaning in our communicative attempts.

THE LOCUS OF MEANING

An assumption quite common among language users is that the meaning of words is contained within the words themselves. When we hear the question, "What does that word mean?" the questioner probably assumed that the meaning of words is contained within the words themselves — that the word has meaning inherent in it. In this sense a word would be a "container" of meaning much like a glass is a container for water, beer, or whatever liquid.

For the sake of illustration, if we assumed that the meanings of words were totally contained within the words themselves, then it would be possible for anyone to understand any message as long as the words/sounds were accurately received. There would be instant understanding since the words would "contain" the meanings—all the receiver would do would be to extract the meaning from the words. To communicate effectively with others, then, all that would be needed is to transmit words to the receiver, for as soon as the transmission is received, there would be instant understanding.

Think now of times when you've heard or perhaps used the phrase, "But I told you...." This phrase is almost always uttered when the "instant understanding" did not occur, when the message sender assumed that the message transmitted would be understood, but somehow it was not. What happened? If you assume meanings are in words, your only conclusion is that the receiver must be stupid. Of course, if you happen to be that person (and don't like to be called or thought of as stupid), you are likely to blame the sender for using the wrong words.

For this reason, we prefer to operate under the assumption that meanings exist largely within an individual so we take the position that **meanings of words are in part in people, not totally in words.** We believe that meaning is the "sense," we make of the sensory information received by our brains. We learn over time that a **verbal symbol** can be used as a convenient substitute or referent for events, people, or objects and we also learn to respond to those symbols. The meaning responses exist within us, though we may also learn certain external responses that are acceptable. As such, no two individuals will have exactly the same meaning for any particular verbal symbol. However, it is possible for individuals to have similar meanings. And, in fact, what we discover is that the more similar the meanings aroused between sender and receiver(s), the more effective the communication will be. If there is very little similarity, the

44

communication will be less than effective and probably very ineffective.

If we assume that meanings are largely in people, then we see why it is difficult to predict just exactly how any receiver will respond to any message, because the meaning that receiver has is so much created within his/her basic processing system. When we attribute meaning similarly, it is usually because of similarity in how we learned the response(s) from a shared culture. We will examine this cultural connection further in Chapter 4, but now will examine various types of meanings.

TYPES OF MEANING

There are at least four types of meaning which we as individuals can learn—connotative, denotative, structural, and contextual. We will consider each of these briefly in this section.

Connotative meaning refers to those personal, internal responses which are idiosyncratic to the individual. What is a "beautiful" person or day or object will depend entirely on the particular person and his/her situation. Thus, you might say, "What a beautiful day!" when the ground is covered with a foot of snow; another might use that sentence only if the temperature were in the 70s and the sky free of clouds.

The importance of connotative meanings for communication is that each of us must remember that our connotative meaning for any given symbol is just that — ours. It is never exactly the same as any other person's and it may actually be very different. We must be aware of the potential differences both when we send messages to others and when we receive messages from them.

Denotative meaning refers to those agreed-upon or conventional meanings for verbal symbols which develop in groups or cultures. Sometimes it is helpful to think of denotative meanings as referential meanings because we learn to use a symbol (along with others in our culture or group) to refer to the particular thing or object or person out there in the world. We can generally agree when we use the symbols "Washington Monument" that we refer to a particular structure which exists in Washington, D.C. And we usually agree that "chair" refers to a kind of object that we use to sit upon.

The referents we agree on are what we then record in our dictionaries as what a word "means." The farther away we are from having a specific referent for a symbol, the more difficult it is for people to agree on a meaning for a term and the more different "meanings" will be cited in the dictionary. For example, think of the symbols, "freedom," "love," "pornography," or even "is," and the many different referents for them.

Even though we agree on a referent, we nonetheless retain our individual feelings about the exhaustive trip up the actual steps of the Washington Monument and the exhilarating view from the top. Or, we remember about the hardness/softness of certain kinds of chairs and the comfort of our "own" particular chair at home. In other words, we always have some degree of connotative meaning associated with our agreed-upon denotative meanings.

Structural meaning was suggested earlier when language was described as structured or arranged in a sequence of recurrent patterns according to some systematic set of rules. As we learn a language, we acquire the necessary rules for putting words together in a meaningful fashion such that others will be able to understand what we say. The grammar of the language supplies us with these rules. The form or syntactical aspect of language, then, is another dimension of meaning.

This type of meaning does not refer to anything out there in reality, nor does it denote or connote anything. It merely helps us understand and sort out meanings for the communication. Thus, we can say that there is structural meaning when one symbol helps us to predict the occurrence of another symbol. One type of structural meaning, for example, is in terms of the agreement in number between words within a sentence, i.e., whether a word is singular or plural. In the sentence "All Xs are Ys," although we may have no denotative or connotative meanings for what "X" is, we do know that there are more than one of them because the pattern suggested by the structure of the suffix "s" means "more than one."

Another type of structural meaning is supplied by the ordering of words in a sentence, as with noun-verb combinations. When the verb precedes the subject-noun in a sentence, such as "Is Sally taking swimming lessons?" we interpret this sentence as a question. Further, the first word "is" helps us predict that a noun will follow and that the sentence will take the form of a question. When the verb follows the noun, as with "Sally is taking swimming lessons," the structure of the sentence indicates that this is a statement. Again, the first word "Sally" helps us predict that a verb will follow and that the sentence will be a statement rather than a question.

Contextual meaning is meaning which can be determined only through the context in which the word or combination of words is used. For example, the sentence, "The glass is broken," would have many different meanings depending upon the context or situation in which the statement is made. On its own, the meaning of the sentence, "The glass is broken," is difficult to determine. However, if a baseball were just hit through the neighbor's front window, we would interpret the sentence, "The glass is broken," as meaning that the window was closed and the baseball broke the window pane. In a different context, the sentence could have another meaning. For example, a child knocks a drinking glass to the floor, shattering the glass, and says, "The glass is broken." There is no way we can determine the meaning intended by this sentence by looking at what the terms refer to or at the structural aspects of the language. The intended meaning of this sentence cannot be determined out of the context in which it appears. The context influences the meaning of a message because of norms, goals, and expectations we have about what should occur in certain situations or contexts.

Thus far in this chapter, we have concentrated on verbal messages in the communication process. This is only part of the story, for remember that our definition of communication includes the use of verbal and/or nonverbal messages. In fact, many researchers argue that the "meaning" of messages is determined primarily through the use and interpretation of nonverbal behaviors. The remainder of this chapter will therefore be concerned with nonverbal symbolizing in the communication process.

NONVERBAL SYMBOLS

What is nonverbal communication? There are many popular definitions, such as "body language" and "body motion." However, nonverbal communication involves more than simply gestures, postures, and facial expressions. The purpose of the remainder of this chapter will be to discuss this important aspect of communication. First, we will define what is meant by nonverbal communication. Second, we will discuss the characteristics of nonverbal communication. Third, we will outline the various types of nonverbal symbols.

DEFINING NONVERBAL COMMUNICATION

Several authors distinguish between nonverbal behavior and nonverbal communication (Burgoon & Saine, 1978; Knapp, 1978; Malandro & Barker, 1983). The key difference is one of intent: for behaviors to be considered communication, the sender must either intend to send the message, or the receiver must interpret the message as intentional, or both. Thus, Burgoon and Saine (1978) define nonverbal communication as:

> those attributes or actions of humans, other than the use of words themselves, which have socially shared meaning, are intentionally sent or interpreted as intentional, are consciously sent or consciously received, and have the potential for feedback from the receiver (pp 9-10).

As with the definition of communication presented in Chapter 1, this definition of **nonverbal communication** emphasizes a purposeful exchange of messages between people who share some degree of similarity in meanings for the symbols used. Therefore, for an action to be considered nonverbal communication, it must involve messages expressed by means other than linguistic within the parameters of our definition of communication. Waving your hand in greeting at someone who does not see you, visualizing in your mind what your favorite kind of pizza tastes like, signalling to your dog to fetch a stick, and rapidly blinking your eye in reaction to a grain of sand in it, would all be considered nonverbal behaviors, but not nonverbal communication.

CHARACTERISTICS OF NONVERBAL SYMBOLS

In many ways, the nonverbal code system is similar to the verbal code system. Nonverbal communication shares some properties with language in that both are conventional, meaningful, structured, and composed of a set of discrete units. That is, like language, groups of people come to an agreement as to how nonverbal symbols are used (conventions), sets of nonverbal symbols have meanings associated with them, there are rules which structure how we use nonverbal symbols, and many nonverbal expressions can be identified as discrete units (frowns, head nods, hand gestures, for example). However, there are several ways in which nonverbal symbols are unique from language or verbal symbols. These unique characteristics of nonverbal symbols include ambiguity, universal forms, spontaneity, and simultaneous multiple message transmission (Burgoon, 1985).

The nonverbal messages we use in our exchanges with others are therefore more **ambiguous** and open to a greater range of interpretations than the words we may use. Whereas with verbal symbols when there is ambiguity or disagreements over denotative meanings, we can refer to a dictionary, there is no dictionary for nonverbal symbols. For example, how do we assign meaning to "lateness"? Suppose Henry has a meeting at 10:00 a.m. with his supervisor but he arrives at 10:30. How will the supervisor interpret Henry's lateness? If you were the supervisor, what would you think? Contrast this with the roles reversed: the supervisor arrives thirty minutes after the scheduled meeting time. How will Henry interpret the supervisor's lateness? As you can see from this simple, but very common, example, we would be mistaken to believe that nonverbal symbols have precise meanings which can be listed in a dictionary.

Although there is no dictionary for nonverbal symbols, there do appear to be some **universal forms** of nonverbal codes which share similar meanings across cultures (Burgoon, 1985; Knapp, 1978). These are nonverbal symbols which are recognized as having a universal meaning in a variety of cultures. Some emotional displays, such as crying in response to physical pain or embracing a long-lost relative, seem to be interpreted in similar ways in many cultures. For example, smiling is universally associated with friendship and goodwill. In this manner nonverbal communication can sometimes bridge cultural differences which language cannot.

Particularly in the larger American cultural context, nonverbal communication is relied on to express emotions. This is partly due to the greater **spontaneity** of nonverbal symbols. While our nonverbal symbol use may be consciously decided and carefully planned, as with our attire for a first date, much of our nonverbal communication involves immediate, rapid, and often automatic responses to particular stimuli. Thus, upon seeing your favorite cousin who has been in Europe for three years, you probably don't think beforehand, "When I see Patti, I'm going to give her a big hug." Rather, that hug is spontaneously given as an emotional response of affection and joy.

Finally, nonverbal communication can involve all the senses, allowing for the transmission of several messages at the same time. This unique characteristic of the nonverbal code system is called **simultaneous multiple message transmission.** With language, we are confined to the visual (reading), aural (spoken), or tactile (Braille) channels of communication, with words presented in a linear fashion. With nonverbal messages, transmission can be via several channels at the same time, and multiple messages may be transmitted simultaneously along the same sensory channel. For example, you may smile, exclaim, "Patti, it's just great to see you!" and hug your cousin all at the same time, using facial expressions, tone of voice, and touch to convey your pleasure at seeing Patti. However, if Patti really isn't one of your favorite cousins, you may give her a hug, yet neither smile nor use an enthusiastic tone of voice in saying hello. In this case, the messages are conveying different meanings, with the hug indicating the importance of this kinship tie, but the lack of a friendly facial expression or energy in your voice indicating that you may be less than thrilled about seeing this relative.

Verbal and nonverbal code systems have several features in common: 1) a group of people agree about how the symbols are to be used and therefore follow **conventions** or like ways in acceptable symbol use; 2) **meanings** associated with sets of symbols are socially shared; 3) **structure** is provided by rules which govern symbol use; and 4) **discrete units** can be identified within the symbol systems. In addition to these similar characteristics, nonverbal communication has some unique properties, including ambiguity, universal forms, spontaneity, and simultaneous multiple message transmission. It is these unique characteristics of nonverbal communication which make it both an interesting and difficult area to study. Distinguishing among the different types or classes of nonverbal symbols will provide a clearer understanding of the immense task facing the student of nonverbal communication.

TYPES OF NONVERBAL SYMBOLS

In any field, discipline, or area of inquiry, colleagues develop terminology, sometimes called jargon, which enables them to more precisely discuss the phenomena under study. We have already introduced you to some of the terms communication scholars and researchers use in exchanging their ideas about how people communicate. This section will introduce you to several key terms which are used to identify the various types of nonverbal symbols individuals use in constructing messages. These types of nonverbal symbols include: 1) kinesics, 2) proxemics, 3) haptics, 4) chronemics, 5) physical appearance, 6) artifacts, and 7) paralanguage. While several of these terms may be unfamiliar to you and sound like unnecessary jargon, they are important in understanding and clearly differentiating among the numerous types of nonverbal symbols we use everyday.

Kinesics

Kinesics refers to the study of body motion (Burgoon, 1985; Knapp 1978; Malandro & Barker, 1983). Many people associate all nonverbal communication with this one class of nonverbal symbols, but as we have noted, kinesics is just one type of nonverbal communication.

Gestures, facial expressions, posture, and eye gaze are included within kinesics. Smiling, head nodding, waving a hand in greeting, slouching in a chair, and making infrequent eye contact with others, are all forms of kinesics. This class of nonverbal symbols has received considerable attention, particularly from those researchers interested in interpersonal communication contexts. For example, researchers have examined nonverbal cues which seem to indicate interpersonal warmth and closeness (Andersen, 1985). Head nods, smiling, an increased use of gestures, and an open, relaxed body position are all ways in which individuals in Western cultures such as the U.S. indicate affiliation and interpersonal closeness.

49

Many of the "popular" books on nonverbal symbols are concerned with kinesics. These authors typically present ways to "read" body language. However, we have already seen that a particular nonverbal cue may result in numerous interpretations. For example, most Americans associate eye contact with self-confidence and demonstrating interest in a conversation. However, in some cultures, holding the eye gaze of another is seen as disrespectful (Burgoon, 1985). In order to interpret kinetic behaviors, as with all nonverbal symbols, it is necessary to know the cultural and contextual norms in which the nonverbal symbols are used.

Proxemics

The study of how we use space in communicating with others is called **proxemics** (Burgoon, 1985; Hall, 1966; Knapp, 1978). Research in this area is concerned with the use and perceptions of social and personal space, particularly the influence of culture on proxemic behavior.

Each of us carries with us in our daily interactions a bubble of space which we keep between ourselves and others. This invisible bubble is called our **personal space** (Burgoon & Saine, 1978; Hall, 1959; Malandro & Barker, 1983). The distance we place between ourselves and other communicaters is not fixed. Rather, it is flexible, depending on our relationship with the other person, setting for the interaction, and cultural norms. Thus, with family members, our personal space may shrink considerably and we probably won't mind if our space is "invaded" by a pat on the arm or hug from Mom. On the other hand, the size of our personal space may be quite large as we walk along an unfamiliar street. Being bumped or jostled by a stranger would very definitely be considered an invasion of our personal space, and a hug or pat on the arm would be considered a serious affront and clear violation of the norms which govern how we use space.

In addition to personal space, proxemics is also concerned with how space is used and defined socially. Hall (1966) has identified four **interaction zones,** labeled intimate, personal, social, and public. These interaction zones are the distances which communicators attempt to keep between themselves in various situations. Hall (1966) suggests that the different zones indicate the relationship between participants and how they feel about each other.

The first interaction zone is from zero to 18 inches and is what Hall (1966) calls the **intimate distance.** We usually reserve this distance for those with whom we are emotionally close: spouse, girl/boyfriend, family members, and close friends. At this distance, we typically discuss topics which we consider quite private and personal, such as our love or caring for the other person. If someone moves within this range without our consent, we usually feel uncomfortable, as in a crowded elevator or bus.

The second interaction zone, the **personal distance** is from 18 inches to four feet. This is the distance within which we usually interact in face-to-face situations with friends and less-immediate family members. For example, Hall (1966) observes that in a public setting, a woman may, and is often expected to, stand next to her husband within the personal distance. The husband's female colleague, however, would not be expected to stand within this distance, and if she did, others would judge her behavior to be inappropriate.

Hall also notes that communicators interacting within the personal distance typically talk about areas of personal interest and involvement. We would expect, for example, two friends to discuss problems they're having with their roommates, and even offer each other advice, within the personal distance of interaction. Test this for yourself: Whom do you interact with in the personal distance? What do you usually talk about? When do you consider it inappropriate for others to enter into this spatial distance? How do you react?

From four to twelve feet is the interaction zone which Hall calls the **social distance.** Much of our daily interactions take place within this distance, particularly at work and school. Employment interviews, exchanges with salespeople, and supervisor/subordinate interactions are examples of conversations which usually take place within the social distance. Communicators interact with others within their social roles, such as bank teller and customer or teacher and student. Conversation centers on topics of less personal interest, such as the task to be accomplished, the weather, or a current issue in sports.

The last interaction zone, the **public distance,** includes exchanges which occur from twelve feet up to the human range of hearing or seeing. Classroom lectures, the keynote speaker at a political convention, and a public hearing on changing local zoning ordinances are examples of interactions which occur within the public distance.

These four interaction zones which Hall identified are not universal. Rather, cultural norms indicate the appropriate distances for various interaction situations in that culture. We will discuss cultural norms in greater depth in Chapter 4. However, the different interaction zones do highlight one way in which we use space in our interactions with others.

Haptics

Haptics refers to those nonverbal symbols which involve touching behaviors or tactile communication. Whom we touch, where and how we touch others, and our intentions in touching or not touching others, convey messages to those with whom we interact. Purposefully not touching someone, such as refusing the offer of a handshake, conveys a message as much as touching someone, shaking the other person's hand, does.

While the interpretation of touching behaviors is generally tied to cultural norms, research has suggested a universal relationship between touching and attitudes (Malandro & Barker, 1983). In expressing emotions, a willingness to touch others with a hug or a kiss, is viewed as an indication of positive attitudes and feelings toward the other person. Refusing to touch the other is viewed as an expression of negative attitudes and feelings.

How much we touch others varies with a number of factors, including culture, age, gender, and ethnic background. Americans are typically described as avoiding tactile contact with others. Malandro and Barker (1983) claim that we live in a "noncontact culture" as compared with other countries such as France. Amount of

"Touch-Me-Not" Has Plenty of Company

Dear Abby: The person signed "Touch-Me-Not" would fit into my family very well. Being Scandinavian, we are not as demonstrative in public as people of other nationalities. Unless we haven't seen each other for a long period of time, even family members do not like to be hugged or kissed. That goes for hugging and kissing children, too. And then we do it only in private.

I have an excellent relationship with my grown children and their spouses, but we seldom touch each other. Being grabbed, clutched or jabbed would be unbearable for us. Luckily most of our friends are of Scandinavian descent, and wouldn't think of doing something like that. — Another Untouchable

Dear Untouchable: Touch-me-not behavior is not a problem, unless, of course, a cool, immovable Scandinavian encounters an irresistible, affectionate, Latin, Semite or European type.

However, conversions have been known to occur, and I dare say it would be easier to warm up a Scandinavian than to cool off a hot-blooded Hungarian.

Dear Abby: The letter about "Touch-Me-Nots" touched me where I live. However, your answer was too gentle. You should advise everyone who is grabbed, clutched or jabbed to punch the jerk in the mouth and knock out his two front teeth, and here is why: A fellow worker playfully jabbed me in the stomach with his thumb with such force that three days later I had to see a doctor, who informed me that I was bleeding internally! It took four pints of blood and a 20-day stay in the hospital, not to mention the hospital bill and a loss of work for a month.

My stupid brother-in-law, when greeting me, punches me so hard on the upper arms, I suffer black-and-blue marks that last for three weeks. If he is behind me, he jabs me in the kidney area and I am in terrific pain for a week.

So, Dear Abby, please encourage victims of these idiots who grab, clutch and jab to fight back by kicking them in the shins and punching them in the mouth to see how they like it.

If, by printing this letter, you save just one person from the torment I have endured, you will have taken a giant step forward for mankind. — Edward D., Springdale, Pa.

What is considered to be appropriate touching behavior varies considerably with cultural, group, and family norms.

touching behavior also changes with age. Babies are usually touched often, while touching the elderly is frequently avoided (Knapp, 1978). Several studies have found that women tend to initiate touch more than men, and that women touch women more than men touch men (Hall, 1985). In comparing the touching behaviors of blacks and whites, researchers have found that blacks exhibit more touching behaviors than whites regardless of the age group studied (Halberstadt, 1985).

Chronemics

How long will you wait in the reception area to see a physician for a check-up you had scheduled two months previously? How long will you wait for a friend who was supposed to meet you at a restaurant for dinner? How long will you wait for an interviewee to arrive for a scheduled job interview? Studying the use of time and how these nonverbal cues are interpreted is called **chronemics.**

The use and meaning of time are very much culture-bound. Some societies are **past-oriented** in that they place a great deal of emphasis on tradition and what has happened in the past (Malandro & Barker, 1983). These cultures, such as the British, look to their history and traditional ways of behaving in order to understand and guide actions in similar present situations.

Present-oriented cultures are concerned with events in the here-and-now and making the most of the present moment. Malandro and Barker (1983) cite Filipinos and Latin Americans as examples of cultures which emphasize spontaneity and the immediacy of events. These cultures do not ignore entirely the past or future, but they place the greatest importance on "living for today" rather than reliving the past or making elaborate plans for the future.

The United States is a good example of a **future-oriented** society. Americans stress the need to work hard today in order to build a bigger and better tomorrow. Whereas past-oriented cultures emphasize the following of traditions, future-oriented cultures view traditions as "stuffy" and constraining, and seek out what is new and different from what was done in the past. The contrast between past- and future-oriented societies can be seen in the traditional Navajo respect for the wisdom of tribal elders and the dominant American culture which prizes the wisdom of youth. Further, Andersen (1985) argues that, "Time is viewed as a commodity in America that can be wasted, saved, spent, and used as if it were money" (p 11).

As with other types of nonverbal symbols, the use and meaning of time is bound to the cultural and immediate context in which communication occurs. How long we will wait for someone then, is a function of cultural norms, the situation, and our relationship with the other person.

Physical Appearance

Clothing, hairstyle, jewelry and make-up are examples of our features which we can manipulate or change in our **physical appearance.** We define this class of nonverbal symbols as including only those aspects of our physical appearance which we can readily manipulate, and exclude those which are considered nonmanipuliable, such as height and body shape (Burgoon, 1985).

"Clothing makes the person," may be a cliche, but how we dress is an important aspect of impression formation. We associate what people wear, hairstyles, and various adornments with social class, political philosophies, religious convictions, intelligence, and numerous personality characteristics. Probably the best example of the role of physical appearance in the communication process is the employment interview. Numerous books and articles have been written which detail how to "dress for success," both in gaining entry to an organization and moving up the corporate ladder.

Artifacts

Anthropologists usually examine a culture's artifacts to learn about the characteristics, values, beliefs, and organization of that culture. **Artifacts** are those objects and environmental features which can be manipulated or changed. These artifacts may convey messages about the designers and/or users of the objects (Burgoon, 1985). Buerkel–Rothfuss (1985) describes three types of artifacts: personal, shared, and public.

Personal artifacts include objects which may be used for our physical appearance, such as clothing, cosmetics, and perfume, and other personal belongings, such as cherished knick–knacks and family photograph albums. Personal artifacts generally belong to one individual and are viewed as reflecting that person's values, interests, and personality. While two siblings may share the same bedroom, it is often possible to determine who has which side of the room from the personal artifacts, such as posters, books, and clothing, of each child.

Shared artifacts belong to more than one individual and include objects such as furniture, household items, and automobiles which we share with others. Thus, the dresser, bunkbeds, and desks in the siblings' room first used by older siblings and eventually to be handed down to the next generation in the family, are shared artifacts. The family car, stereo, television, and home computer are other examples of shared artifacts.

The artifacts that a group or a culture shares are called **public artifacts.** Objects which are for public use or observation, such as schools, restaurants, national parks, and shopping malls, are considered public artifacts. These artifacts convey information about a particular group or culture. In addition, public artifacts, as objects in our environment, influence communication. For example, classrooms in which chairs or desks are bolted to the floor inhibit interaction among students, whereas moveable chairs or desks allow students to interact with greater ease.

Paralanguage

Paralinguistics is the study of vocal cues in the communication process. **Paralanguage** refers to vocal behaviors in oral communication other than the words used. Paralanguage, or vocalics, includes **voice qualities** such as pitch, pauses, articulation, and tempo, and **vocalizations** such as laughing, crying, "umm," and "uh-huh." The nonverbal aspects of the human voice convey messages about our emotional states and the strength of our emotions. Exclaiming, "I'm so happy you called!" in a cheerful tone of voice conveys a much different message than sarcastically saying, "I'm so happy you called." Voice qualities and vocalizations are more than simply how we say something, for as Knapp (1978) argues, paralinguistic cues "frequently...are what is said" (p. 361). Speaking loudly, whispering, laughing, and crying are as much the content of our messages as the words we may use.

Paralinguistic cues are also used to identify demographic and various other characteristics of the people who use them. Rate, inflection, and enunciation in speaking vary not only from culture to culture, but also within cultures. Broadcasters, such as national television news anchors, usually speak without a noticeable regional accent. This is thought to broaden the newscaster's appeal, in that s/he is not associated specifically with, for example, New England or the South. We also use paralinguistic cues to identify whether a person whose voice we hear over the phone is old/young, female/male, black/white, well-educated/uneducated, etc. In addition we evaluate the competence of speakers based on their paralinguistic cues. For example, public speakers who frequently use vocalized pauses such as "errr," "uhh," and "umm," are viewed as less competent and more anxious than those whose speech flows more smoothly (Malandro & Barker, 1983).

Classifying nonverbal symbols provides us with terminology for identifying and discussing types of nonverbal cues. However, it is somewhat misleading to treat verbal and nonverbal symbols separately in that interpreting the meaning of the messages we exchange usually involves consideration of verbal and nonverbal cues. The final section of this chapter will therefore examine the ways in which verbal and nonverbal symbols are related.

RELATIONSHIP OF VERBAL AND NONVERBAL SYMBOLS

Verbal and nonverbal code systems are interrelated in several ways. Nonverbal symbols can repeat, substitute for, complement, accent, regulate, or contradict verbal symbols (Knapp, 1978). These relationships may exist singly or several may occur simultaneously.

Nonverbal symbols may **repeat** the words which are used in an interaction. When Carla says, "The picture I need a frame for is 16 by 24 inches," and uses her hands to demonstrate the approximate size of the picture, her hand gesture repeats what she has said. The sales clerk who responds to Carla by shaking his head as he says, "I'm sorry, we don't have the size picture frame you need," is also using nonverbal symbols to repeat what was said.

Sometimes we use nonverbal messages in place of verbal messages. In this case, nonverbal symbols **substitute for** verbal symbols. Nodding your head in agreement, waving at a friend on the other side of the cafeteria, or shrugging your shoulders in response to a question are all ways in which nonverbal cues may substitute for words.

Nonverbal symbols which indicate the relationship between interactants serve to **complement** or add to the meaning of verbal symbols. That is, they need not repeat the verbal cues, but instead they function to better fit the message to the situation. In this manner, nonverbal cues provide information about degrees of liking, dominance, and interaction interest between communicators. For example, an employee who speaks to his/her supervisor softly and hesitantly with downcast eyes, slouched shoulders, and few hand gestures is indicating little interest in the interaction and less power than the supervisor. The supervisor, standing behind a desk, speaking in a loud, clear voice, and looking steadily at the subordinate indicates both higher status and greater interest in the interaction. When the supervisor ends the conversation by offering to shake hands and the employee ignores the extended hand and leaves the supervisor's office, the employee's nonverbal cues suggest a disliking of the supervisor.

We also use nonverbal cues such as gestures, tone of voice, and facial expressions to underscore, reinforce or italicize verbal cues or to **accent**. Emphasizing particular words by raising your voice, pointing to yourself to stress that what you are saying is your own opinion, and hugging your best friend as you say, "It's great to see you," are all ways in which we nonverbally accent what we say.

How do you know when it's your turn to talk in a conversation? Usually, the other person doesn't say, "I'm finished with my utterance, now you can speak." We rely on nonverbal cues to **regulate** the flow of talk in our interactions. Initiating, ending and turn-taking in conversations are controlled primarily through nonverbal means. A shift in posture, pausing, increasing or decreasing eye contact, and change in vocal volume serve as cues for regulating conversation. For example, when we can't quite think of what to say next, we may use vocalizations such as "umm," or "ah" to indicate to the other person that we do not yet wish to relinquish the floor. In ending a conversation, we may decrease eye contact, glance at our watch, and begin tapping our fingers on the table to convey the message to the other that it is time to leave.

Finally, nonverbal symbols may **contradict** verbal symbols. Researchers have found that when nonverbal cues are perceived as contradicting the accompanying verbal symbols, communicators will rely on their interpretations of the nonverbal cues for the meaning of the message (Malandro & Baker 1983). This stems from the belief that it is easier for us to control our words than our actions. Thus, we focus on nonverbal symbols in attempting to detect when others are trying to deceive us (Zuckerman & Driver, 1985). For example, most Americans interpret the avoidance of eye contact, while claiming one's innocence, as an indication of lying. As another example, if a husband says to his wife, "Of course I care about you," in a loud, sharp tone of voice and stomps out of the room, his wife will probably doubt the truthfulness of her husband's words. Asserting, "I'm not nervous about speaking at the conference," with a quaking voice, a slight grimace, and trembling hands, is another example of nonverbal cues contradicting the verbal symbols used.

In our interactions with others, nonverbal symbols, then, serve six functions in relationship to verbal symbols: nonverbal symbols may repeat, substitute for, complement, accent, regulate, or contradict verbal symbols. Examining the relationships between verbal and nonverbal symbols in the communication process is important in understanding how we interpret the meaning of messages.

SUMMARY

In this chapter, we have discussed the verbal and nonverbal symbolic foundations of the communication process. All languages as verbal code systems share the characteristics of: 1) being composed of a set of sounds or phonemes, 2) arbitrarily linking sound combinations and referents, 3) structure, 4) convention, 5) completeness, and 6) meaningfulness. The characteristic of meaningfulness is particularly important when examining the exchange of verbal messages in communication. Because the meanings of words exist primarily within each person, no two individuals have <u>exactly</u> the same meaning for a particular word. This can make it difficult to predict how others will respond to our messages and attempts at interaction. Furthermore, complexity of linguistic meaning can be seen in the four types of meaning discussed: connotative, denotative, structural and contextual.

Nonverbal code systems are also structured, conventional, meaningful, and composed of discrete units, but they are considered more ambiguous, spontaneous, universal and also multiple nonverbal messages may be transmitted simultaneously. While words may have multiple meanings, we can consult a dictionary for the denotative meaning or meanings of a particular word. We have no "dictionary" for nonverbal symbols.

Although verbal and nonverbal symbols are often discussed separately, we have seen six ways in which the verbal and nonverbal messages we use may be related. Nonverbal cues may repeat, substitute for, complement, accent, regulate, and contradict verbal messages.

Much of our discussion of symbolic processes in this chapter has included the necessity of understanding the cultural context in which communication occurs. The next chapter will be concerned with cultural foundations of communication.

KEY TERMS

verbal symbols	kinesics
phoneme	proxemics
referent	chronemics
phonological structure	physical appearance
grammatical structure	artifacts
denotative meaning	paralanguage
conotative meaning	personal space
contextual meaning	interaction zone
structural meaning	haptics
nonverbal symbols	

CHAPTER 4

CHAPTER 4

CULTURAL FOUNDATIONS OF COMMUNICATION

Much of our information-processing is influenced by expectations we have developed from our experiences as part of one or more cultures. A culture provides each of its members with: a set of shared beliefs, attitudes, and values about the world around it; a language or a particular accepted way to use a language; and a set of rules for how we are expected to behave and to communicate in various situations. The size of the culture is not important, for a culture may include a very large number of people, such as a whole nation, or a very small group. The geographic boundaries are also not important, for one geographic area may actually involve many different cultures as in large metropolitan areas. **The key factor is a shared set of beliefs, language, and rules for interacting — all of which are learned and internalized individually.**

Sometimes we learn about our culture very explicitly. Our parents, teachers, or friends may say clearly things like "good girls don't do that" or "don't pick your nose in public" or "we don't say 'ain't'." Other times we learn about our culture implicitly; that is, we only infer what is appropriate from watching how other people react to us or someone else. Much of what we learn to accept as appropriate nonverbal behaviors we learn only in this implicit way. Furthermore, we may not be aware that we have these cultural expectations until we come up against someone who doesn't do things the way they're "supposed to be done" which is, of course, the way we've learned them in our own culture.

In our daily lives we encounter situations which vary in the degree to which they are "scripted" or defined by our culture. For example, the procedures for ordering a Big Mac at McDonald's are highly ritualized or scripted. There is little variation in how customers and counter personnel interact. Other situations, however, are less clearly defined, as with first meeting one's future in-laws. Here, communication is less scripted and the cultural rules which guide interaction are more open to negotiation by the participants.

This chapter focuses on those cultural factors which influence how we process information and communicate with others both as senders and receivers of messages. The two key concepts which will serve to frame our discussion are **cultural scripts** and **speech events.** In examining these terms, we will see how our culture provides us with a shared system of beliefs and rules which guide our communication with others. Without this shared system, communication would be both troublesome and anxious.

CULTURAL SCRIPTS FOR COMMUNICATION

Our culture provides us with beliefs about everything from the nature of God to the proper way to drive cars, eat, and drink. Anthropologists and sociologists usually study the full range of influences of culture on thinking and behavior. As people studying communication we are most interested in those features of culture that influence the way we speak to one another.

Whenever we talk about the influence of culture on our communication we need to remind ourselves how the very language used by a particular culture or group influences not only how they communicate with each other but how they process information. Whorf (1956) described this connection as so pervasive that we can't legitimately separate our language from the way we perceive, think, and experience our environment. We have come to call this the **Whorf-Sapir hypothesis.** The notion then, will obviously make it difficult for us to communicate effectively whenever they communicate with people whose native language, culture, and experiences are different from our own.

In addition to the influence of language on thinking, we need to examine those cultural rules that govern how we use language in communication. These rules are organized, in part, in terms of different speech events which occur in cultures. A **speech event** is a frequently occurring and important context for communication in a culture organized by shared rules for how communication is to be conducted in that context (Coulthard, 1977; Hymes, 1972). In American culture the sermon, the lecture, and social conversation are all familar speech events.

What is most important here is that the culture in which we've grown up and the various institutions (church, school, etc.) in which we've developed provide us with guidelines about how to communicate in a speech event. We call this set of shared rules or guidelines **cultural scripts.** These scripts indicate appropriate ways in which we are to communicate in a particular speech event. For example, we would expect people to communicate differently in the speech event "political rally" than in the speech event "committee meeting." This is because we have different cultural scripts or set of shared rules for appropriate communication behavior in a political rally and in a committee meeting. The cultural script for a speech event, such as a committee meeting, will vary from culture to culture.

COMPONENTS OF SPEECH EVENTS

A speech event is organized around nine components: setting, channel, participants, relationships, purpose, key, topic, norms of interaction, and norms of interpretation (Coulthard, 1977). Cultural scripts provide us with guidelines for each of these components of a speech event. Considering the components separately will illustrate the critical role of culture in our everyday communication with others.

SETTING

The **setting** of a speech event is the time and place in which the speech event occurs. For many speech events there are clear cultural rules for the very setting in which the event occurs. Lectures are expected to occur in classrooms or lecture halls. So if a professor lectured regularly in a small seminar room s/he would be stretching the rules for lecture settings. Furthermore, if the professor were to try to lecture while at a party, even if the others present were students, people would not only regard the activity as inappropriate, but also would try to explain the behavior (s/he must be drunk) and perhaps even impose sanctions (not invite the "weirdo" to any more parties).

CHANNEL

There are many channels for communication: spoken or oral, nonverbal, written, television, and/or even tribal drums. The **channel** used in a speech event is the form, mode, or medium for transmission of the message. In America we expect Presidential State of the Union messages to be communicated through the channel of television. We do not expect the President to send that message in a personal letter mailed to each of us. To use a channel that is not expected would likely arouse our attention. For example, in business environments most types of upper management-to-employee communication are done in writing, so that if the boss stops by for a verbal chat, we assume "something big is up." Thus, cultural scripts not only provide us with shared rules concerning the setting of a particular speech event, but also the channel of communication which is to be used.

PARTICIPANTS

Some of the most powerful and interesting rules governing speech events define how many participants are needed for the event as well as who can be acceptable participants. Conversation as a speech event in American culture requires at least two participants. Very young children, egocentric in nature and relatively unsocialized, routinely violate this rule and carry on conversations outloud with themselves. An adult, however, who consistently violates this conversational "rule" may find him/herself referred to a psychiatrist.

Some speech events require participants of a particular age, gender, kinship, status, or profession. In middle-class American culture the disciplining of children is done by parents, although the rules can be stretched at times to allow other kin, like grandparents, to do so. However, woe to neighbors who take it upon themselves to severely discipline another's child. Likewise, sermons are typically delivered only by some official of a church, who is identified by a title, special education, ordination, and, until recently, male. Some churches have speech events called "lay" sermons conducted by regular church members, but the very need to provide a separate label for such events defines it as an exception to the typical "sermon" event.

In other speech events the script allows anyone to participate as long as s/he will adopt a certain role and behave in a certain way. Anyone can be a student in the speech event called "teaching" as long as s/he functions primarily as a listener and does not take over the stage at the front of the room, a role presumed only for the teacher.

RELATIONSHIPS

Cultural scripts for speech events often not only define who is to participate but the kind of **relationship** that is to exist between the participants. The degree of intimacy, equality, competitiveness or cooperativeness, dominance, trust, affection, etc., that participants are expected to create in their relationship as they conduct the event is often highly rule-governed. For example, in most "selling" speech events in our culture the salesperson and buyer are expected to create and maintain a competitive, non-intimate, neutral, non-trusting relationship.

PURPOSE

Speech events also imply a particular **purpose** or goal. Participants share an understanding of why they are communicating. An old-fashioned revival is held to save souls. A person who attends and then complains to others because s/he learned nothing new about the historical evolution of the scriptures or a preacher who concludes the revival by passing a petition to save historical landmarks in the community is ripe for excommunication from the cultural community. The shared perception of purpose is important because participants will interpret most everything that occurs in light of or in relation to that expected purpose.

KEY

The **key** of a speech event is the tone or manner in which participants are to communicate. Many speech events are expected to be conducted in a certain key or tone, with different degrees of reverence, seriousness, formality, joviality, even anger. The cultural requirements for key are met largely through nonverbal channels. We dress a certain way, speak in a certain tone of voice, assume certain postures and facial expressions, all to create the appropriate key for the event. The student who offers his/her contributions to class discussions in a sarcastic, angry tone of voice, while sprawled out in the chair with feet propped on the seat in front of him/her is asking for sanctions from the professor and fellow students who are properly socialized about the appropriate key for classroom discussions.

TOPIC

For some speech events there is a **topic** or specific range of topics seen as appropriate for discussion. Violation of topical rules typically causes embarassment, anxiety, and even anger. Consider the event of a "funeral ceremony." The topics for communication in such an event are expected to be the deceased's life, accomplishments, relations with family and friends, etc. However, at a recent funeral the minister began on topic but quickly changed the topic to the salvation of the souls of those attending. "She was ready to meet her maker, are you?" he said, and launched into a hell-fire-and-brimstone oration.   Not only did he introduce an inappropriate topic, his new key (loud and aggressive) violated the reverent one expected for this event. Family and friends moved uneasily in their seats and afterwards expressed considerable anger about the minister's behavior.

They, like most of us, were not consciously aware of all the rules provided by the cultural context for this speech event. But, like all of us, they certainly noticed and responded to the violation of those deeply ingrained rules. In fact, largely because these "rules" have become ingrained in us so we don't need to talk about them explicitly, our reaction is likely to be very emotional — the other person has violated us.

NORMS OF INTERPRETATION AND INTERACTION

These last two components of speech events are grouped together because they are somewhat different in nature from the others. While generally there are different rules for topic, participants, etc., for different speech events, some norms of interpretation and interaction are applied across varieties of speech events. Others are, like the rules for the other components, specific to a particular speech event. Here we will explain both types of norms. In Chapters 5 and 6 we will point to their significance for interpersonal interactions.

Norms of interpretation are shared guidelines which help each of us determine the meaning of particular communication messages and behavior. Some of these norms take the following form: if person A does/says X in speech event Y, then interpret X to mean Z. Such a norm is tied to a particular speech event. We have a shared **speech event-specific norm of interpretation** for a behavior. For example, if a person raises his/her hand in the air, how would we interpret the behavior? If a student does so during a classroom interaction, most likely the student wants to speak. Seeing the same behavior by people in a film of a Nazi rally during World War II, we would employ an entirely different norm of interpretation. Similarily, if the bride's father began crying during the wedding ceremony, we would probably interpret that behavior as "tears of joy" rather than "tears of sorrow." That same crying behavior during a funeral ceremony, however, would be interpreted much differently.

Other norms for interpreting the meaning of messages seem to cut across many, if not all, speech events. These shared guidelines for determining the meaning of particular communication behaviors are termed **universal norms of interpretation.** For example, there is a universal norm of interpretation which tells us when to interpret a statement, wherever it occurs, as a request for us to do something.   That norm tells us to hear a statement as a "request" if we think the person speaking believes: 1) there is a need for the action requested; 2) we would not do the action without the request; 3) we have the ability to comply; 4) we have an obligation or are at least willing to comply; and/or 5) the speaker has the right to make the request. If any of these conditions are not met, then we typically will not interpret the statement as a request. For example, if someone asks us to do something they know we cannot do (violating condition 3), we most often would hear that not as a request but as a put down. If an employee requests something of the boss that s/he has no right to request (#5), the boss will not hear the statement as a legitimate request but most likely as an act of insubordination.

Norms of interaction are cultural guidelines which govern when, how, and how often we should speak. As with norms of interpretation, there are universal norms of interaction which apply in many or all the speech events of a cultural community, and there are norms of interaction which are specific to particular speech events.

Some **universal norms of interaction** govern how often we speak in speech events within a culture. For example, the norms of some cultures, as with the American middle-class, greatly value speaking and encourage its use in a wide variety of situations. Other cultures do not value speaking, especially if done in great quantities, because they view it as demeaning or even dangerous to the maintenance of social harmony. These types of norms of interaction cut across speech events within the culture, influencing <u>when</u> and <u>how often</u> people even engage in communication. So, if a person from middle-class American culture attempts to communicate with someone from a culture such as the Navajo which does not value quantity of speech, the participants may experience many problems in communication.

Other norms of interaction which seem to cut across entire cultural communities refer to <u>how</u> the participants should interact. For example, many studies have shown members of particular cultures to prefer a particular physical distance, volume, and use of touching behavior in their interactions. Differences between cultures in these norms of interaction can lead to serious misunderstandings. One study (Watson & Graves, 1966) compared the interaction norms of Arab and American students and found that Arab students preferred being closer to one another, speaking more loudly and touching more than American students, interaction behavior which the American students then interpreted as abnormal and aggressive.

Other interaction norms seem to be tied to **specific speech events.** For example, consider how we end informal conversations with others. This "closing" or "leave-taking" is very patterned in middle-class North American culture. You know that it is not appropriate just to "stop talking" when the time comes to close a conversation. You, in cooperation with your partner, must negotiate a closing consistent with norms of appropriateness for this situation. Failure to follow these rules and patterns can lead others to see you as rude, abrupt, or, at the very least, a strange and unpredictable conversationalist.

In closing a conversation, you typically should do three things verbally. First, provide some comment <u>summarizing</u> the conversation. The summary comment may be a simple statement of some adage or truism with which the other person can agree as with, "Well things always work out for the best, I guess." A more detailed summary of what has been said in the conversation may also be given, such as, "We seem to have covered all the important points for preparing for the meeting tomorrow. I'll be opening the discussion, then you'll present the proposal, and I'll close with a demonstration of the impact this ad campaign can have. I think we have everything in order."

Second, closings usually involve some indication of the <u>degree of access</u> to one another communicators will have in the future. "I think we should talk again before the week is out;" or "I'm going to be tied up for a while, maybe lunch before I leave on vacation?" indicate to the other when and under what general circumstances future communication will take place.

Finally, some statement of <u>supportiveness</u> about the conversation or the relationship with the other person is usually called for. "This has been great. I always enjoy our chats," and "It's been good to see you. We should get together more often," are statements which indicate support for the conversation and the participants' relationship. This type of statement is very much a part of the American middle-class leave-taking ritual.

Not all closings must have all these verbal components, but a closing which lacks all three will typically be seen as abrupt because it violates the norms of interaction for verbal behavior in conversational closing. Closings also frequently involve the use of internal and external legitimizers for ending the conversation. These are regularly used when summary, access, and supportiveness statements fail to bring the conversation to a close. An **internal legitimizer** provides an explicit reason for ending. This reason is something for which that person is solely responsible. For example, the statement, "Well, I've got a 2:00 o'clock appointment, so I guess we'd better wind this up," provides an example of an internal legitimizer.

External legitimizers offer reasons for closing that are external to the person wishing to end the conversation. Often the reasons are relevant to the other person such as, "I know you are busy so I won't take up any more of your time." This type of legitimizer is often used by people of lower power or status who want to end a conversation with a higher status person. For a "low" to use an internal legitimizer is often seen as an affront to the "high" and thus a violation of relationship rules.

In addition to the norms for appropriate verbal behavior in closings, there are norms governing appropriate nonverbal behavior. In setting the stage for closing you typically will: 1) decrease the amount of eye contact with the other person; 2) increase the physical distance between you (if you are standing); and 3) engage in increased head nodding. When you are seated during a conversation you typically begin to close by making major shifts in body position, such as leaning forward in the chair, or by making sweeping movements with your hands while planting your feet squarely on the floor, often placing your hands on your knees or the arms of the chair as if to rise.

Again, not every closing involves all of these cues, but some combination is required to set the stage for closing. People who violate these verbal and nonverbal norms of interaction for closing conversations will be noticed. Particular attributions made about the person will vary depending on the situation but they are most often negative and they are likely to result in some kind of sanction against that person.

It is possible to break the rules intentionally to accomplish some purpose. For example, you may use an internal legitimizer with a teacher or boss because you <u>do</u> have a 2:00 o'clock appointment. However, since this may be seen by the other person as a norm violation, you may need to go to some length to justify your use of the internal legitimizer: you may, for example, emphasize the importance of the appointment or offer to meet again at the boss' or teacher's convenience, so as not to insult him/her.

The key issue is to be aware of the norms. Unintentional violation can disrupt conversation and hinder your efforts to accomplish your goals in the situation.   It should be clear, though, that the cultural context provides many shared rules for how to interpret the meaning of behavior (norms of interpretation) and rules for when and how to communicate with one another (norms of interaction).

THE FUNCTIONS OF CULTURAL KNOWLEDGE

Given that we all think of ourselves as individuals with specific goals and feelings, we would, no doubt be amazed to realize how much of our communication behavior is influenced by specific cultural rules and how often the entire nature of an encounter is dictated by a cultural script for the event. Part of the reason for that strong influence is the way we use those particular rules and general scripts in dealing with others. The <u>force</u> or power of a rule is, in part, dependent on the frequency with which members of cultures use it to predict, explain, and evaluate their own and others' behaviors.

PREDICTION

The first function rules serve is to allow us to **predict** behavior so we can know what to expect from others and what they probably expect from us. As we enter a classroom setting for a lecture, we expect the person in the front of the room to assume the role of teacher-lecturer and we plan to take the role of student-audience member.   We also assume the instructor and other students are predicting the same thing.

These predictions often become **self-fulfilling prophecies** in that our expectations for what will happen make us perceive them in just that way. For example, if all the students assume the predicted roles and consistently cast the instructor in the lecturer role by only speaking when a direct question is asked and then only after a long silence, refusing to initiate active discussion with other students, and directing all talk to the instructor, the instructor will find it difficult not to conform even if s/he would like to create a different sort of speech event, such as a group discussion.

If the instructor does conform to the students' expectations, the students will come away convinced that their predictions were accurate — not realizing that it was the combination of their predictions and the way they behaved based on those predictions that insured that the predictions, or prophecies, would be fulfilled.   In this instance the students are like the large group of stockholders who predicted that stock prices were going to fall and so all of them tried to sell their stocks. When this resulted in stock prices falling, the stockholders came away feeling smug about how good they were at predicting stock prices and even more confident about their ability to predict events at future times.

EXPLANATION

In addition to using cultural knowledge to predict behavior, we also use it to **explain** behaviors after the fact. Why did your parents talk to you as they did after finding out about your poor grades? Because parents are "like that" — i.e., there are shared rules defining the parent-child relationship which your parents, like all other parents, follow in that type of situation. As such, your parents have engaged in **rule-following behavior.** A good deal of research suggests that when you or others follow a rule or set of rules seen as operating in a situation, no one even thinks that much about why someone behaved as they did. The reason seems obvious because the reason is the rule itself.

However, what happens when people do not conform to the rules? How do we explain the behavior of the waitress who interrupts us in the middle of our order to say, "Excuse me, but you look worried — is something bothering you?" Or, consider the reaction of your mother who says, "So you flunked out of school. You have your own priorities and I respect them. Don't worry about the tuition money, your Dad and I can afford it." Even here we use cultural knowledge as a backdrop against which to explain behavior. We define behavior that does not conform to the rules in one of three ways — rule-breaking, rule-violating, or rule-ignorant (McLaughlin, 1984).

Nonconforming behavior that is seen as an intentional rule violation is termed **rule-breaking behavior.** This kind of explanation will lead you to actively interpret many more features of the situation because you will try to see motives which might explain such intentional behavior. For instance, you begin to notice things such as how old the waitress appears to be, whether she wears a wedding ring, the type of restaurant this is, and how other waitresses interact with the restaurant's customers. Based on this information which you have attended to, perceived, and comprehended, you might conclude that either your waitress is lonely and wants to get to know someone or she believes something is bothering you and is genuinely concerned about your welfare.

On the other hand, your fully activated information-processing system may lead you to conclude that the script was violated unintentionally, i.e., **rule-violating behavior.** Thus you might interpret your mother's response to your flunking out as the product of being in shock and not knowing what to say. She just blurted out the first thing that came to mind. You might then expect a script-following argument later when she recovers. For now, however, you interpret her violation of the rules as unintentional.

Finally, you may decide that this is an instance of **rule-ignorant behavior** in that the person did not conform to the rule because s/he did not know it. For example, to explain the waitress's behavior, you may conclude that she is obviously a foreigner who just "doesn't know" that a waitress in America isn't supposed to do such things.

Whether behavior follows or does not follow the rules, we use the rules to help us explain the behavior. Nonconforming behavior produces more arousal and activates more of the psychological structures discussed earlier in Chapter 2. These determine whether we categorize the behavior as rule-breaking, rule-violating, or rule-ignorant. Furthermore, how we define and explain the behavior will affect how we react to the person as well as how we will evaluate the behavior.

EVALUATION

Evaluation is the third function served by cultural rules. Most cultural rules and scripts not only tell us how to act but also how we ought to act. That is, they have a moral force — to follow the rule is good, moral, polite, etc., and to violate the rule may be seen as bad, even evil, unethical, rude, or as suggesting a number of other negative qualities. The evaluative function of rules leads each of us to impose **sanctions** on those who do not conform. The nature of the sanctions will vary depending on whether we see the behavior as rule-breaking, rule-violating, or rule-ignorant.

Rule-ignorant behavior usually receives the mildest sanctions. At the very least we let the other person know what s/he has done and we most often go on directly or indirectly in attempts to educate that person in the appropriate ways to behave. Rule-violating behavior, on the other hand, may or may not be excused. For example, it is possible to excuse or to overlook the rule-violation of an employee who, in a pressure situation blurted out the boss's first name unintentionally even though s/he knew there was a strict rule about addressing superiors by title. But, it is also possible not to excuse such a behavior: for example, "I don't care how drunk he is, if he touches me one more time while he's talking to me, I'm going to let him have it."

We reserve our most severe sanctions for rule-breakers. If a professor believes a new student is calling him/her by a nickname intentionally (for whatever reason), sanctions are almost inevitable. The only aspect likely to vary is just how severe the sanction will be. Usually the severity of the sanction depends on the reasons which the professor attributes to the student's intentional rule-breaking.

In sum, because we use rules and scripts provided by our culture for communication to predict, explain, and evaluate communication behavior, they have enormous force in affecting our communication with others.

SUMMARY

Our culture provides us with a set of shared beliefs, language, and rules for interacting which we learn and internalize through our communication with others in that culture. We are concerned here with those aspects of culture which influence and serve as a foundation for communication.

Cultural scripts provide a set of shared rules about how we are to communicate appropriately in different speech events. These rules or guidelines are organized around the components of a speech event: setting, channel, participants, relationships, purpose, key, topic, and norms of interaction and interpretation.

We use cultural knowledge to predict, explain and evaluate our own and others' communication behaviors.

In these first four chapters, we have discussed the biological, psychological, symbolic, and cultural foundations of the communication process. These are the fundamental building blocks of human communication which are the basis for the different contexts for communication. In chapters 5-10 we will examine the interpersonal, small group, organizational, and mass media communication contexts.

KEY TERMS

Whorf-Sapir hypothesis
cultural scripts
speech event
speech event components:
    setting
    channel
    participants
    relationships
    purpose
    key
    topic
    norms of interpretation
    norms of interaction
prediction
explanation
rule-following behavior
rule-breaking behavior
rule-violating behavior
rule-ignorant behavior
evaluation
sanctions

CHAPTER 5

CHAPTER 5

INTERPERSONAL COMMUNICATION CONTEXTS:
COMPONENTS AND CONCEPTS

Interpersonal communication processes are central to the success or failure of our most important communications with others. Creating and maintaining relationships with family and friends, job interviews, visiting the doctor, our efforts to persuade, comfort, and inform others — all of these features of humans as social beings frequently are accomplished in interpersonal contexts where the ability to apply your understanding of interpersonal communication largely determines whether you achieve your goals.

DEFINING INTERPERSONAL COMMUNICATION CONTEXTS

The clearest case of an interpersonal context for communication is where **at least two people are mutually aware of one another and both have a communicative goal.** While this may seem like a very broad definition, let's look at the types of contexts it suggests as "interpersonal" in nature. If I look across the street and see a man with pink hair, dressed in black leather, and think "There's one of my kind of people," am I involved in interpersonal communication? No. First, the two of us are not mutually aware of one another. To be mutually aware I would have to be aware of "Pinky," know that he is aware of me, that he is aware that I am aware of him, and he would need to know the same things about me.

But let's assume he notices me. For that moment we are both aware of one another and each of us knows we are thinking about each other. However, that is not enough to define an interpersonal communication context because there is no communicative goal. By **communicative goal** we mean a desire to make something private (known only by one person) into something "public" and shared by both people or to make an individual perception of a piece of factual information, a feeling, desire, attitude, or opinion available to the other person. Thus, if I desire to get to know the person across the street or to find out if he plays in a band and then act on that desire by crossing the street and talking with him, then we have met the minimum requirements for creating an interpersonal communication context.

Beyond the minimum requirements of mutual awareness and acting on communicative goals, the most typical interpersonal contexts involve a great degree of **immediacy.** Speakers are face-to-face, able to use both verbal and nonverbal channels of communication, and both are involved in sending and receiving messages. However, here we are forced to think in "more or less" terms. That is, rather than describing a context as either interpersonal or not, we describe it as more or less interpersonal depending on many factors. This is consistent with our view of communication as a process, which assumes an avoidance of a two-valued, either-or orientation, as we discussed it in Chapter 1. For example, consider two people communicating through computer terminals who are mutually aware of one another, who have communicative goals and yet their immediacy is lessened because the nonverbal channel is severely restricted because the people are not face-to-face. Or, consider telephone talk in which the communicators are also not face-to-face. Can these count as "interpersonal" communication contexts? Well, they have more elements typical of interpersonal contexts than of other contexts.

Furthermore, you will see in the discussions of other communication contexts (small group, organizational, and mass) provided in later chapters, interpersonal processes still operate, but the different contexts for communication add new complexities to interpersonal communication processes, change the way these processes are conducted, and/or make certain interpersonal processes more important, less important, or even irrelevant.

ORGANIZATION OF INTERPERSONAL INFORMATION

Interpersonal contexts and communication within them are organized around each communicator's **definition of the situation.** These definitions are made up of several components. The component parts of the definition of the situation look much like the components of the "speech event" discussed in Chapter 4. In fact, you can even think of a speech event as a culturally-scripted definition of the situation. **A well-defined speech event provides each speaker with a shared or ready-made definition of the situation.**

However, in most interpersonal communication contexts, communicators are provided only with a partial, and often minimal, script. They are left to "negotiate" or to figure out the definition of this situation using those cultural guidelines they see as relevant to this communication situation. So, while you see definite similarities between the components of the definition of the situation and those of the speech events, the emphasis will be on those components most subject to negotiation in typical interpersonal contexts and how they are negotiated when the cultural script is less than complete.

COMPONENTS OF INTERPERSONAL COMMUNICATION CONTEXTS

For every interpersonal communicative interaction each person has an **expected definition of the situation** at the beginning of the encounter. This expected definition includes definitions of: the identities to be assumed by each participant; the type of relationship that exists between them; the purposes or goals of the interaction; and the setting.

Each also expects the communication to follow the **norms of interaction** which each learned from his/her culture. These norms govern such things as turn-taking in conversation, topic management, and sequences for appropriately beginning and ending interactions (as we discussed in Chapter 4). They are less subject to negotiation (except perhaps in cross-cultural communication) and constitute taken-for-granted features of the communication. Failure to follow these norms can seriously hinder successful negotiation of identities, relationships, and practical goals.

Three aspects of the definition of the situation are especially important objects for negotiation in many interpersonal contexts — the nature of identities of the participants, managing identities, and the nature of their relationship. The remainder of this chapter will discuss these key components in greater detail.

THE NATURE OF IDENTITIES

In trying to define interpersonal contexts nothing concerns people more than creating an appropriate identity for themselves. The term **identity** refers to the specific image we present in a particular context. When we share a cultural script or set of expectations for what our identity should be in a type of situation, we call that a **role.** We may negotiate our identities to more or less conform to those role expectations (McCall & Simmons, 1978).

People tend to think of identities as a static entity. That is, if we were to ask ourselves, "Who am I?" we would expect to answer directly, "I am X type of person." We often think of the self as some sort of sculpture, set in concrete, and perhaps even partially hidden from us by a blanket of ignorance. We strive to lift the blanket to see who we really are. A large body of research in interpersonal communication suggests, however, that this whole approach to understanding the self is misguided.

This research claims that we do not consist of a single self. Rather, we consist of **multiple selves,** each self created in response to social role expectations, expectations of specific others, and our own goals in the variety of communication situations in which we are involved. The identity you present when you communicate with your parents is probably very different from the one you present to your date. You may even create different identities for yourself depending on the particular types of encounters you have with your dating partner. Moreover, in future communication you may create an identity different in some respects from any you have ever presented before: i.e., a "new you" to add to the many other "yous" with which you are already familiar.

This does not mean that in each situation we "start from scratch" in constructing an identity. From situation to situation each of us carries a **self-concept,** a more or less organized and complex set of beliefs about who we are. From observing ourselves and others' perceptions of us in thousands of situations we selectively abstract from these observations beliefs about ourselves which we organize into a theory about who we are. Like any theory, this is highly subject to bias, inaccuracy, and change. Nonetheless we use this theory as a resource from which to create expectation(s) for the identity we can or should present in a given situation — i.e., our **identity goal(s).**

We may not be aware that we even have identity goals. In a job interview you are very conscious of the particular identity you wish to present. But at the outset of a casual conversation with a friend, the goals are not likely to be so apparent. In this casual context we may not have a specific identity goal but rather a **range** of acceptable identities, one of which you expect to use in

76

this situation. However, if your friend starts the conversation by accusing you of revealing a secret, implying you are a disloyal friend, your reaction will make clear that you <u>do</u> have identity goals and the identity s/he is ascribing to you is in conflict with those goals. This would be outside the range of identities you are willing to assume. Since our self-concept — our theory of self — greatly influences specific identity goals in communication, we will examine it in more detail.

One way to divide the self-concept is in terms of our beliefs about our material, social, and ideal selves. The **material self** consists of beliefs about our physical appearance, way of dressing, possessions, etc. Often identity goals in communication are aimed at presenting (and having others validate) particular beliefs about the material self, such as that we are physically attractive or at least not unattractive.

The **social self** embodies beliefs about our personal qualities (intelligence), the way we interact with others (talkative, insecure), as well as what we think others think we are. Cooley (1902) long ago labeled this aspect of the social self the "looking glass self;" i.e., in observing how others communicate with you, you peer into the looking glass. The image you see often greatly influences what you think you are. We may choose to reject the image. For example, people may think you are self-indulgent, but you know you are not, so you reject their image. Children are particularly susceptible to the looking glass self. What they see in the looking glass (based on family, peer group, and classroom communication) has a tremendous influence on the way they will see themselves several years in the future. Think, for instance, of how your own looking-glass self has affected your self-concept today.

The **ideal self** includes all that we would like to be, both materially and socially. Many of our identity goals in communication are aimed at presenting an identity consistent with some part of our ideal self. Furthermore, we seek to mask those qualities which we feel are inconsistent with that ideal.

Goffman (1959) suggested that much of our ideal self is culturally defined. He argued that our culture provides both positive idealizations we attempt to "live up" to and negative idealizations which certain people are expected to "live down" to. One positive idealization which recently has emerged on the American scene is that of the "yumpy" (Young Upwardly Mobile Professional). Many books on the market now tell people how to live up to this positive idealization. Conversely, many groups of people, such as ethnic minorities and women, are faced with negative idealizations which they are expected to live "down to." Young girls as they approach adolescence may learn to hide their abilities — to act dependent upon and less intelligent than boys. For a long time in America (and in some regions even today) black Americans were expected to assume deferential roles suggesting they were slow-moving, less articulate, and less intelligent than whites. Typically, however, the ideal self is thought of as a set of positive beliefs about what you want to be which you seek to actualize in your communication and have validated by others.

Our self-concept serves as a resource, a reservoir of beliefs from which we create our identity in a given situation. Of course, the other person also has a self-concept and identity goals. Communication is the medium through which each of you work to create your identities. In the next section we will examine this negotiation process.

MANAGING IDENTITIES

Identity management in communication is the product of each communicator's efforts at self-presentation and his/her response to the identity s/he is cast in by the other person. These two processes occur simultaneously throughout the interaction. Your success at presenting and having others accept an identity desirable for you is closely tied to how you respond to their self-presentation. We will examine several strategies you and the other person each use to manage your identities—self-disclosing, disclaiming, repairing, and altercasting.

SELF-DISCLOSING

Self-disclosure is the process through which we reveal information about ourselves to others. Self-disclosure may occur at different levels and you need to follow strategies for appropriate self-disclosure if you and others are to successfully use self-disclosure to achieve your identity goals. Each of these features of self-disclosure needs further explanation.

Levels of Disclosure

The information you self-disclose nonverbally as well as verbally varies in its **level** or depth. Garner (1980) distinguished between four levels of verbal self-disclosure. The first level includes **cliches** or surface information exchanged in greeting rituals or when you simply want to pass the time with a conversation of little substance. For example, consider how much information is disclosed by these statements: "Hi, how are you doing?" "Oh, I'm fine, how about you?"; "Hi, how are the kids?" "Growing up too fast. Are yours in school yet?". The second level involves **facts** about your life including your occupation, where you grew up, your major, activities you engage in, etc. The third level consists of **opinions** or personal attitudes toward things, such as whether you think baseball is boring to watch, the President's foreign policy is dangerous to our future, or sex before marriage is immoral. The deepest level involves **feelings** or your emotional reactions to events. Statements such as, "I really feel frightened when I hear the President talk about 'winning' a nuclear war" and "I experience overwhelming guilt every time I visit my grandmother in the nursing home," are examples of information shared at the feeling level of self-disclosure.

Norms for Disclosure

Usually self-disclosure progresses from surface information to deeper levels over time in a relationship. However, that is not always true. In some cases you may never go beyond cliches; in others deep feelings may be revealed before many facts

78

are known.   There is no ideal model. However, there are certain guidelines to follow for appropriate self-disclosure:

Self-disclosure should be symmetrical.   This means both persons should participate and should disclose at approximately the same level. When you continue to self-disclose without the other person reciprocating or when you disclose "feelings" when the other person only wants to disclose facts, your self-disclosure will probably be seen as inappropriate.

Self-disclosure should be conversationally relevant.   Whether you self-disclose facts or feelings, it should be clear how they are relevant to the topics currently being discussed. "Coming out of left field" with current family conflicts during a conversation about possible questions on the next communication exam, would be seen as inappropriate to the topic of conversation.

Self-disclosure should be believable.   Obviously, if others believe you are putting up a false front, they are unlikely either to self-disclose or to accept the identity you are presenting. It is important to be as specific as possible.   For example, to say, "I took two courses on interpersonal communication processes last year with Dr. Applegate," would be more believable than, "I've read all the latest research on interpersonal communication."

Appropriate self-disclosure requires observing these guidelines and a careful monitoring of the other person's perspective, especially his/her view of you currently and his/her definition of the relationship which exists between the two of you.   Mistakes are frequently made: unintentional cues may lead to false impressions or information may be revealed at an inappropriate level or at an inappropriate time given the topic of conversation. Self-disclosure, then, has direct effects on the way identities are managed in communication.

DISCLAIMING

In addition to disclosure you use other methods to manage your identity. Often you will recognize, before you say it, that something you are about to say or do may lead the other person to see you in a way that is inconsistent with the identity you wish to present. You may then use certain strategies to prevent the other from inferring you have some undesired quality. These strategies are called **disclaimers** (Hewitt & Stokes, 1975).   There are many types of disclaimers but we will describe here only those three most often used: hedging, credentialing, and sin licenses

One type of disclaimer is called **hedging.**   When you suspect a statement may cause others to view you negatively, you often hedge in order to test their reaction before committing yourself to the statement. Prefacing statements with phrases like, "I'm no expert, but," or "I'm not really sure how I feel about that yet but I do think," is hedging. Hedges allow you to disclaim the idea if your statement is received negatively.

Happy Couples Accentuate the Positive

Contrary to myth, couples don't tell each other everything. They stress the upbeat and downplay their daily miseries, a new study reveals.

Those who aren't content with their relationships spend more time baring their anxieties, fears and weaknesses.

Unhappy and happy couples do about the same amount of self-disclosing. But in better matches the partners do more sharing of hopes and dreams and analyzing their strengths, says Kenneth Sereno, head of the communications department at University of Southern California at Los Angeles.

Sereno and co-author Melanie Rich studied the self-disclosure habits of 148 men and women who were married or who lived with a person of the opposite sex for at least six months.

They found that a happy marriage was strongly linked to higher "communicative competence."

Compared to people with less rosy relationships, these couples were more polite, had higher empathy ratings, listened more attentively and were less likely to interrupt others.

"When there's too much negative communication," Sereno says, "it just becomes a continual downer for the other spouse, and that creates stress in the relationship."

And the value of no-holds-barred self-disclosure has been exaggerated, he says.

"It may be more important how information is handled than how deeply it goes."

"Are spouses really listening, trying to understand each other's point of view? That's what seems to lead to happier marriages," he says. "We're talking about a more selective type of self-disclosure."

USA Today, 12-11-86, p.D

Appropriate self-disclosure is important in interpersonal communication contexts.

Another type of disclaimer we use often is **credentialling**. In this type you disclose features of yourself ("credentials") to show you are not the kind of person the statement you are about to make suggests you would be. For instance, if you preface a negative remark about Blacks with, "Now my roommate in college was Black and so are many of my friends, but...," you would be credentialling to prevent being seen as a racist.

Sin licenses are a third type of disclaimer. Sin licences let people know ahead of time that you _know_ you are breaking a rule or norm and you may even provide a reason for doing it. That is, you don't want them to think you are an irresponsible type who goes around breaking rules. Ending a phone conversation with, "I'm sorry to cut you off, but...," or introducing a job problem at a party with, "I know you're not supposed to mix business with pleasure, but...," can be seen as using a sin license so as not to be thought of either as rude or as a workaholic.

REPAIRING

While disclaimers are strategies used to prevent others from casting us into undesired identities, sometimes we do not recognize in advance that some statement or behavior could disrupt our efforts to manage our identity. Then, we are forced to use **repair strategies** after an apparent failure, impolite statement, or unintentional self-disclosure of undesirable information in order to salvage our image in the eyes of others.

Like disclaimers, there are several types of repair strategies, including excuses and justifications. In using **excuses,** you admit your statement or behavior was wrong, impolite, etc., but you offer reasons why you should not be held responsible and thus not be perceived in a negative way. Telling a professor that your paper is late because the dog ate your rough draft admits your wrong in being late but suggests that it wasn't your fault so you should not be treated as an irresponsible student who doesn't hand in papers.

Justifications are strategies in which you admit responsibility for your behavior but you argue that the other person is wrong in seeing that behavior as negative. Suggesting to your mother that moderate marijuana use is no different from social drinking after she sees a joint accidentally left in the ashtray of your car would be considered a justification.

Both disclaimers and repair strategies are useful tools for identity management. A word of caution is in order, however. Research suggests that overuse of these strategies may lead others to see you as lacking in competence or character. An occasional hedge can be useful in preserving your identity. On the other hand, frequent hedging, may lead to an overall perception that you lack decisiveness. Research has found that females are more likely than males to be negatively perceived when they use disclaimers and repairs (Pearson, 1985).

ALTERCASTING

In your communication with another you use self-disclosing, disclaiming, and/or repairing in an effort to manage your identity. You also influence the identity assumed by the other person and, in turn, they influence your presentation of self as well. This mutual influence process is called **altercasting** (Weinstein & Deutschberger, 1963). We always talk with other people "as if" they are some type of person. When you discuss your marital problems with your friend John, you cast him in the role of "confidant." If you ask for advice, you further altercast him as counselor, even though this altercasting may not be intentional.

Sometimes you intentionally altercast another into an identity in order to aid in accomplishing some task or to allow you to assume the identity you want in the situation. One common altercasting strategy is to treat others as if they are special friends or allies in order to get their help on some project. If the other person accepts the role into which s/he is cast, s/he may find it difficult as this "special friend" to turn down your request for help.

Not all altercasting need be so selfishly manipulative. If you want to assume the identity of a friend or advisor for someone having trouble, you may first need to altercast that person as a strong but open and honest individual, so that s/he will talk about his/her problems free of the fear of being seen as weak or incompetent.

To understand the identities people assume in communication, we must look not only at their identity goals and strategies for identity management, but also at the effects of the altercasting being done by the people with whom they are communicating.

THE NATURE OF RELATIONSHIPS

Every time you communicate, whatever the topic, you present an identity for yourself and you altercast, or attempt to altercast, the other person into one. Similarly, in every communication situation you negotiate or try to work out the **definition of the relationship** existing between you and the other person. Friends, strangers, acquaintances, roommates, boss-employee, parent-child — all these relationships are defined in the way people communicate with one another. In this section we explore the nature of interpersonal relationships, how they develop, how they dissolve, and the communication strategies associated with development and dissolution.

BONDS IN RELATIONSHIPS

Relationship bonds are the glue which hold relationships together. These bonds are created by the support each person in the relationship receives for the various identities each presents. For example, a bus driver and passenger form a bond as they communicate and provide support for the other's identity. The bus driver asks, "Where are you going today?" The passenger responds, "I'd like to go to Krogers, but I'm not sure that this is the right bus." "It sure is," says the bus driver, "and I'll have you there in a jiffy." The bus driver and passenger have thus provided support for the identity each participant has presented. This identity support is one of the important rewards we receive in relationships.

The nature and extent of the identity support provided by others varies with relationship partners. Therefore, the relationship bonds created, or the kinds of glue which holds our relationships together are not all the same. One way to characterize relationships is by the types of bonds which link relationship partners. While there are many kinds of relationship bonds, we will discuss three of the most important ones: ascribed, commitment, and attachment bonds (McCall & Simmons, 1978).

Ascribed bonds hold people together by virtue of the role positions the communicators occupy in society, independent of any individual qualities people may have. Kinship bonds are like this. Brothers are brothers whatever else they may be. In the same way teacher-student, boss-employee, and husband-wife relationships are defined by role expectations given to them by society. The bond between the bus driver and passenger is an example of an ascribed bond. They are linked together by their societal roles of "bus driver" and "passenger." Thus, the content and nature of their interpersonal tie or bond is to a large extent culturally defined.

Commitment bonds are created when you commit yourself to engage in certain activities, seek certain rewards, and display and seek support for certain identities primarily with a particular other person. This commitment may be public, such as forming a business partnership or announcing a marriage engagement, or private, such as two high school students agreeing to remain friends when each leaves for college. Further, the commitment may be explicit, as with marriage vows, or implicit and not talked about, as with an understanding between friends (McCall, 1982). With commitment bonds, you come to weigh this other person's opinions of your identities and activities more heavily because the identity support you receive from the other is nearly exclusive. For example, if the passenger commented to the bus driver, "I don't see why any young man like you would want to have long hair. You look like a 1960's hippie with that ponytail," the driver probably wouldn't be too concerned. This is because any number of people who ride the bus may serve to support the bus driver's identity as "bus driver," and therefore support for this identity is plentiful. However, if one of the bus driver's friends said to him, "Don't you think it's time you gave up on the 60's and got a decent haircut?" the comment would be taken more seriously, since the relational bond is not due to socially prescribed roles but is one of commitment, based on an agreement to rely on the other person for certain rewards and for supporting specified identities. The identity support, then, that the bus driver receives from his friend is available from fewer sources than that received from the passenger, which leads to the increased value of importance of the friend's opinion.

Attachment bonds are created when you begin to feel the relationship you have and the rewards you receive are nontransferable. That is, without the other person you would be unable to find the particular kinds of identity support and other rewards s/he provides. This belief provides a strong reason for holding the relationship together because that specific person is crucial to the contents of the identities associated with him/her. The other person becomes a part of your self-conception and is therefore "attached" to particular identities you present (McCall, 1982). Thus, while any passenger may support the bus driver's identity as "bus driver," and several friends may provide support for the driver's identity as "friend," only the bus driver's mother can provide the rewards and identity support for the bus driver as her son. We may be able to seek out other acquaintances and friends, but we cannot so easily go looking for another mother or child. The less transferable your relationship, the more attached you are and the more vulnerable you are to the other person (McCall & Simons, 1978).

Relationships vary in the strength and type of bonds that hold them together. Obviously, when your communication with another person involves introducing multiple selves into the relationship, it creates commitment and perhaps attachment bonds. It also functions to manage the relationship so that each of you successfully and dependably provides the expected support. Thus, there is strong reason to expect the relationship will be maintained.

However, successful and long-term relationships between people who simply conform to ascribed role expectations are possible and common: neither commitment nor attachment is needed, each simply fulfills the role expected of them by society. Think, for example, of your relationships with your doctor or dentist, with your boss at work, or the janitor in your dorm or apartment building. **The key to success in both situations is that each person shares the same goals and definition of the relationship.**

Your communication with others creates, reflects, and occasionally changes the types of bonds included in the definition of your relationship. If your communication primarily involves exchange of rewards (goods, information, identity support) tied to the social roles each of you occupy (for example, those rewards associated with the typical teacher-student relationships), then you have created a relationship primarily held together by ascribed bonds. If, however, you come to rely on Professor Jones for insights (information) into the meaning of your life which you feel no one else can provide (a ontransferable reward), then the relationship definition includes attachment bonds. The bonding process, then, is accomplished in communication.

Bonds are not the only features of relationship definitions which are negotiated in communication. Justice, relational dominance, and the breadth and depth of the relationship are other important features of any relationship definition.

RELATIONAL JUSTICE

"All's fair in love and war," according to one popular adage. But how is "fairness" determined? As with relational bonds, relational justice is negotiated by the participants as they define their relationship. Relational partners use various systems of justice to decide what is fair in a relationship: social obligation, equity, parity, or need (Roloff, 1981).

Often you assess what is fair to get or give based on **social obligation.** Traditionally men were supposed to pay for dates and husbands to provide financial stability for their wives. Under a system of social obligation, fairness in the relationship is based on cultural and societal norms governing that relationship. We consider it "fair" that children are provided food, shelter, and clothing by their parents. Children, in turn, may feel socially obligated to care for their parents as their parents age.

At other times you assess justice on the basis of **equity:** things are fair when each person gets as much as they give to a relationship. For example, if I make the car payments, I get to decide who uses the car. Equity is most clearly dominant as a form of justice early in the development of a relationship.

Parity is a form of justice in which the key to fairness is for each person to receive equal rewards, regardless of how much they give. For example, a husband and wife may feel it doesn't matter how much effort each puts into their relationship as long as both are equally happy and satisfied.

Need as a principle of justice suggests that things are fair when each person's needs are met, even if that requires unequal distribution of effort and/or rewards. You may know your partner is very insecure and needs a lot of identity support. It would only be fair, then, that you fill that need even though you receive little support in return for your efforts. That is fair because you do not need equal support.

People usually employ different systems of justice in different areas of their relationships to decide what is a fair allocation of resources. Roommates, for example, may agree that one should have more control over use of the apartment because s/he pays most of the rent (equity rule), one helps the other with a calculus problem because s/he is a math whiz and the other has a lot of trouble with math (need), grocery money leftover at the end of the month (regardless of whose it is) goes toward a night of pizza and beer in which they share equally (parity), and, finally, neither loans out the other's belongings (social obligation).

Problems often arise in at least two ways as you negotiate what is fair and just. First, partners can be using two different forms of justice in making their decision. Your roommate may feel it's fair that you help him/her with schoolwork because s/he needs help and you do not. You, on the other hand, may assess the situation using the principle of equity. What are you getting of equal value in return for all the help you are providing? If the two of you fail to come to agreement on the appropriate system, you will feel more and more used. Then, when you start reducing the amount of help you provide, your roommate will likely feel that you are being unfair. And, given that s/he is using the need principle, you are.

Second, even if you are in agreement that one form of justice is the appropriate one, you still must agree that the way resources are distributed is fair given that system. You may agree that equity is the form to use in deciding who controls use of the apartment, but how much extra control should you get for the additional 50 dollars a month you pay in rent?

As with many of the other aspects of interpersonal relationships, we are not always fully aware of either the forms of justice or the need to negotiate it. However, the success of a relationship depends on the partners' abilities to communicate effectively about the forms of justice to be used in different areas of the relationship and how systems of justice should be applied.

RELATIONAL DOMINANCE

No discussion of the nature of relationships would be complete without examining how dominance or control is allocated in communication between relational partners. **Relational dominance** refers to control over the very definition of the relationship, including the types of bonds created, systems of justice employed, and degree of intimacy sought and achieved. The definition of dominant and submissive roles in a relationship usually follows one of three patterns: complementary, symmetrical, or parallel.

In **complementary** relationships one person adopts the dominant role while the other accepts or seeks the submissive role. Hence, each person's behavior complements the others. The wife says she thinks extra money should be invested in mutual funds to which the husband says, "Fine, you're the financial expert in the family." Such a pattern reflects a complementary relationship between them in the financial domain of their relationship.

In some relationships such as teacher-student, doctor-patient, and boss-employee, the entire relationship may be defined by a complementary pattern with one person always in the dominant role. Typically, however, dominant and submissive roles vary across different areas of a relationship with partners assuming both roles at different times.

Symmetrical patterns of control are typical when both partners see themselves as equals. Here dominance or control is less clearly defined by societal roles and thus more in need of negotiation. Two common symmetrical patterns are found. **Competitive symmetry** occurs when both partners vie for control of the relationship. For example, two physicians on a health care team may compete with each other for the team's leadership position. **Submissive** symmetry, on the other hand, results from each partner trying not to dominate or control. This can lead to exchanges such as, "What movie do you want to see tonight?" "You decide." "No, you decide." "It's really up to you." "I'll go to whatever show you want to go to." In both types of symmetrical patterns someone should eventually assume control. If no one does and the communication continues, the relationship takes on the character of either a war (competitive symmetry) or a stagnant pond (submissive symmetry).

The final pattern of relational dominance is the **parallel** pattern. Here communication involves both complementary patterns, with the person in the dominant role varying, and symmetrical patterns in some areas of the relationship as well. Some research suggests that relationships defined in this more complex way are less rigid and thus healthier for the partners. However, there is no clearly ideal model. One key to success appears to be communication which can both: 1) allow partners to negotiate mutual agreement about how and in what areas dominance or control is to be granted; and 2) leave the option for change in roles open.

BREADTH AND DEPTH OF RELATIONSHIPS

Each of your relationships differs in the amount and quality of activities and information you and the other person share. Altman and Taylor (1973) analyzed these differences in terms of the breadth and depth of the relationship. **Breadth** refers to the amount of information shared between partners and the number of activities they engage in together. **Depth** of the relationship is measured by the centrality of the information and activities shared to each person's self concept.

Breadth and depth may vary across different domains of your life. Figure 5.1 shows different levels of breadth and depth in two different relationships. Think of the circle as everything you care about and do in your life. Each slice of the

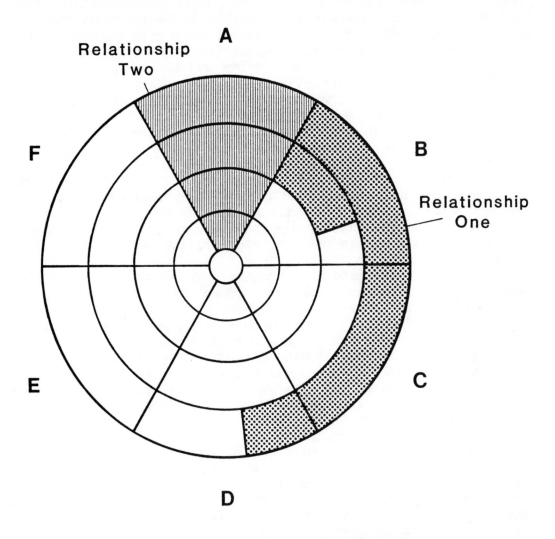

Figure 5.1 Breadth and Depth of Two Relationships

Adapted from Altman and Taylor's Analogue of Personality Structure (Social Penetration, New York: Holt, Rinehart & Winston, 1973, pp. 129–135).

circle is a different area of your life: area A may be school-related activities, abilities, interests, anxieties; B your family life; C your religious life, etc. Using the breadth and depth ideas to analyze the nature of the two relationships, you can see that Relationship One is characterized by great breadth, but little depth. Here each person knows a lot of surface information about the other. For example, they may know each is a Methodist and go to church together, both like sports and regularly jog together, both are communication majors, take classes together, and help one another on exams.

Relationship Two, on the other hand, has great depth in one area but little breadth. An example of this type would be two people who meet at a graduation party near the end of their college career and quickly "fall in love." They spend much time together sharing their feelings for one another, their deepest desires and fears about their future after college, their sexual likes and dislikes. However, neither has much breadth of knowledge about the other. They only know they love one another, are sexually compatible, and share similar plans after college. In this relationship there is depth, but overall there is little breadth.

Many perfectly satisfactory relationships have neither much breadth nor depth. You and a co-worker may share only those activities and information about yourselves necessary to work together effectively. If that is what you both want for the relationship and you work together well, then you have effectively negotiated and managed the definition of your relationship.

Of course, you or the other person may work to change the definition of your relationship. If you invite your co-worker out to dinner and begin talking about your "life after divorce," you are making a bid to increase the breadth and depth of the relationship. Your co-worker can accept the re-definition and share similar information about his/her personal life or s/he may beg out of the invitation altogether or change the topic at dinner back to work projects, trying to keep the relationship at its current level of breadth and depth.

Differences in two people's perceptions of the breadth and depth of their relationship and/or in their future goals for increasing, maintaining, or decreasing breadth and depth create potential problems. Each must be able to communicate effectively enough to allow recognition of their differences and negotiation of mutual agreement on this issue.

As researchers have examined how these various dimensions of relationship definitions are negotiated in communication, they have found that most relationships go through particular stages as they develop and other stages as the relationship dissolves.

THE PROCESS OF RELATIONSHIP DEVELOPMENT

In this section we describe the process of relationship development and the typical patterns relationships follow. Not all relationships progress through all these stages, nor is there any reason that they should. Nevertheless, understanding these stages and the way people decide to continue or discontinue development through these stages may help you see how and why many of your relationships develop as they do.

RELATIONSHIP ESCALATION OR DEVELOPMENT

As you learned from the discussion of attraction in Chapter 2, if a person is conveniently located in proximity to you, similar in social desirability, similar in at least their external qualities, and reciprocates your interest, you are likely to pursue a relationship with that person. Your relationship is likely to develop through a series of stages or phases identified by Knapp (1984) and based on the study of a wide variety of relationships.

In the **initiating stage**, both partners limit their communication to highly ritualized or scripted forms of communication. Any topics beyond greeting rituals, the weather, etc., are limited to what is clearly relevant to the immediate situation. On the first day of this class, before the class session began, as you talked to a stranger/classmate, you probably focused on ritual communication — this class, your walk to this building, the heat in the room, etc.

At some point you and/or the other person may decide to enter the **experimenting stage.** Here "small talk" begins. You disclose bits and pieces about yourself in search of topics of common interest that you and the other person can pursue in your communication. Knapp (1984) points out that small talk serves several important functions both very early in the relationship and later on when partners are trying to expand and solidify the focus of their relationship. Small talk can be useful in finding areas of shared interest and openings for more penetrating topics, in providing an "audition" for a future friendship, in giving greater breadth and depth to the current relationship, and in providing a safe means for reducing uncertainty about who each of you is.

Communication in this experimenting stage is casual and nonjudgmental. You are less concerned with ironing out differences of opinion and more concerned with gathering information to help you assess the future potential of the relationship. Many relationships continue to exist without going beyond this experimenting stage while others may terminate at this stage.

As you experiment with one another as potential relationship partners, one or both of you may decide to intensify the relationship. In the **intensifying** stage partners increase the breadth and depth of the relationship by disclosing more intimate information across a wider variety of topics. They begin to use informal terms of address often developing special terms of endearment for each other. We also note other verbal changes including: more use of statements referring to "we" and "us" rather than "I" or "me;" more talk about the future; and frequent reciprocal affirmations of the worth of the relationship and the value of the other person. Nonverbally, spatial distance decreases, touching increases, and nonverbal behaviors are more frequently substituted for verbalizations, especially about feelings.

At some point in the process of intensifying, the fourth stage of development, the **integrating stage,** begins. Then we may see the individuals change habits, religion, attitudes, and interests, so that they fit together better. Areas of

Americans Still Have A Love Affair With Romance

Nearly one out of two marriages may end in divorce, but romance seems to be alive and well.

More than three-quarters of Americans think they are "very" or "somewhat" romantic, according to a recent survey of 1,000 men and women commissioned by Korbel premium champagne. Slightly more men consider themselves romantic than women. Eighty percent of men polled and 77 percent of women described themselves as either "very" or "somewhat" romantic.

The most romantic people live in the Northeast region of the country, according to the study, with the South and West virtually tied for second and the Midwest coming in a close third.

If you want to make an impression, don't bring a box of candy. When asked what things signify "romance", the Top 10 items in descending order were flowers, wine, romantic meals, champagne, food in general, candles, perfume/cologne, jewelry, candy and clothing.

Southern respondents were most apt to believe that romance is "on the rise." They attribute it to changes in lifestyle, more emphasis on morals and values, and the effect of the media, particularly soap operas and commercials.

The Detroit News, 3-10-87, p. 1D

Cultural norms influence our expectations concerning relationship development and de-escalation.

commonality are emphasized, especially those that allow them to see their relationship as somehow unique and special from all others. The commitment and attachment bonds discussed earlier become evident in the relationship. Because integration and bonding are the focus, differences and individuality are de-emphasized. [Often those invididual differences must be reasserted later in the relationship as each partner feels the need to express those parts of themselves not part of the particular relationship. If individuality is not eventually allowed to surface, each may begin to feel "suffocated" or "trapped" by the relationship.]

If integration goes smoothly, relational partners often desire to engage in some public ritual to institutionalize the relationship. We call this the **institutionalizing stage.** Marriage, going public about "living together," and going through fraternity initiation rituals are all means of institutionalizing relationships. Partners take on social obligation bonds which provide legal (or at least publically-defined) guidelines for the relationship. Stabilizing the relationship by institutionalizing it makes it harder to dissolve the relationship without risking social and legal sanctions.

Your relationships may not progress in order through each of these five stages. Some relationships begin at the institutionalizing stage, as when you sign a contract for a new job with your employer, and never go beyond fulfilling the social obligations implied by the institutionalized roles of the relationship partners. Other relationships may move backward and forward at various times in their history. For example, troubles with integrating may lead to more experimenting and attempts to re-intensify the relationship. Still others may never get past the experimenting stage, as with many workplace relationships. In fact, Knapp (1984) argues that most of our relationships remain within the experimenting stage.

RELATIONSHIP DE-ESCALATION OR DISSOLUTION

At any time in the course of a relationship one or both partners may decide either to de-escalate or dissolve the relationship. **De-escalating** a relationship involves re-defining the relationship so that it has less breadth and depth, is less demanding or involving, and is an attempt to halt the course of relationship development. De-escalation may or may not result in **dissolving** or terminating the relationship. While relational development is a mutually-negotiated process in which both partners must agree to changes, dissolution can and often does occur underlineally. That is, it takes only one person to end a relationship. That aspect alone makes the two processes very different in character.

At some point in every relationship one or both relational partners experience dissatisfaction with the relationship. Duck (1982) provides a model of what happens when dissatisfaction brings thoughts of relationship dissolution. In Duck's model, as with Knapp's stages of relational development, relationships do not necessarily move through all of the stages or in order. They may move back and forth between stages or skip stages depending on the communication (or lack of it) between the partners engaged in de-escalating, dissolving, or re-negotiating their relationship.

Whatever the source of dissatisfaction, it often initiates the initial **intrapersonal stage** of relationship dissolution. In this stage you: become very reflective about the relationship, carefully evaluating your partner's behavior to identify the sources of and justify your dissatisfaction; become more hostile, evaluative, and concerned with immediate equity in the rewards and costs exchanged; feel the need to express your discomfort with confidants other than your partner (some have called this a third-person "leakage"); become more negative in your descriptions of both yourself and your partner; try to indirectly change your partner's behavior without directly addressing the sources of dissatisfaction; change your communication style; and/or even begin to convince yourself that leaving would be better than staying. All of this can occur before you even communicate your dissatisfaction to your partner — hence the label "intrapersonal."

Sometimes relationships are broken off immediately following the intrapersonal stage. However, if and when you decide to discuss the problem with your partner, your relationship enters the **dyadic stage.** During this stage: you try to get your partner to go along with redefining the relationship; the two of you engage in increased amounts of private discussion about the relationship, often withdrawing temporarily from contacts with outside friends; and/or you talk a lot about future forms the relationship might take as you weigh its possibilities. Ultimately this stage ends with a decision either to repair the relationship or to dissolve it. If dissolving is the decision, the two of you move on to the social stage.

The **social stage** of dissolution involves "going public" with the decision to dissolve. First, the two of you may work privately to create a picture of what the state of the relationship and each person will be after dissolution. You may develop separate or mutual accounts for why the break-up occurred. You "try these out" on friends, parents, children, etc., in an attempt to get them to understand and agree that dissolving is the right thing to do. Many people get to this point only to find the realities of breaking up — the real costs for each person, the negative reactions of friends and family — are much more than they bargained for. The result is often a move back to the dyadic phase and renewed effort to repair the relationship.

The final phase of dissolution is the **grave-dressing stage.** Here partners work together or separately to finalize their stories about the break-up and get it all behind them. They may re-interpret events from long past to show that the relationship was "doomed from the start" or that they just "outgrew the relationship." In an extensive analysis of the accounts and stories people create during the social and grave-dressing stages, McCall (1982) found two points especially clear. First, the accounts seldom have much to do with the actual process of dissolution. In addition, the best accounts are acceptable to both partners and their social networks, and they provide reasons for dissolution that allow each partner to save face in the eyes of others and to maintain self-esteem. The creation of accounts clearly is crucial to successful dissolution in easing both immediate pain and long-term problems associated with dissolution.

Duck's model of relationship dissolution points to the importance of communication in the process. How you communicate affects whether you decide to repair or dissolve during the dyadic phase and also the degree of success in resulting attempts to repair the relationship. The quality of communication also affects your ability to create functional accounts of what happened during the social and grave-dressing phases that enable you, your partner, and your social network to adjust to the dissolution.

SUMMARY

An interpersonal context for communication involves at least two people who are mutually aware of each other with both participants having a communicative goal to make something private, public and shared. For every interpersonal communication context, each person has an expected definition of the situation. Most interpersonal contexts require participants to negotiate the definition of the situation. Two key components of this expected definition are the identities of the participants and the nature of the relationship.

Each of the participants needs to be aware of his/her own range of identities (material, social, and ideal self) and identity goals for this situation as well as to be aware that the other person will be doing the same for him/herself. Strategies of self-disclosing, disclaiming, repairing, and altercasting can be used to manage these identities in the communication.

The nature of the relationship is also key in interpersonal communication. Each relationship is held together by relational bonds (ascribed, commitment, or attachment) and is based on a system of relational justice (social obligation, equity, parity, or need). In addition, relationships are created, maintained, and changed over time in our communication with others, so it is important to understand the various stages of relationship escalation (or development) and de-escalation (or dissolution).

This chapter has outlined the fundamental concepts of interpersonal communication contexts. Chapter 6 will provide a practical application of these concepts by identifying skills and strategies important in interpersonal communication competence.

KEY TERMS

immediacy
definition of the situation
identity
self-concept
identity goals
material self
social self
ideal self
self-disclosure
disclaimers
repair strategies
altercasting
bonds
relational justice
relational dominance
breadth of relationship
depth of relationship
relationship escalation (development)
relationship de-escalation (dissolution)

CHAPTER 6

CHAPTER 6

INTERPERSONAL COMMUNICATION CONTEXTS: STRATEGIES AND SKILLS

This chapter will highlight several keys to interpersonal communication competence. The guidelines should help you in accomplishing your relationship goals whether they be developing, repairing, de-escalating, or effecting a tolerable dissolution that minimizes the pain for all involved. Their usefulness is not limited to accomplishing relationship goals, however. Acquiring the knowledge and skill necessary to follow these guidelines should help you in managing your identity and achieving all the other practical goals you pursue in communication (e.g., interviewing well, teaching, persuading, comforting, or leading others).

Becoming a competent interpersonal communicator includes: the ability to take the perspective of others; developing active listening skills; maintaining a supportive communication climate while avoiding defensive communication in both yourself and others; and managing interactions effectively.

PERSPECTIVE-TAKING

To be a competent interpersonal communicator you first must be able to understand similarities and differences between your own and another's definition of the situation. The definition of the situation is your perspective on a communication event which includes three different levels. First, each communicator has his/her own **direct perspective.** Your definition of identities, the relationship, and the goals of the interaction provide your direct perspective.

The mutual awareness characterizing interpersonal contexts described at the beginning of Chapter 5 suggests you also have some definition of the other person's definition of the situation, i.e., how that person is defining identities, the relationship, etc. This level is your **meta-perspective:** what you think the other person thinks.

Often communication is affected by yet a third level: What you think the other person thinks you think. For example, you may think I think you think of yourself as more intelligent than I. This third level perspective is the **meta meta-perspective.**

Your communication will be affected by all three levels — your direct perspective, your understanding of my definition of the situation (meta-perspective), and/or how you think I understand your definition of the situation (meta meta-perspective). Figure 6.1 presents these levels focusing just on the perceptions two people, Jack and Jill, have of their relationship. The presence of these levels of knowledge reflects what is referred to as **interpenetration of perspectives** in interpersonal communication.

As the figure indicates, when you compare Jack and Jill's direct perspectives you are identifying points of **agreement** or **disagreement.** Clearly, Jack and Jill disagree about the relationship they have. When you compare one's meta-perspective with the other's direct perspective, the primary concern is whether there is **understanding** or **misunderstanding.** Jill understands there is disagreement; Jack does not. Comparing one's meta meta-perspective with the other's meta-perspective tells you whether there is **realization** or **failure to realize** if they understand or misunderstand one another. Here Jill realizes Jack misunderstands her, while Jack realizes Jill understands him. If you look at each person individually and compare his/her own meta meta-perspective and direct perspective, you discover whether the person is **feeling understood.** In this case, Jill feels misunderstood; Jack feels understood.

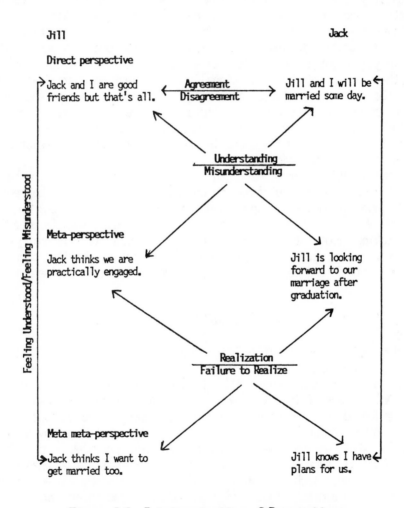

Figure 6.1 Interpenetration of Perspectives

Typically, you expect communication to go most smoothly when you have agreement, understanding, realization of understanding, and the feeling of being understood from both people. This is seldom the case, however, for every feature of both communicator's definition of the situation. The model identifies places for a variety of "mismatches," any one of which may or may not cause communication problems. Fortunately, successful communication does not require a perfect match at all levels between our beliefs about the situation. Typically only certain beliefs are **communication-relevant,** that is, important to the accomplishment of the primary goals the communicators have in a particular situation. For example, Jack and Jill may be able to communicate and work very effectively together in preparing for an exam, because the primary goal is a task goal to which their differences about the future of their relationship are not relevant.

Understanding both similarities and differences among the three levels — direct, meta-, and meta, meta — is called **perspective-taking.** This process of perspective-taking is essential for effective interpersonal communication.

Accurate perspective-taking allows you to know what issues need to be addressed in your negotiation of identities, relationships, and task goals. Being aware of the need to step back occasionally and reflect on communication-relevant differences between perspectives and being accurate in your perspective-taking about those communication-relevant beliefs is central to effective interpersonal communication. Despite Jack and Jill's success at preparing for an exam, if they are unable to negotiate differences in the definition of their relationship, it will cause serious communication problems in many other situations.

Many communication problems can emerge when you fail to be a good perspective-taker: when you fail to understand you agree or disagree; fail to realize you understand or misunderstand another; or when you feel understood or misunderstood when the opposite is the case. And, knowing when to move into this perspective-taking mode of thinking is the product of active listening as much as anything else. For, even if you have perspective-taking ability, poor listening can make you blind and deaf to the cues which alert you to the need to use that ability.

LISTENING

Listening involves a set of skills which are learned. We are born neither "good" nor "bad" listeners. Rather, listening is a learned response behavior. Considering the fact that over 50% of our communication with others involves listening (Adler, Rosenfeld, & Towne, 1986), the skills we have developed as listeners are indeed very important in our effectiveness as communicators.

As with other communicative behaviors, listening is affected by many factors: how we feel, what we believe is important, our previous experiences, our attitudes, physical surroundings, etc. Think of some situations when you scarely heard what went on, such as when a friend tells a story you've already heard several times or in a class right before an important job interview. You may only "float" in and out of the conversation or class lecture, perhaps being mentally absent much of the time, or what we termed "ideational attention" in Chapter 2.

Contrast these instances of poor listening with examples of when you listened carefully and well. For example, when we wake up in the middle of the night because we've heard a noise, we listen especially hard for several minutes in order to quiet our fears. When you listen to a person whom you have great respect for, you may find yourself listening very carefully to topics you'd never even thought you would be interested in yet you do listen. Or perhaps the review before an exam leads you to concentrate closely on details which may have escaped you before.

If you think about those times when you listened well, you'll note some generalizations about your activity, your behavior, at that time. You are interested in the subject and/or speaker, the outcome of the message is important to you, and most crucial to effective listening, you focus your attention closely. In order to be an effective listener and enhance your interpersonal competence, you must learn to **actively participate** as a listener in the communication process.

Effective listening does not mean passively absorbing what others say. To the contrary, competent listening requires both mental and behavioral work. To better understand the listening process we will first define listening and discuss each of its components. Then we will discuss different types of listening and outline the skills involved in active listening.

A DEFINITION OF LISTENING

Based on research and observations of human listening behavior, we have developed a general definition of listening: **Listening is the selective process of attending to, hearing, and retaining aural stimuli.** We will briefly discuss each of the key terms in this definition to help you better understand the listening process.

Process

In Chapter 1, we discussed the assumptions underlying the notion of "process" in communication. Listening, as one aspect of communicative activity, is also viewed as a process. That is, listening behaviors are on-going, with no precise beginning or end. The listening process is seen as dynamic, changing, and continuous, rather than a passive, static, and discrete phenomenon.

Selective

As we saw in Chapter 2 we cannot process all the sensory information in our environment, so we select out, at varying levels of consciousness, only certain stimuli to pay attention to. In this case the selectivity refers to the fact that only a small portion of what we are capable of hearing will actually be processed further.

Hearing

Listening and hearing are <u>not</u> the same. Hearing is the physiological function of receiving auditory stimuli. Sound waves impinge on the eardrums causing vibrations. As with the processing of information from each of senses (as discussed in Chapter 2), these vibrations are transmitted by means of an electro-chemical process to the brain. Hearing involves getting the information through to the brain; listening involves making sense and assigning meaning to the sounds we hear.

Comprehending

Once our brain has received the auditory information, we try to "make sense of" what that information means. As we learned in Chapter 2, we employ schemas or cognitive frameworks in our attempts to understand the stimuli in our environment we first attend to and then perceive. In the listening process, comprehension is the assigning of meaning to stimuli we hear.

Retaining

Beyond comprehending auditory stimuli, listening involves the storing of meaningful information for later recall. In Chapter 2, we discussed two types of storage systems: short-term memory, which lasts for up to 60 seconds, and long-term memory, which is storage of information after one minute and which may be retained for a lifetime. Bostrom and Waldhart (1980) identified similar components in listening (i.e., short-term and long-term listening) and also two others: short-term with rehearsal time and interpretive listening which includes consideration of paralinguistic cues.

Most of us would agree that it makes little sense to hear, attend to, or comprehend sounds in our environment unless we remember or retain the information in some way. However, whether we retain that information quite briefly, or remember it for years is a function of a number of factors. For example, in a short conversation with an acquaintance, it is probably not important to retain every detail of the exchange. In contrast, remembering what a supervisor said during an employee training session may be so important that we may use memory aids such as tape recorders and extensive note-taking to assist us. That is, the kind of listening varies from situation to situation.

TYPES OF LISTENING

In addition to understanding the basic components of the listening process, we can also identify different types or kinds of listening we engage in. Actually, these types of listening stem from different situations which influence how we listen. The four types of listening we will discuss are casual, obligatory, argumentative or defensive, and active listening.

Casual listening

This type of listening is really hardly listening at all. We use this term to refer to those times when we are aware of sounds uttered by another person, but we are so passive that we scarcely pay attention to what is being said. "Listening" to a friend tell a story we've heard several times before is a case which would probably involve casual listening.

Obligatory listening

Obligatory listening refers to those situations in which we should pay attention (usually because of our relationship with the other person), but we either don't hear the specific words or don't process the message as the speaker intended. We feel obliged to be there and thus to look like we are listening, yet often we are actually faking our attention. Unlike casual listening where we feel it is unnecessary to listen closely, with obligatory listening or whenever we are "obliged" to remain where we are, we only appear to listen.

At an early age children learn to engage in this type of listening with their parents. When a parent begins the "you-must-clean-up-your-room" lecture, the daughter or son may give all the appropriate responses which indicate active listening, such as head nodding, stating agreement and making eye contact, when in fact, s/he is processing little of what the parent is saying. Parents can also be guilty of obligatory listening, asking the standard, "How was your day at school?" yet paying only minimal attention to the child's response. This type of listening is **pseudo-listening**, in that the receiver is only pretending to listen (Adler, Rosenfeld, & Towne, 1986). While this type of listening may seem to be a polite way to handle a situation, it is frustrating to both the sender and the receiver because in essence both have wasted their time.

Argumentative listening

Argumentative listening (which is also called defensive listening) occurs when we perceive what others have said as being a personal attack on the identity we have presented. In argumentative listening, we attend primarily to possible weaknesses in the other person's position and then use the rest of our time plot our attack or what we want to say all the while we appear to be listening. In other words, we usually do not listen to the full message. Rather, we marshall our defenses and think about what we're going to say when it's our turn to talk. This type of listening is also frustrating because meaningful interaction cannot occur when the full message of neither participant is being comprehended. In addition, argumentative listening is likely to lead to an increasingly defensive communication climate, as we shall see later in this chapter.

Active listening

In interpersonal, as well as small group, organizational, and mass communication contexts, active listening is an essential aspect of becoming a competent communicator. With this type of listening, we are not passive receivers but are very actively involved in the communication process. Active listening meanings "working at" understanding the meaning intended by the speaker. We try to listen to the entire message, to make sense of what the speaker is saying, and to respond appropriately.

Active listening requires both the **mental or cognitive work** necessary to accurately and efficiently process what you hear and see in a communication context and the **behavioral work** necessary to let others know you are listening. This type of listening takes a great deal of effort on the part of the receiver. But as with anything learned, we often have developed some less-than-desirable habits over the years. So, in order to improve our listening skills, we may have to "un-learn" those habits which hinder effective listening. It will take time and effort, but the goal is worth achieving. Below are suggested several strategies in which we can improve our skills as active listeners in interpersonal as well as other communication contexts.

Mental Work. First, let's look at the mental work involved in active listening. You should constantly work to **motivate** yourself to listen. Find some reason that it would benefit you or the other person (or both) to accurately understand one another. Typically when you enter a communication situation, you are dominated by motivations to talk — to get in your "two cents worth." You must learn to feel rewarded by the creation of an accurate understanding of others. Creating that motivation will not be easy given our inclination to value talking over listening, as we saw in Chapter 4.

Second, you must "listen" with both your ears and eyes — **attend to both verbal and nonverbal cues.** Often the message you should respond to is indicated as much by what people communicate nonverbally as by the words that are used. If as you discuss problems in a class with your professor, he draws back in his chair, begins to glare at you as he talks, and raises his volume and rate of speaking, it may mean he feels something you have said was an attack against him personally. Her words may continue to refer to class issues, but the active listener will understand there is another message — another issue — that must now be dealt with if the communication is to be effective.

The active listener also works mentally to **summarize major themes and ideas** in other people's messages. Functioning like a video-recorder — simply memorizing every word and behavior emitted by the other — is not being an active listener. Since you can process information at a rate faster than anyone can speak, use that extra time to look for multiple messages provided through both verbal and nonverbal channels. Try to identify the main points the other makes so you can avoid responding to some specific statement that is, in fact, a relatively unimportant part of what the other person is trying to say.

As you process information in this way, try to **withhold evaluation** of the other person and/or his/her comments until all the information is in. Often we may fail to listen to others actively because we are "sure" they don't know much or because we think we already "know" what they are going to say (since we know them so well). If we do listen at all, it is with an evaluative set that insures that we will hear only what we expected to hear.

At other times, we may make premature evaluations when the other person uses a buzz term. **Buzz terms** are words or phrases that, like sitting on a buzzer, creates an immediate reaction — an evaluative, often emotional, response to others. Each of us has our own buzz terms that short circuit our listening skills. For example, suppose that you are a dedicated fraternity member and while discussing college life with a classmate, s/he mentions those awful "frat rats." You are likely to immediately shift to an argumentative listening mode and prepare a defense of sorority and fraternity members for this "typical independent." Racist or sexist language commonly provides buzz terms for many people. While such terms are justifiably offensive, as an active listener you should work to avoid letting them lead you to immediate evaluation and poor listening. If for no other reason, do this so you can accurately understand and effectively disagree with the person who uses the terms. You might try to list your personal buzz terms as a first step in preventing them from making you a poor listener.

Behavioral Work. In addition to all the mental work described, active listening involves a lot of behavioral work to let others know you are listening. If you don't believe the latter work is important, think of your reaction when you feel someone is not listening to you especially if you are trying to discuss something important to you. The competent communicator is careful to avoid creating that reaction in others.

Active listening has at least two important behavioral components: being nonverbally responsive and using the verbal strategy of paraphrasing. To be **nonverbally responsive** involves: giving your complete attention to the other and not engaging in other activities (such as reading or talking) while you are listening; maintaining relatively constant eye contact; and leaning toward the other person, so it looks like you are orienting yourself directly to him or her. In addition, the active listener provides backchannel responses such as head nods and facial expressions that show understanding or misunderstanding, as well as occasional verbal affirmations of the other person's statements such as, "I see," "yes," "uh-huh," "right," or "OK." These are called "back-channel" responses because they are not attempts to take the floor and gain control of the main channel for communication. Of course, as we discussed previously, merely "looking like" you're listening does not guarantee that you are listening well, but active listening behaviors do provide important nonverbal cues to the speaker.

As an active listener, while the other person is speaking you should exhibit behaviors which show the speaker you are listening. When it is your turn to talk, you should often use the verbal tactic of paraphasing. **Paraphrasing** is the act of summarizing your interpretation of what the other person has just said and checking to see if your interpretation is correct before offering your response.

And, if your interpretation is not accurate, then the other person needs to be given an opportunity to restate his/her ideas before you speak.

For example, you may think you hear Jack say, "Woman without her <u>man</u>, is <u>nothing</u>." Before accusing him of sexism or worse, you should paraphase and ask him if he is implying that women have no value except that provided to them by men. You might find out that he heard himself saying or least intended to say, "Woman, without <u>her</u>, man is nothing." Through paraphasing you have prevented a very unpleasant encounter based on a simple misunderstanding. In addition, through it you have shown the other person that you were listening to what s/he said and were trying to understand it as that person meant it.

Not all statements need to be paraphased. However, it is generally a good idea to paraphase frequently to make sure that your mental work as a listener has produced an accurate representation of what the other person intended to say. In some situations it may even be wise to invoke a "paraphasing rule" requiring each person to parapharase accurately and to the satisfaction of the previous speaker before responding.

FACILITATING A SUPPORTIVE COMMUNICATION CLIMATE

Effective perspective-taking and active listening will help you uncover the particular areas of disagreement and misunderstanding that hinder your efforts to communicate effectively. As you assess communication-relevant similarities and differences between your own and others' perspectives, you should be particularly alert to beliefs that might lead you or the other person to communicate defensively.

Defensive communication has been defined by Gibb (1961) as those behaviors which occur when an individual anticipates or perceives a threat from others to the identity s/he is presenting in a particular situation. We become defensive when we perceive that our identity in the situation, the image we are trying to project, is being challenged or attacked by others. It doesn't matter if the challenge was intended as such; it only matters if we <u>think</u> it is. For example, in a group discussion, suppose another responds to your proposal by saying, "I think if you had read the materials more closely, you would see that . . . ." In this case, you may not even hear the other person's counter proposal. What you hear instead is only the attempt to altercast you into the role of a less than diligent person who hadn't read the materials carefully.

In such situations you typically begin to devote most of your energies to defending your identity and "winning" the point. Understanding and negotiation of differences and arriving at the best solution suddenly becomes secondary. Furthermore, your defensive reactions spawn defensiveness in others. Very quickly a **regressive spiral** develops: with each comment the interaction spirals further down into more intense defensive efforts to protect identities and attack the other person. Each person becomes less willing and able to engage in perspective-taking and active listening skills are forgotten in favor of defensive or argumentative listening.

How do you avoid this unhappy state of affairs? First, as you do your perspective-taking work before and during communication with others, be on the alert for evidence of defensiveness-producing behaviors. Gibb (1961) identified six general characteristics that create a **defensive climate** for communication: evaluation, control, hidden agenda, neutrality, superiority, and certainty. He contrasted each with an opposing characteristic that encourages a **supportive climate**, that enhances your ability to negotiate differences with others: description, problem-orientation, spontaneity, concern, equality, and open-mindedness.

Evaluation vs. Description. When you feel you are being **evaluated**, judged, or tested by others, you often engage in defensive communication. Your main goal is to pass the test or to challenge the right of the other person to evaluate you. On the other hand, when you believe the other person is simply **describing** in an attempt to make his/her feelings and ideas clear and understandable, a climate of mutual supportiveness is created.

Control vs. Problem Orientation. Often perceptions that others are trying to **control** or influence your thoughts and behavior will cause defensive reactions, especially if the attempts at control are coercive in nature. In contrast, perceptions that each communicator is trying to achieve a mutual definition of the problem and mutually agreed upon solution create a **problem-orientation** and encourage supportive communication.

Hidden Agenda vs. Spontaneity. Believing that others have **hidden agendas** and motives, i.e., that covert manipulation is their goal, often spawns defensive communication. On the other hand, **spontaneity** in conveying thoughts, feelings, and desires honestly and openly makes people more willing to seek to understand and be supportive of others.

Neutrality vs. Concern. Sometimes people feel another person is neither concerned about nor values their feelings, goals, or anything else about their contribution to the interaction. They perceive the other person as **neutral** or indifferent toward them. While in many aspects of life neutrality (in the sense of not taking sides), is positively viewed, in communicating with others to show neutrality in the form of ignoring or being indifferent to the other person is likely to arouse the other's defensiveness. Instead, competent communicators will use both verbal and nonverbal cues to demonstrate that they are **concerned** and are trying to listen and understand that person's point of view. This doesn't mean they must always agree with the other person; rather it means that they are concerned enough to try to understand them.

Superiority vs. Equality. Feeling that others see themselves as **superior** to you, that their ideas and goals are inherently better and more valuable than yours, typically creates defensive reactions. When both communicators treat each other as **equals**, at least in terms of the attention and consideration their communication deserves, they are much less likely to feel the need to defend themselves or attack the other person.

Certainty vs. Open-Mindedness. Feeling that you are "up against a brick wall" with another person or that they are **certain** of their position and will entertain no others may lead you to attack them and their ideas all the more fiercely. You also begin to defend your own position with an equally dogmatic, closed-minded attitude. In such situations the communication often degenerates into a shouting match. By working to engage in perspective-taking and active listening, you can convey **open-mindedness** to others and encourage a supportive climate for communication.

Obviously, the competent communicator attempts to create and maintain perceptions of spontaneity, concern, a problem orientation, description, equality, open-mindedness, as a part of both his/her own and the other's definition of the situation. Sometimes, of course, you _are_ trying to control or influence others or evaluate their behavior as in a job performance appraisal, and not all communication is among equals, as with teacher-student communication. In these cases the defensiveness potential is naturally higher and you must work to compensate by encouraging perceptions that maintain a supportive climate.

Despite your best attempts to manage your own and others' perceptions, you or they can slip into defensive communication before you are aware of what is happening. For that reason you need to be alert for behaviors that are the early warning signs for defensiveness. While these vary for each individual, anytime you see frequent interruptions, attempts to steal the floor from others, people trying to talk at the same time, and/or obvious evidence that people are not listening to one another, you should step back and check for the presence of perceptions creating a defensive climate.

In addition, you might keep a diary account or a "defensiveness record" of situations in which you and people you interact with become defensive (see your **Course Manual**). Knowing the causes and behaviors that characterize defensive communication in yourself as well as in those around you is an important first step in learning how to avoid or break regressive spirals in which each person's defensive behavior creates increasingly intense defensive reactions from others.

INTERACTION MANAGEMENT

In Chapter 4 you read about norms of interaction — cultural rules that define how communication, and conversation in particular, should be carried out. A competent interpersonal communicator must be aware of these rules in order to **manage** interaction and produce smooth and coherent conversations. As a socialized member of your culture you have learned and follow many such rules even though you may not be consciously aware of them. Norms of interaction define appropriate ways of opening and closing conversations, introducing and changing topics within a conversation, turn-taking, and many other important features of communication. They govern both your verbal and nonverbal behavior. Violations of these rules, even if unintentional, can lead others to make negative attributions about the person who breaks the rule and/or to void communication with them.

We do not have the space to define even a small part of the norms of interaction that govern communication in American culture, much less point to differences in norms across cultures. We leave that task to instructors in other courses focusing specifically on language, culture, and communication. The key issue is to be aware of the norms because unintentional violation can disrupt conversation, hinder your efforts to accomplish your goals in the setting, as well as lead others to evaluate you in negative terms.

The task of becoming a competent communicator is not an easy one. One course, or even an entire college experience devoted to it, is not enough. To develop and

---

LADY CHATTERLY?

Study Says Cheating Wives Want Conversation

NEW YORK (UPI)—A lust for talk — not sex — causes women to cheat on their husbands, a study shows.

The study supported other research that found the failure by spouses to communicate is a primary cause of marital problems, the Ladies' Home Journal said in its September issue.

It also said that the search for new partners was not a result of the desire for more sex, but rather the need to communicate.

The study reported in the Journal was headed by Lynn Atwater, an associate professor of sociology at Seton Hall University in New Jersey.

One researcher traced 100 couples who had been married for five years and found they spent only about 30 minutes a week talking with each other, the Journal said. Journal readers surveyed by the magazine in 1983 found women's second-biggest complaint about their marriages — after money fights — was: "We don't talk any more."

Family counselors said the fast pace of life and changes in lifestyles are among the reasons why families talk so infrequently.

"People are preoccupied with solitary pursuits - running, aerobics, working out," said Richard Dublin, associate executive director of Jewish Family and Community Service of Chicago.

The result, the Journal said, is that "our stomach and leg muscles have never been tighter, our conversational skills never flabbier."

Adding to the lack of talk among family members is the disappearance of the family dinner hour and the ubiquitous presence of television, the Journal said, citing a 1986 Nielsen report that found televisions were turned on in American homes for a record seven hours and 10 minutes a day.

The Detroit News, 8-13-86, p. 3A

Competent communication skills are central to the development and maintenance of our interpersonal relationship.

---

maintain a competent level of communication ability is a **lifetime effort.** The effort required, though, is no greater than the importance of the task. Whether you plan to be an engineer, a farmer, a lawyer, a doctor, or whatever, the ability to manage smoothly your relationships with your clients, co-workers, family, etc., is crucial to your practical successes and to your happiness and satisfaction.

All of this discussion is but the "tip of the iceberg." There is much more involved in each of the topics covered here as well as other important issues tied to effective interpersonal persuasion, cultural effects on interpersonal communication, etc. In subsequent chapters in this book you will see how factors present in small group, organizational, and mass communication contexts further add to the complexity of the task of communicating effectively with others.

SUMMARY

This chapter has discussed the strategies and skills necessary for competent interpersonal communication. Perspective-taking, active listening, fostering a supportive communication climate, and effectively managing interaction are the key areas which contribute to achieving communicative goals in interpersonal contexts. In the chapters which follow, we will see how these strategies and skills may also apply in small group, organizational, and mass communication contexts.

KEY TERMS

direct perspective
meta-perspective
meta meta-perspective
perspective-taking
causal listening
obligatory listening
pseudo listening
argumentative/defensive listening
active listening
buzz terms
paraphrasing
regressive spiral
defensive communication climate
supportive communication climate
interaction management

CHAPTER 7

CHAPTER 7

SMALL GROUP COMMUNICATION CONTEXTS

What constitutes small group communication? How many people are needed for a "small group"? Exactly what is meant by a small group communication context is something which has been debated by those in the field of communication. How would you define a small group? Test yourself by placing a check beside each of the following descriptions which you think involve small group communication.

1) Ten people standing on a street corner waiting for the light to change so they can cross the street.
2) A monthly bridge group.
3) Five law school students who have formed a study group.
4) Any group of 3-20 people.
5) A self-help therapy group for children whose parents have recently divorced.
6) The seven-member grievance committee for a local factory.
7) Several friends getting together to watch the final game of the World Series.
8) Four people who commute to work together every week day.
9) A communication research team which has eight members.
10) Six employees from different departments in a local television station who have been assigned the task of designing a new set for the daily newscasts.

DEFINING SMALL GROUP COMMUNICATION CONTEXTS

While it is possible to include most, if not all, of the above as examples of small group communication contexts, our discussion will focus only on those **small groups that solve a problem or make a decision.**

So, in examining small group communication contexts, we will not be discussing groups such as friendship groups (#2 & #7) whose primary purpose is social. And we will not be concerned with groups whose primary purpose is psychologically help for group members such as self-help therapy groups (#5). Nor are we concerned with social groups or groups which are simply a collection of people who are in the same location (#1, 4, & 8). Instead, we will focus on groups whose explicit goals are to solve a problem or to make a decision. As such, the study group (#3), grievance committee (#6), communication research team (#9), and the tv station set designers (#10) fit our definition of a small group since they must resolve a problem or make a decision.

The most useful way to think of a small group is as a whole system, with group members being parts of the system. Through their communication, face-to-face, written, via the telephone or other channels, group members are able to coordinate their activities in such a way that the group can successfully reach its goal

(Stech & Ratliff, 1976). It is this communication among group members which is critical in achieving the goal of resolving a problem or making a particular decision.

The numerical boundary of the small group communication context is arbitrary, but most researchers consider a small group to include between three and twenty people. What is important is that the group is of a size which allows each group member to communicate with the other group members in order to achieve their goals.

INDIVIDUAL VS. GROUP DECISION-MAKING

The old adage "two heads are better than one" suggests the appeal of groups over individuals when it comes to making decisions. While this can be true, the superiority of groups over individuals actually depends on several factors. Obviously, compared to individuals, groups are much slower in making decisions. It takes a great deal of time to listen to different opinions and ideas and then to try to reach consensus on a particular course of action. So, **when the decision to be made is a simple one or one with time constraints, it is probably best to leave that decision to an individual, rather than a group.**

Some decisions, however, seem to be made more effectively by a group than by an individual. Even a very insightful individual benefits from the interaction provided by other group members. Groups provide a critical exchange of ideas, a sounding board, and a context where creativity can be encouraged. Generally, tasks for which there is only one right answer are not best served by a group. However, **on tasks where there is more than one right answer, or where creative solutions are desirable, groups surpass individual efforts.** The communication research team and the television employees who need to design a newscast set, require creativity for their tasks. Thus, a small group is appropriate in both these cases.

As groups develop and interact over time, they become more than just the individuals who comprise it. This is called the **principle of nonsummativity** which says that the whole is greater than the sum of its parts. The thinking that occurs in a group is greater than the thinking of any one individual and cannot be broken down into individual parts or contributions. This is also referred to as the **assembly effect.** In solving problems or making decisions where this assembly effect is achieved, productivity exceeds the simple sum of the individual efforts if the members were working alone. The members of the study group certainly recognize the importance of the assembly effect in working together to prepare for their law classes and exams.

One phenomenon that seems to occur in groups is called the **risky shift phenomenon.** That is, a group is more likely to make a decision which takes greater risks than the members would have done if they were making the decision individually. When choosing from several alternatives, groups tend to select an alternative with a bigger payoff but with a smaller chance of being realized, i.e., one which is more risky. This would be an important factor in a group such as a grievance committee which may have to make decisions with which other

113

organization members may disagree. The interaction among group members appears to make them feel comfortable taking greater risks and being less conservative than they would be if each acted alone. Several possible explanations for why this happens have been offered by researchers. The explanation that has received the greatest support suggests that group members feel less individual responsibility because they are able to share, or diffuse, the responsibility among all the group members. Obviously, though, if conservative decisions or ideas are desirable, a group context may not be appropriate.

In summary, groups are more effective than individuals when time is not a consideration, the problem or decision is a complex one, creativity and the assembly effect are desired, and conservative decisions or ideas are not appropriate.

NETWORKS

As group members interact with each other over time, patterns of interaction develop. These patterns emerge as a result of the frequency of the communication links between group members and are called **networks.** Group members' interaction patterns become structured in a way that can facilitate or impede the group's effectiveness.

Throughout the 1950's and 1960's, researchers conducted laboratory studies where they manipulated group structure to try to understand how it affected the group process. They looked at how group structure affected the group's efficiency in solving a problem and how an individual's position in the group structure affected morale and satisfaction with the group. It is important to keep in mind that these laboratory studies were conducted with groups of people who had never met and would probably never interact again once the experiment was completed (sometimes called "zero history" groups). Also, rather than sitting face-to-face, these group members sat in cubicles separated by partitions with slots that could be opened or closed, depending on the particular network the researcher was investigating — i.e., slots would be opened or closed to allow or prevent interaction among group members. Interaction was not oral but rather took the form of passing written notes through the open slot in the cubicle. Given these manipulations, it is not clear how well the conclusions of the studies apply to every day kinds of problem-solving or decision-making groups.

Bavelas (1950) identified small groups into several communication networks and labeled them the circle, wheel, chain, and all-channel, designations we still use in describing group networks (see Figure 4.1). Each group member was given certain information that had to be shared with all other members in order to successfully complete the task. This study looked at how much time was needed for the group to reach the correct solution, how many messages were exchanged, how many errors were made, who group members perceived as the leader, and how satisfied members were. Bavelas concluded that highly centralized networks (like the wheel) were superior for routine tasks but decentralized networks like the circle were better for less routine tasks, where adaptation and innovative thinking were required. He also found that with less routine tasks when only centralized communication was allowed (i.e., the wheel or chain), the task was seldom completed successfully. Performance improved when decentralized communication (the circle) was allowed.

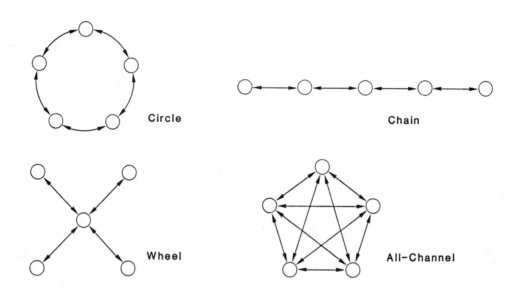

Figure 7.1 Communication Networks

Leavitt (1951) followed up on Bavelas's work but also looked at the amount of time it took for the group to reach the correct solution and the number of errors they made. He found that the wheel network was considerably faster than the circle for solving problems. But in the circle network, the group made fewer errors than in the wheel. One explanation for this was that in the circle all group members can check the solution and find possible errors, while in the wheel only the person in the center can.

Gilchrist, Shaw, and Walker (1954) also contributed to the small group network research by looking at independence and saturation. **Independence** refers to how free individuals felt to participate in the group. **Saturation** refers to an individual's amount of overload. These researchers found that members felt greater independence in decentralized networks (the circle or all-channel) regardless of the type of task, and that group members who felt more independent in the group were more satisfied with the group experience. In addition, the more overloaded, the more saturated with input and output demands the individual was. They found a negative relationship between saturation and efficiency in solving group tasks. In other words, when group members were saturated (overloaded), the group was less efficient in solving its task. In addition, the person in the center position of the wheel experienced saturation most often.

ROLES

As a small group continues to meet and its communication networks become more stable, members often begin to fill a need within the group by taking on certain roles. A **group role** is a set of behaviors developed through interaction with group members. Sometimes an individual fulfills only one role throughout the life of the group. In other groups, a group member may play several roles either simultaneously or alternately, and more than one person may fulfill a given role in a group. In this section we will discuss the three broad classifications of roles taken by group members — task, maintenance, and individual roles — as well as leadership roles (Benne & Sheats, 1948; Fisher, 1980).

GROUP ROLES

Task roles are those roles which emphasize the group's coordination of selecting and defining the problem and the solution for it. These roles are geared toward completing the task in the best or most competent manner. Within the task area there are three roles: information-manager, analyzer, and expediter (Benne & Sheats, 1948; Buerkel-Rothfuss, 1985).

Group members who fulfill the **information-manager** role provide or seek information and opinions in group interaction. For example, in the law student study group, Anita provides each group member with a detailed outline of a case she was assigned to research. She asks other members for their opinions, and Daniel suggests one additional reference the others may want to read. Both Anita and Daniel have fulfilled the information-manager role in this instance of group interaction.

An **analyzer** in a group tests evidence and opinions by questioning inferences and generalizations others may have made. The analyzer reveals faulty reasoning in the group's problem-solving process. During one meeting of the study group, Zachary says, "Professor Gold is a woman who gives difficult exams, so I guess it's something female professors do — give difficult exams." Thomas then fulfills the analyzer role when he points out Zachary's incorrect reasoning by stating, "Zachary, I agree that Professor Gold does give tough exams. However, Professor O'Neal, who is also a woman, is known for giving very easy tests. And remember the exam from Professor Parrish last semester? You thought she asked questions which were neither too difficult nor too simple." In fulfilling the analyzer role, Thomas has shown how faulty reasoning can lead to incorrect conclusions.

Finally, the **expediter** is concerned with the group's problem-solving and decision-making procedures. The expediter tries to coordinate the activities of the different group members and keep the group focused on the task at hand. This may involve reminding the others of the meeting agenda, questioning the direction the group's discussion is taking, or summarizing what has been talked about thus far. For example, Anita says to Zachary and Thomas, "While this discussion of the kinds of exams different law professors give is interesting, we've got to get back to the cases we'll be expected to know for class tomorrow. We've talked about the case I prepared notes on, but we still have to hear from Belinda." Anita has brought the group back to its original agenda and thus functioned in the role of expediter.

In small group communication contexts, task roles are crucial to getting the job done and achieving the group's goals in an effective manner. However, there is more to small group functioning than simply "getting the job done." **Maintenance roles** are those roles that are concerned with the relationships among group members. Many of the concepts and skills involved in interpersonal communication contexts (which were discussed in Chapters 5 and 6) also apply to small group interaction. This is particularly evident in group maintenance roles which serve to develop, maintain, or change the nature of the group's interaction in order to facilitate how the group works. As with task roles, more specific roles have been identified within the general category of maintenance roles (Benne & Sheats, 1948; Buerkel-Rothfuss, 1985). The encourager, harmonizer, and negotiator are roles which are concerned with the socio-emotional aspects of group interaction.

The primary goal of the **encourager** is fostering a supportive climate. Group members who fulfill the encourager role urge others to participate by offering praise or agreeing with their contributions, by being sensitive to others' desires to participate, and by helping others to communicate by expressing interest in the views of other group members. When Thomas perceives that Belinda is hesitant to present the court case she has researched, he fulfills the encourager role by saying, "I agree with Anita that we need to listen to what Belinda has prepared to present. I found this case very confusing. And, from the help you provided in other cases, we can use your explanation and analysis." Thomas has not only encouraged Belinda to participate in the group, but has also encouraged Anita to contribute by agreeing with what she said.

The **harmonizer** plays the mediating role. This person tries to relieve tension in the group and preserve smooth working relationships among group members. When disagreements or conflicts arise within the group, the harmonizer will steer the discussion away from personality issues. The harmonizer's objective is to soothe hostile or defensive group members and keep differences of opinions from becoming interpreted as personal attacks. For example, Zachary complains that Thomas is dominating the group and Thomas responds by stating that Zachary is such a mousey person he'll never survive law school. Daniel fulfills the harmonizing role by observing that law school is indeed a zoo, the instructors are the zookeepers, law students are the caged animals plotting their escape, and the study group has to work together to outwit the zookeeper/professors. The group members laugh and agree with Daniel's analogy, and tension which had built up may be relieved.

The third maintenance role is that of the **negotiator.** While the harmonizer attempts to diffuse emotional tension through any relevant means, such as telling an appropriate story or joke and commenting on areas in which group

117

members agree, the negotiator is directly concerned with the management and resolution of conflict situations. Group members who fulfill the negotiator role facilitate the use of compromise and collaboration in resolving group conflicts. For example, in the second meeting of the study group, Belinda, Thomas, and Daniel sharply disagreed over how the topic areas should be assigned to each group member. Anita, in the role of negotiator, suggested that rather than competing with each other, the group work together to determine a fair way to make topic assignments. Group members collaborated to develop a systematic method to solve the problem, deciding to have two people work together on some topic areas. Thus, Anita was able to facilitate the group in managing a conflict situation.

Effective group work is characterized by members fulfilling the various task and maintenance roles we have discussed. In contrast, **individual roles** hinder or interfere with effective group processes. Group members who assume individual roles are more concerned with satisfying their own needs and achieving their own objectives, rather than the group's needs and goals. Specific roles within this category include the aggressor, recognition-seeker, joker, and withdrawer (Benne & Sheats, 1948; Fisher, 1980).

The **aggressor** deflates others' status, attacks the group or the problem the group is working on, and expresses general disapproval. Thomas was fulfilling the aggressor role when he said that Zachary had a mousey personality and would fail in law school. A group member fulfilling the aggressor role expresses disapproval of other members' values, behaviors, or feelings in an attempt to demonstrate his/her superiority and the others' inferiority.

The **recognition-seeker** wants to impress the group with how much s/he knows. This person calls attention to him/herself by boasting, bragging, or citing personal achievements. For example, if Belinda told the other law students in her study group, "My strategies for studying for the semester exams must be superior to all of yours since I scored better than any of you last term," she would be fulfilling the recognition-seeker role.

While humor is essential in maintaining effective interpersonal relationships within small groups, using joking behavior to call attention to oneself can hinder the group in accomplishing its goals. The **joker** is cynical, nonchalant, or engages in horseplay that disrupts group processes. During one group meeting, Daniel first played a practical joke on Thomas then insisted on relating parts of the previous night's monologue from "Late Night with David Letterman." Daniel continued to crack jokes and make fun of the others while the others wanted him to stop. As long as David assumes this role, he interferes with the group's accomplishment of its goal.

Last, the **withdrawer** demonstrates an attitude of indifference and refuses to participate in group problem-solving and decision-making. An individual assuming this role displays a clear lack of involvement in group interaction. For example, in the study group's first meeting, Belinda ignored all opportunities to state her opinion as to how the group should proceed. When asked directly, she said, "I don't care. Whatever the rest of you decide." She made little eye contact with other group members, slouched in her chair, and doodled on a piece of paper. Belinda was fulfilling the withdrawer role in the group by expressing her indifference and apathy toward the group's task.

Obviously group task roles and group building and maintenance roles function in very important and useful ways to aid a group's effectiveness. The individual roles, however, can jeopardize the group, especially if group members reinforce them. Indulging the member in his/her performance of an individual role wastes valuable group time and may set a dangerous precedent. The aggressor for example, may interpret the group's lack of resistance to his/her domination as tacit approval to continue this sort of behavior. It is important for group members to recognize that roles do develop and that these roles frequently act to impede the group's movement toward its goal.

LEADERSHIP ROLES

Leadership roles refer to the ways an individual influences others to behave so as to move the group towards its goal (Shaw, 1976). Leadership roles clearly involve group maintenance functions — promoting participation, regulating interaction, promoting cooperation, arbitrating conflict, protecting individual rights (especially of minority views), providing exemplary behavior, and promoting group development. In addition, leadership roles involve group task functions — informing, planning, organizing, integrating information, coordinating, clarifying, evaluating, and stimulating information exchange (Baird & Weinberg, 1981). These are not different from the task and maintenance roles discussed earlier. However, when we consider leadership roles, we key in on the coordination of these functions. That is, leadership roles require simultaneously coordinating both the group members and the group's efforts toward accomplishing the task.

It is not enough for the person who occupies the role of leader to be appointed or emerge in this role. Once in this role, there are four "basic realities" the leader must face. First, **the leader must earn the role.** The leader must, to some extent, earn the leader role each time the group meets. As long as the leader behaves in ways that are perceived by group members as competent, fair, and trustworthy, s/he will probably continue to be accepted as the leader.

Second, **the leader must reconcile individual member's goals with the group goal.** The leader must make individual members feel that reaching the group goal will benefit them and will not endanger their own personal goals.

Third, it is critical that **the leader must recognize that each task of leadership is different.** Leadership style has been studied in a number of different ways, but, generally we think of "style" as the pattern of behaviors a leader uses to influence others in the pursuit of the group's goal(s). Having a "style," however, doesn't mean the leader uses the same pattern of behaviors with every group or group member in every situation. Some theories of leadership (e.g., Hersey & Blanchard, 1972; House, 1971) prescribe different behaviors depending on the needs of the situation. For example, Hersey and Blanchard's situational leadership theory suggests that a leader should provide more direction, structure, and guidance for a less competent, inexperienced group than for a competent group with more experience on the given task. In other words, leadership style should vary depending on the group being led, the task being dealt with, and even with the different phases of development the group is going through.

Fourth, it is important to realize that **even a good leader cannot make every group successful.** Leadership is only one of several influential factors in the success of a group. Personalities of individual group members, vested interests, and other factors the leader has no control over may result in an ineffective group, in spite of quality leadership (Scheidel & Crowell, 1979).

In the previous section, we suggested that communication networks emerge and become relatively stable in the context of the group process. Likewise, as members perform the various roles — task, maintenance, individual, and leadership — specific performances are either encouraged or discouraged by other group members. As a result, these roles become relatively stable through the group process. Of course, both networks and role performances can change in the process of group interaction. To understand some of the changes that occur as the group process unfolds, we now turn our attention to developmental phases.

DEVELOPMENTAL PHASES

Small group researchers have studied numerous types of groups, including problem-solving, decision-making, therapy, and friendship groups. Some of these groups were composed of people who had never met before and, after meeting for the researcher's study, would never meet again. Some of these groups had been meeting for a long time and would continue to meet after they were studied. Even with all the differences in terms of the types of groups and the extent to which members knew each other or knew they would meet again, there seemed to be four phases all of these groups experienced.

Tuckman (1965) called these phases forming, storming, norming, and performing. He reviewed other studies and synthesized their findings and reported that in these four phases, groups must simultaneously deal with both task and interpersonal issues and problems. The four phases and the problems associated with each phase are summarized in Figure 7.2.

In the **forming phase,** group members are literally forming opinions about both the task and each other. They need to discuss precisely what the task is, what type of information is needed to complete the task, and how best to get that information. Their communication is likely to be somewhat tenative and polite because they need to get a better idea of the other group members before they feel ready to openly assert their real opinions. Each of the members is also trying to fit this task to his/her own personal needs and goals. Interpersonally the group members are going through a testing and dependence stage. They try to determine what behavior will and will not be appropriate and acceptable or to figure out to what extent they can actually depend on the other individuals in the group.

As the group proceeds to the **storming phase,** conflict develops. The politeness and lack of assertion found in the forming phase changes as the group members become more secure in expressing their opinions and feelings honestly.

Phase	Problems	
	Task	**Interpersonal**
forming	orientation to the task	testing and dependence
storming	emotional response to task demands	development of intra-group conflict
norming	open exchange of relevant information	development of group cohesion
performing	emergence of solutions	functional role-relatedness

Figure 7.2 Phases and Problems in Small Group Contexts

The group has to deal with emotional responses to task demands. Members may argue about the approach to the task, the best way to complete the task, and who should be responsible for what. Obviously this involves some "storming" and conflict as members show their concern that all members carry their own weight in the group's activities. At the same time that these task concerns are occurring, the group has to deal with conflict among the members themselves. Individuals may appear to be hostile, angry, defensive, or even resistant to conforming to the group norms. Each may be trying to assert his/her individuality. Clearly this conflict has to be resolved before the group can continue to the next phase.

While this phase is a difficult one to get through, it is a critical one. It is only through the open sharing of different ideas that members will hear each other out so that later they will be able to generate shared solutions. Furthermore, once the group has successfully worked through their conflict, the relationships among the group members typically become stronger and the group becomes more committed both to each other and the task. While it would be easy for a group to become discouraged during this phase and individual members may even want to leave the group, it is essential that they stay and try to work through their differences.

In the **norming phase,** the group's task efforts are centered on the open exchange of relevant opinions. By this point the group has become comfortable about sharing opinions openly and freely and is ready to work toward the completion of the task. At this point the group is able to express opinions in ways that are helpful to the group and that are not threatening either to individual members or the group as a whole. And, as the communication becomes more open and frequent, interpersonally the group is developing cohesion and a sense of commitment to each other and the group. Getting along with each other becomes very important in this phase.

121

As the group reaches the final phase, the **performing phase,** they begin to deal with solutions to the problem/task. Members offer their own suggestions and then work actively together to reach the best possible solution. Interpersonally we describe this phase as one of functional role-relatedness. That is, the group members become able to maximize their relationships with one another and to effectively utilize the various roles members have taken on in the course of the group's development so as to complete the group's task most effectively. Once a decision is reached, group members typically can be counted on to defend both that decision and the group.

Scheidel and Crowell (1979) noted that there are also differences in the general ways of thinking that occur in the development of effective groups. During both the forming and storming phases groups tend to think in **diverging** or individual ways. Many ideas are being generated and tested, members are actively participating, and ideally the group is coming up with more ideas than it may ever be able to use. In the phases of norming and performing, however, thinking is characterized as **converging** since members try to narrow their ideas and pull them together (converge) in order to arrive at a solution.

It may sound like groups go through a very orderly progression of phases until they finally complete their task. While these phases are considered to be sequential, there is likely to be some overlap or even regression to earlier phases as each group develops. Often during the performing phase some conflict may develop and the group will regress to the storming phase. This time, though, the group is likely to be less threatened by the conflict and to see it as necessary for them to adequately assess all possible ideas. Just like in any relationship, the first time you encounter conflict, it is very risky because the outcome is so uncertain. As group members become more confident in a positive outcome, however, the risk seems less so they may be willing to take it. Also, groups may go through these phases repeatedly such that diverging and converging thinking may occur throughout the group process.

There must be enough time for the group to be able to go through these phases; however, presently research does not tell us exactly how the phases work depending on the amount of time a group meets. Some disagreement exists among researchers as to whether these phases occur if a group only meets once (Tuckman, 1965; Fisher, 1970), if they take place during the ongoing meetings of a group that meets often (Bennis & Shepard, 1956), or if all of the phases occur in every meeting and keep occurring throughout the life of the group (Bales & Strodtbeck, 1951). What is important to recognize, though, is that these phases tend to occur in this general order.

Furthermore, these phases are essential for a group to function effectively, both in terms of completing its task and in terms of developing successful interpersonal relationships among the group members. Through the interaction within each phase individual agendas and goals are brought out into the open and group goals, norms, roles, operating strategies, and networks emerge or are negotiated. Without the "testing" of the forming stage, the conflict/negotiation of the storming phase, and the compromise and shared agreements of the norming phase, the group may never reach a level of operating effectiveness of the performing phase.

PRODUCTIVITY AND COHESIVENESS

So far, we have been emphasizing the importance of the interdependence between the task and interpersonal dimensions in a problem-solving group. The effectiveness of these two dimensions should maximize the group's ultimate productivity and cohesiveness. The extent to which the group successfully and effectively accomplishes its task is the group's **productivity** level. The extent to which interpersonal relationships develop among group members refers to the **cohesiveness** of the group. Members of cohesive groups feel a sense of loyalty and commitment to the group as well as to group members.

Just as the task and socio-emotional dimensions of the group are interdependent, so are productivity and cohesiveness. We describe the relationship between productivity and cohesiveness as curvilinear as is shown in Figure 7.3. That is, up to a certain point, as cohesiveness increases so does productivity; after that point, however, as cohesiveness increases, productivity decreases. Thus, a low cohesive group is also likely to be low in productivity. A moderately cohesive group is likely to be very productive. But, an extremely cohesive group will probably be only moderately productive (or perhaps even very unproductive).

There are several possible reasons for this relationship. As groups become more cohesive, they are more likely to communicate frequently and to be friendlier. However, becoming too cohesive and too friendly can actually backfire if the friendly interactions of the group become more important to the group than the completion of the particular task. They then seem to enjoy just getting together more than accomplishing the task, it is also possible that groups which are very cohesive may have what we call "reserve productivity." That is, the group may be capable of being productive, but they may not give the kind of effort required for the group to be productive. As a result their productivity is dormant or in reserve (Shepard, 1964).

When cohesiveness reaches a high level, groups often experience a great deal of conformity among members. Members feel pressured to go along with the group and accept the norms of the group. Often the group influences individual members to conform in subtle ways, sometimes in such a way that they may not be consciously aware of it. While conformity can serve some useful functions, like keeping a deviant from disrupting the group, it can also inhibit the group. Two classic studies point to the important influence group members can have on getting individuals to conform to something that they may not believe is right or desirable.

The first study by Sherif and Sherif was done in 1936. They conducted several experiments where they looked at a phenomenon called the autokinetic effect. If you were to look at a stationary point of light while in total darkness, it would look like the light was moving. In fact, the appearance of movement is only an optical illusion. The light actually does not move at all. However, all people think it is moving. In addition, the estimates of how much it moves vary quite a

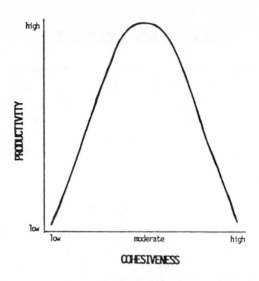

Figure 7.3 The Relationship between Productivity
and Cohesiveness in Small Groups

bit.   Sherif and Sherif found that if individuals looked several times at the
light alone, they would develop their own standard of movement and would estimate
the amount of movement within their own standard range. But, when a group of
people first looked at the light, the group (not the individual) developed the
standard.   Then, when the individuals looked at the light again, they tended to
estimate the movement of the light in terms of the group norm. Even more
interesting, if a person first viewed the light alone but overheard other people
estimating the distance the light moved, the individual tended to correct his/her
estimate so that it was more in line with what the others described.

A second classic study was done by Asch (1956) in which he asked subjects to
look at a picture of three lines of different lengths and choose the line that was
the same length as a target line. He had several confederates "planted" to give
incorrect answers.   When subjects heard these "planted" opinions before giving
their own, approximately one third of them were the same as (or at least in the
direction of) those incorrect responses.   Only about one half of the subjects
maintained their judgment independent of the others.

In both studies **participants felt pressured to conform to the group to avoid
expressing a deviant opinion.**   Interestingly, when Asch did some follow-up
interviews, he found that only a small percentage of those who went along with the
confederates really believed the majority opinion had been correct! So publicly
they had appeared to agree with the majority, while privately they did not. The
significant influence the group can have on the individual has important
consequences for small group communication contexts.

As a group becomes highly cohesive and conforms to group norms, there is a
tendency for **groupthink** to develop. Groupthink, as first described by Janis

(1972), is a "model of thinking that people engage in when they are deeply involved in a cohesive in-group, when the members' striving for unanimity override their motivation to realistically appraise alternative courses of action" (p.9). That is, the group becomes so loyal to itself and its ideas and/or values that it is no longer able to function effectively to arrive at the best decision or solution. Because the group thinks of itself as such a tight unit or in-group, group communication is not likely to be characterized as open (and perhaps not even honest). The more the group sees itself in this way, the less tolerant it becomes of any differing views, so the group begins to exert pressure on any individual who might try to bring up a dissenting or differing view, to censor itself to minimize the importance of any possible doubts, and to develop a "shared illusion of unanimity" of opinions conforming to the majority view.

Furthermore, the group begins to develop an unquestioned belief in its own inherent morality which can lead them to ignore ethical consequences of their decisions. An illusion of invulnerability may lead the group to excessive risk-taking behavior and excessive optimism because members feel invulnerable to the external consequences of their behavior. In addition, the group often stereotypes opposition leaders as either too evil to warrant genuine attempts to negotiate or as too weak (or even stupid) to be a threat. Along with these distortions of the opposition, there is frequently a development of "self-appointed mindguards" within the group who set themselves up to protect the group from conflicting information that might jar the group's uniformity and in doing so may censor information or distort it to maintain the group's complacency.

Janis (1972) also suggested several ways that the group, and especially the group leader, can work to **counteract groupthink.** First of all, it is very important throughout the discussion that each group member retain the role of critical evaluator, working consciously to avoid any excessive group pressure or influence because s/he likes the others in the group and doesn't want to

displease them. It also helps to get as many different or diverging ideas as possible to work with, whether this comes from having someone in the group play the role of "devil's advocate" or by inviting individuals known to have divergent interests to come to talk with the group. It is important that individuals avoid stating their own personal views too early in the process since doing so could inhibit others from expressing different views. Sometimes it may even be important for the group to meet without its leader to avoid the group being unduly pressured or dominated by that individual. Finally, it is a good idea once a tentative decision has been made to schedule a "second chance" meeting in which each member would be required to express as strongly as possible any residual doubts before finally committing the group to a particular decision.

Group members may not be aware of the occurrence of groupthink in their group and may not recognize that they have given up their ability to critically evaluate ideas in a preference for reaching consensus. Groupthink results in inferior decision-making and keeps the group from engaging in productive conflict in becoming an effective group. As such, it is important for each group member, and especially for the leader, to continually look out for development groupthink.

COMMUNICATION SKILLS IN SMALL GROUPS

The four keys to competent communication which were identified in the previous chapter — perspective-taking, active listening, avoiding defensive communication, and interaction management — are as important for effective small group communication as they are for one-on-one interaction. There are also several specific factors for effective communication in small groups: make the group goal your goal; be knowledgeable about the topic; participate actively; encourage others' participation; observe and listen carefully; be open-minded; and evaluate issues rather than people. As we discuss each of these specific factors in this section you will see how they build on the four general interpersonal skills by focusing on small group contexts in which the goal is to accomplish the particular task in a way that allows for maximum group participation and that leads to member satisfaction. These factors are important for every group member, regardless of who is designated as leader.

MAKE THE GROUP GOAL YOUR PERSONAL GOAL

We have already discussed how individual roles and goals which are purely self-serving can damage the group process. It is important whenever you are part of a decision-making group that you become group-oriented and that you remain so throughout the existence of the group. This means that you need to understand clearly what the goal is and that you make it important for yourself that the goal be accomplished. You need not only to be sensitive to the task and maintenance roles but also to be willing to perform any of these roles which can facilitate the group's functioning. Many of the suggestions offered here follow logically from this one.

BE KNOWLEDGEABLE ABOUT THE TOPIC

Group decision-making typically takes longer than making the decision individually. This is especially true if meeting time must be spent informing members of relevant facts. So it is important that you find out what topics are on the agenda for discussion and then that you prepare thoroughly in advance. Spending time in preparation means that you need to think through carefully your own ideas. This does not mean that you must formulate a rigid position which you then must defend to other group members. Rather, what it encourages you to do is to think about the information in advance and not depend only on what is mentioned on the spur of the moment by the group. This "thinking" time can also be valuable for providing you with time to consider various perspectives or positions the topic raises, so that during the discussion you will then be able to consider others' contributions from a base of knowledge rather than ignorance.

PARTICIPATE ACTIVELY

A group cannot fully realize the benefits of the assembly effect unless each member contributes. This does not mean that each person must talk exactly the same amount of time; it does mean that the ideas of each group member should be heard. Thus, it is important for you to identify opportunities where your ideas might be helpful — and then to contribute them!

ENCOURAGE OTHERS TO PARTICIPATE

Just as it is important for you as an individual member to actively participate in the accomplishment of the group goal, it is important that all members do so. You can aid this accomplishment by being sensitive to the others in your group and by explicitly encouraging them to add their ideas or concerns to the effort. Obviously this means you need to be alert to both verbal and nonverbal cues.

LISTEN AND OBSERVE ACTIVELY

In order to determine what sort of contributions might be most helpful to the group at a particular time, it is important that you be attentive to both verbal and nonverbal messages from other members. You need to pay particular attention to whether members seem to be responding positively or negatively to particular changes in the group process or whether some member appears to miss the point of a piece of information or a specific line of reasoning. You need to be continually alert to others' responses if you are able to address those issues most important to the group's progress.

BE OPEN-MINDED

Even if you have prepared thoroughly (and perhaps especially if you have done so), you need to be open to the possibility that you haven't thought of everything — which is one of the basic reasons why group decision-making often has the advantage over individual decision-making. You need to be prepared to clarify aspects of any point you have made. However, there is no need for defending each position you raise especially if you do so only to "win" an argument rather than to help in the group's decision. As such, it is important not to get too emotionally attached to an idea as **yours**; instead think of any idea as one that could be of potential use to the **group's** efforts.

EVALUATE ISSUES NOT PEOPLE

Disagreement in group contexts is inevitable. It is very important, though, when disagreement occurs that the focus is on the issue and not on the person who brought up the idea. Whenever issues and the people who talk about them become too tightly linked, it is highly likely that any talk will become very emotional and defensive and lead to a long (and perhaps boring) session for the whole group.

LEADERSHIP SKILLS

If you are designated the leader of the group, you will need to take the previous suggestions into account both for yourself and for each group member as you try to guide the group to accomplish its task and to achieve satisfying interaction among the group members. There are some specific things, however, to which you will want to pay close attention as the leader of a group (Rardin, 1982). For instance, consider the physical setup. A circle, semi-circle, or "U" arrangement of chairs in which all members (including the leader) can see and directly interact with all other members will be much more likely to encourage all to participate.

It is also important that everyone be aware of the purpose of the discussion. You need to introduce the discussion by reiterating its specific purpose or task and then briefly describe how the topic and purpose apply to and are important to all group members. This introduction need not be long but it is critical that it be made, even if you think that the group must already know this information.

In addition, the group's efforts must be focused on that topic and purpose throughout the interaction if the task is to be accomplished. Prior to the discussion you need to prepare a set of possible questions (or an agenda of items to be considered) which functions as a guideline for the discussion. It is important, however, to remember that this agenda is only meant as a "guide," as one possible way through the problem. You must be prepared to be flexible so that during the discussion if a point which was not on the "list" is raised and if the group finds it important, then at that moment you must be ready to digress from the original "guide." At the same time, however, if a point is not something that seems directly relevant or if it seems to drift away from the main point/purpose/agenda, it is up to you to keep the group's efforts "on track." It is this determination of when to let the group go and when to ease gently back to the agenda that is one of the most important skills of the group leader. Sometimes it is helpful to summarize what the group has done up to that point to provide a way back to the main task.

Throughout the group's interaction, you must pay close attention to the verbal and nonverbal behavior of all the group members. You are responsible for seeing that no one dominates (and, of course, that includes you). And you will need to fight the tendency to answer questions too rapidly yourself when silence occurs. Sometimes silence, even it feels a bit awkward, is needed for some "thinking" time. At any rate, you ought not to jump in too quickly to provide answers. It is also important that the leader not put group members on the defensive and thus disrupt group interaction. This is especially important when the leader asks questions, for the group needs to feel that the discussion is on topic.

The leader needs to monitor the participation of group members, encouraging those who have been quiet perhaps by a direct question asking them for their opinions and also trying to downplay efforts by any who might try to dominate the discussion. While not everyone needs to participate in exactly equal amounts, it is important that each member feels that s/he is important and is free to make a contribution whenever needed. This general atmosphere of supportiveness is especially important in having the group feel satisfied or comfortable about its efforts.

The leader is also responsible for closing the discussion. Not all discussions end with the task completed. However, rather than ending on a negative note, the leader needs to summarize what has been done so the group can see where they will need to begin at the next session. It is up to the leader to explicitly tie these ends together at the close of a session.

It may be helpful to think of a leader of a small group as the conductor of an orchestra. The conductor prepares him/herself carefully in advance by looking over the script written by someone else (i.e., the task at hand, the agenda which can guide the accomplishment of the task) and at the moment of performance (the actual group interaction) works to bring out all of the harmonies (various inputs from all group members, observations of their reactions and feelings) in such a way as to produce the best possible music from the particular group (a combination of completing the task and of achieving maximum group satisfaction).

SUMMARY

This chapter acquainted you with the context of small group communication. When group decision-making is appropriate, small groups can be very effective. Through regular, on-going interaction, small groups develop networks and roles that enable them to proceed through the forming, storming, norming, and performing phases of group development. These four phases include both task and interpersonal dimensions within the group and help the group become productive and cohesive. However, too much cohesiveness can result in a decrease in productivity and can also result in groupthink. It is important for effective small group communication that the group retains the ability to think critically and to monitor itself. We also identified several areas for you to work on to increase the effectiveness of your communication skills in small group contexts.

KEY TERMS

principle of nonsummativity
assembly effect
risky shift phenomenon
networks
independence
saturation
task roles
maintenance roles
individual roles
leadership functions

forming
storming
norming
performing
diverging thinking
converging thinking
productivity
cohesiveness
groupthink

CHAPTER 8

CHAPTER 8

ORGANIZATIONAL COMUNICATION CONTEXTS

There is little question that organizations pervade our lives. Recent studies reveal that over 110 million persons in the United States work for or in organizations. Students are members of educational organizations, volunteers are members of nonprofit organizations, many people belong to religious, social, or political organizations and most Americans are affected, in one way or another, by government organizations. The extent to which organizations are a part of our lives makes communication in this context an especially important issue. Through communication, organizations are created and maintained. That is, communication is the "cement" which holds the organization together and communication is the vehicle through which people come to understand their own and others' roles in the organization.

Organizational communication is the study of the communication patterns and processes (both formal and informal) through which members of organizations get their work done. New members are hired or recruited through communication, decisions are made through communication, and almost every other work-related activity is somehow affected by or accomplished through communication. Some people argue that communication is organizing (Weick, 1979). Others claim that "without communication, organizations could not exist" (Bradley & Baird, 1983, p.xi). To accomplish a goal through the coordinated efforts of others — which is a definition of an organization — demands communication.

The purpose of this chapter is first to provide an overview of organization theory to show how notions of organizations affect organizational communication and then to focus on four different topics about communication in organizations which are currently being studied: information flow, communication climate, networks, and organizational cultures. Each of these topics will be discussed with the purpose of helping you: develop a better understanding of your own and others' behavior in organizations; improve your abilities to diagnose and solve organizational communication problems; and to increase your knowledge of what makes for successful organizations and successful organizational members.

ORGANIZATION THEORY AND
ORGANIZATIONAL COMMUNICATION

During the early part of this century, organizations were viewed as machines. Members of organizations were considered supplements to machines, primarily designed to keep the machines running smoothly and efficiently (Taylor, 1923). Communication was considered something of an unnecessary luxury, and when it was studied, only formal written messages were considered important to examine. Management efficiency was seen as the key to organizational success (Taylor, 1923). Thus the communication behavior of managers was the central focus of many organizational communication studies influenced by this **mechanistic approach.**

The development of a more **humanistic approach** to organizations recognized the significance of informal communication in the functioning of an organization. This approach claimed that the importance of participation and supportive relationships increased the importance and need for effective organizational communication. That is, from the humanistic perspective, the organization's "climate" was considered an important determinant of employee satisfaction and performance. The influence of Likert (1967) and others stimulated interest in climate issues such as the quality, quantity, accuracy of and satisfaction with communication (Goldhaber, Yates, Porter & Lesniak, 1978). However, both the mechanistic and humanistic views of organizations take a micro-approach to organizational communication; that is, they focus more on the individual and his/her perceptions of communication.

The **systems approach,** however, is more macro in focus (Katz & Kahn, 1978; Farace, Monge & Russell, 1977). From this perspective interdependent work groups (or subsystems) are viewed in terms of how they process information internally and monitor the organization's environment to gather information about such things as the economy, politics, consumer behavior, government regulations, social concerns, etc. To achieve an overall view of the organization demands consideration of both internal and external communication. With its focus on structure, the systems approach provided the theoretical foundation for studies of communication networks as well as of information overload and underload.

More recently organizational scholars have characterized organizations as cultures. This **cultural approach** focuses on a shared sense of values, norms, and similar attitudes, beliefs and behavior among organizational members. Martin (1980) defined an organization's culture as "the way we get things done around here." From this perspective, communication is viewed as the vehicle through which organizational cultures are created and maintained (Putnam, 1982). Stories, language, rituals, and documents are studied as indicators of an organization's culture.

These four perspectives of organizations have influenced our notions of organizational communication, both what it is and how it is to be studied. The mechanistic approach encouraged a preoccupation with management issues. Research from this perspective focused on information flow studies, especially downward and formal communication. The humanistic approach encouraged studies of communication climate, especially in regard to superior-subordinate information exchanges and communication satisfaction. The systems approach encouraged a focus on communication network structures and properties. And the cultural approach has encouraged a focus on organization stories, heroes, values, rituals and language usage among organizational members. Each of these major topics — information flow, communication climate, networks, and organizational cultures — will be reviewed in the remainder of this chapter.

INFORMATION FLOW

One of the major communication topics studied in organizational contexts is the flow of information. Information flow refers to the direction (upward, downward or horizontal) in which information moves through the organization's hierarchy. Communication that flows in each of these directions is vital for the success of the organization. Since each type functions for different reasons and each usually carries different kinds of information to the various members of an organization, we will consider each type in more detail.

UPWARD COMMUNICATION

Communication traveling up the organizational hierarchy can take many forms. The more traditional topics include grievances, complaints, suggestions, and reports on organizational and individual job performance, but even a sales clerk asking his/her store manager for pricing information counts as **upward communication.** Employees often give their managers information about themselves, their job performance, the job performance of others, and information about what has been done. Each of these forms of communicating involves a person with less status, position, or power sending information to someone with more status, position or power. Organization members have reported that upward communication is the most satisfying yet the most difficult type of communication in which one participates (Berkowitz & Bennis, 1961).

DOWNWARD COMMUNICATION

Communication which flows from higher levels of the hierarchy to members in lower levels defines **downward communication.** There are basically five types of downward communication: job instruction, job rationale, policies and procedures, feedback about performance, and information about organizational goals (Katz & Kahn, 1978). These topics, of course, only represent the more formal types of information communicated downward. Those in higher positions also might talk to those in lower levels about such things as the economy, recent movies, jogging, recently read novels, or the decor in one's office. These informal topics were once considered superfluous to the work day and, in many cases, forbidden between superiors and subordinates and even between employees at the same work level. However, a more humanistic view of organizational life points to the importance of informal communication in getting tasks completed as well as in satisfying employees.

Most organizational theorists argue that effective communication must start at the top. Managers set the climate and norms for communication, and as a result openness in sending and receiving downward communication is considered essential (Jablin, 1979). Managers are expected to be accurate, timely, consistent, and confident in sending downward-directed messages.

HORIZONTAL COMMUNICATION

Horizontal communication is communication between peers or workers at the same level in the organization. As such, status and power differences between communicators are considered to be minimal (or even absent). Horizontal communication functions to coordinate work-related activities as well as to increase cohesiveness, fulfill social needs, and/or clarify role expectations.

To coordinate activities, members in various types of organizations must communicate with their coworkers. For example, horizontal communication is necessary for UPS delivery persons to pick up the appropriate packages for their distribution district. Likewise, horizontal communication makes it possible for an advertising staff to design an ad, or for fundraisers for the March of Dimes, American Cancer Society, or Greenpeace to accomplish their goals by communicating with their coworkers about details and procedures.

In addition to making task coordination possible, horizontal communicaiton also helps fulfill organizational members' social needs. Some time ago Likert (1967) argued that member satisfaction was the key to productivity. He also suggested that fulfilling members' needs was a responsibility of the organization if those members were to be satisfied and committed to the organization. Today we consider the encouragement of horizontal communication as one indication of an organization's concern for its employees' social or affiliative needs.

However, too much horizontal communication can become a problem because of its potential to interfere with or even become more important than communication flowing vertically through the organization. It is especially troublesome if organizational members actually allow horizontal communication to substitute for communication in other directions. For example, consider the situation in which a contented and competent worker who dislikes his/her boss consequently avoids interactions with that boss. Other organizational members may become so engrossed in peer-related communication that they neglect the efforts needed for organizational success. A manager who is more concerned about staying on good terms with all the other managers and forgets to keep his/her subordinates informed is guilty of letting horizontal communication substitute for downward communication.

A neglect of any one of the directions in which communication can flow is likely to seriously affect both the organization's performance and the individual member's satisfaction. Consequently, many studies have focused on the barriers to effective upward and downward communication (Huseman, Logue & Freshley, 1974).

FORMAL AND INFORMAL COMMUNICATION IN ORGANIZATIONS

Organizational communication can be considered either formal or informal depending on who sends and who receives the information. **Formal communication** is described as communication that flows between persons designated by the organization's hierarchy. Superior-subordinate communication is one example. Written communication (such as memos, and reports), presentations, slide or graphic displays, and scheduled meetings are all forms of formal organizational communication.

Although formal communication is vital to the functioning of most organizations, informal communication is often considered to be more effective in stimulating responses and generating ideas (Bradley & Baird, 1983). Informal communication is a necessary supplement to the more formal means of disseminating information. **Informal communication** is communication that is not necessarily specified by the organization's hierarchy or its "chain of command" rules. This can be an interaction between persons who do not have direct authority over one another or it can be any nonwork-related exchange of information between persons regardless of their relationship as specified by the organizational hierarchy. Usually this communication occurs in face-to-face situations including such situations as coworkers talking about sailing, students talking about Kentucky basketball, or superiors and subordinates discussing lunch food. Even communication concerning merit increases, fund raising possibilities, and budgetary concerns would be considered informal if neither of the persons interacting had official authority over the other.

Informal communication is sometimes called **grapevine communication.** The term "grapevine" has somewhat negative connotations because of its association with rumors. Rumors are messages which have no evidence of accuracy yet are passed from one organizational member to another. Rumors have often been considered communication to be avoided. However, researchers have conceded that not only are rumors inevitable but more importantly, they may provide a healthy contribution to an organization. Rumors have been considered negative because people seem to remember sensational or catastrophic ones. Davis (1973) reported, however, that rumors actually occurred much less frequently than was imagined. Furthermore, in more than 80 per cent of the organizations that he studied the rumors were accurate. Goldhaber and his associates (1978) reported that rumors were less likely to occur when communication from superiors was considered trustworthy and satisfying.

Informal communication offers organizational members a network for diffusing information which cannot or would not normally be sent through formal networks. Mintzberg (1973) found that managers spend as much as 80 per cent of their time in face-to-face communication which also emphasizes the importance and necessity of informal communication. Over 60 per cent of the top corporate executives responding to Cox's (1982) survey said that communication in their organizations was more (or mostly) informal.

Both formal and informal communication are needed to organize activities, motivate employees, contribute to the organization's image, and help members better understand behavioral expectations. Both formal and informal communication can move in any of the three directions discussed earlier.

COMMUNICATION CLIMATE

Likert (1967) first pointed to the importance of an organization's climate when he posited that job satisfaction is a key to organizational and individual performance. Studies in communication have focused on the role of communication in contributing to an organization's climate. In general, organizational communication is considered a part of the overall feeling members hold about their organization. Thus, the term **communication climate** refers to "the measurement of employees' perceptions and attitudes of selected [communication] behaviors" (Jablin, 1980, p. 328).

An organization's communication climate is viewed favorably when coworkers, especially supervisors, are thought of as open and responsive, willing to interact, sensitive to emotions, trustworthy and skilled in communication. In many studies **communication satisfaction** (and thus communication climate) has depended on such things as information accessibility, information adequacy, and content factors such as accuracy, utility, appropriateness and timeliness of information received. All of these factors are somewhat dependent upon the supervisor, and not surprisingly, superior-subordinate relationships were found to be the single most important influence on how one evaluates an organization's communication climate (Goldhaber, et al., 1978).

There are several factors that appear to influence one's perceptions of communication climate — superior-subordinate relationships, adequacy of information, information content, certain demographic factors, and job satisfaction. We will now look at each of these factors in more detail.

SUPERIOR-SUBORDINATE RELATIONSHIPS

Employees report being more satisfied with communication when they have good relationships with their supervisors. These findings led Goldhaber and others (1978) to conclude that "maintaining an effective relationship with an employee's immediate supervisor is, thus, the most important correlate of job satisfaction" (p. 84). They found the following factors predicted satisfying superior-subordinate relationships: when the boss understands you; when you trust your boss; when your boss is warm and friendly; when the boss is honest; and when you are free to disagree with your boss.

It is not yet clear whether opportunities for message sending or adequate amounts of message receiving most affects this relationship. However, it is clear that supervisors hold the key to satisfying employees both in terms of communication and the job. Some studies revealed that adequate downward-directed messages appear to be a stronger predictor of communication satisfaction than does upward communication freedom (Goldhaber, et. al. 1978). Even though accessibility and/or approachability of superiors is considered important, employees report stronger desires for their superior to keep them informed of such things as expected behavior or job responsibilities, feedback on performance, information about organizational goals, and advance notice of changes, among other things (Redding, 1972).

INFORMATION ADEQUACY

Information adequacy refers to how well the amount of information employees receive meets their expectations or desires. Adequate amounts could include information flowing in all directions or it could mean information flowing mainly one way. The actual amount of information desired will depend on the kind of work involved and the type of organization and individual.

Reaching the optimum level of information is another factor contributing to communication satisfaction. Most findings suggest that "too much" information can be as dissatisfying as "too little" information. There tends to be a naive belief among employers that more communication leads to more satisfied employees, but most studies reveal that this indeed is not the case. In fact, increased amounts of communication can lead to decreased communication satisfaction (Wiio, Goldhaber, & Yates, 1980).

Receiving too much information is often referred to as **information overload.** When employees are overloaded with information, they are unable to process and make use of it. This is often the problem with written communication. When organization members get too many memos, letters, announcements and bulletins, they end up ignoring all of them. One organizational member received so much information that she found herself becoming confused and frustrated. She said, "I wish they would only give me what's pertinent, so I can use my time to focus on the important and forget what's unimportant."

Mid-level managers and secretaries often complain of information overload. They receive more information than they can use or desire. Waiters, waitresses, bus drivers, top level executives, and university faculty members also may be subject to information overload. The nature of one's role in the organization, one's position in an organizational network, and particular communication skills and abilities all are likely to influence the degree to which information overload (and underload) will be experienced. Obviously persons differ in their capability and desire to process information whether they are in an organizational, interpersonal, or mass communication context.

Information underload, on the other hand, occurs when one does not receive enough information to be able to perform one's job in a competent or satisfying manner. This is especially likely to happen whenever (either by choice or through physical distance) some persons are excluded from the communication networks. For instance, people who work second or third shifts often complain of not receiving enough information.

INFORMATION CONTENT

The content of the communication is also considered an important predictor of an organizational member's feelings about communication climate. Information related to the organization as a whole rather than information related to one's specific job best predicts job satisfaction. Of course, task-related information is also considered necessary and satisfaction is related to receiving adequate task-related information.

DEMOGRAPHICS AND COMMUNICATION SATISFACTION

Early research findings found a sex difference for communication satisfaction; that is, relatively more women than men reported satisfaction with communication. More recent studies (such as Wiio, Goldhaber, & Yates, 1980) reported that the age of the individual and his/her type of work were related to communication satisfaction. Younger employees (20-34 years old) were more dissatisfied with communication than were older employees (over 50). White-collar employees were more dissatisfied with communication than were blue-collar employees. In this study the employees most satisfied with communication were managers and older women; those most dissatisfied with communication were male, blue collar, union members and young, well-educated lower and middle managers.

COMMUNICATION SATISFACTION AND JOB SATISFACTION

Numerous studies have found a significant positive relationship between communicaiton satisfaction and overall job satisfaction. In the early 1960's evidence began to accumluate suggesting that employees who were more pleased with the communication in their organizations also liked their jobs better. Findings from subsequent studies have not been as overwhelming about the relationship between communication and job satisfaction, but they generally have concluded that communication satisfaction and job satisfaction are linked.

The strength of the relationship between communication and job satisfaction appears to depend upon the type of organization and the level of the individual's position. In some types of organizations, communication may be more crucial and thus a stronger predictor of job satisfaction. In organizations demanding less communication and employing members with fewer communication needs, the relationship between comunication and job satisfaction is likely to be weaker. More recent studies have revealed that this relationship appears to be strongly influenced by the organization member's level in the hierarchy; that is, communication satisfaction contributes more to job satisfaction at higher levels in the organization where people seem more satisfied with their jobs overall than is true of those in lower levels.

In summary, communication climate refers to an employee's attitudes about such things as superior-subordinate relationships, information adequacy, information content and methods of transmitting information, and demographics. Communication satisfaction provides one measure of communication climate.

NETWORKS

In addition to studying the direction in which organizational messages flow, researchers have also been concerned with the structure or pattern of information exchanges. This work is called network analysis. A **network** is a pattern of information flow within an organization. This pattern or structure identifies the links between members of an organization based on the regularity with which they interact informally with each other (Farace, Monge, & Russell, 1977; Taylor &

Eagle, 1980).

Links with others in the organization may develop for a variety of reasons. For example, your office may happen to be located near someone else's. You see them every day and gradually may increase your interaction from simple greetings to talk about work and/or social activities. You may share a common interest outside of work or you may find the other person attractive. Whatever the reason, your communication relationships develop with certain people, and this ultimately results in an informal communication network.

Links between individuals vary depending on the content of the talk. The content may focus on **production** concerns, such as the job, work in general, etc. It may focus on the **maintenance** of social relationships in the workplace, with talk focusing on social activities and non-work-related information. Or, the content may emphasize **innovation**, the sharing of new ideas and new ways of doing things.

The strength of the link is also important in describing communication networks. The more frequent the communication, the stronger the link. For example, if you communicate with someone several times every day, your link with them is stronger than someone you typically communicate with only twice a week.

In network terms, each organization member is called a **node.** Each node can be described by its communication role. Richards (1975) identified these roles as:

> **group member**—a node whose communication primarily (more than 50%) occurs within the group;
>
> **bridge**—a node who is a member of a group but who also links two or more groups together;
>
> **liaison**—a node who is not a member of a group and links two or more groups;
>
> **isolate**—a node with either no links or only minimal links with others; and
>
> **other**—a node who does not fit any of the above criteria.

Figure 8.1 illustrates these roles in an organizational communication network.

Two linking roles — the bridge and liaison — are critical to the flow of information throughout the network. If these linkers were removed, the organization would have no way to transmit information between groups. Thus, even when these linking roles do not have very strong ties (frequent communication) with other organization members, they are essential to the transfer of information within the organization (Granovetter, 1973).

Network research has primarily looked at the roles of the participant (combining group members, bridge, and liaison roles) and the isolate. In general, findings have suggested that isolates tend to be poorer performers and tend to be less satisfied with their supervisors and coworkers than participants. Isolates also tend to: hold a higher rank, have been in the organization longer, be less productive, perceive their information as less accurate, and use the phone and written modes of communication more often than do those in participant roles. Participants tend to be less educated, be more satisfied with their job, perform better, and to be more committed to the organization (Roberts & O'Reilly, 1974).

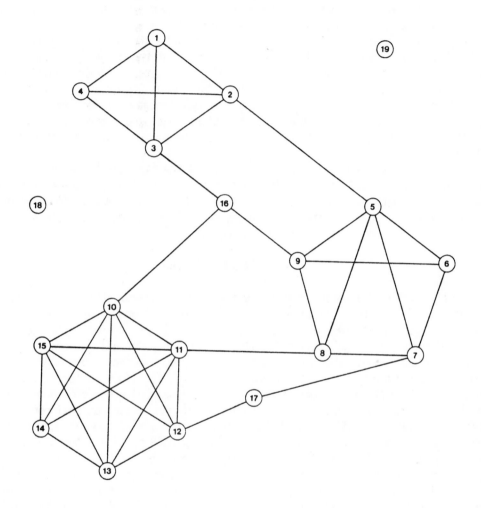

Group 1:   1, 2, 3, 4
Group 2:   5, 6, 7, 8, 9
Group 3:   10, 11, 12, 13, 14
Bridges: 2, 5, 8, 11
Liaisons: 16, 17
Isolates: 18, 19

Figure 6.1   Organizational Communication Network Roles

Other network research has found that key communicators (linkers) perceive themselves as more similar to management, identify more with their jobs, are more satisfied with messages directed downward, and perceive their jobs as more central in the overall organization. Non-key communicators (group members or isolates) identify less with their jobs and managers and their perceptions toward management are more varied. In general, key communicators perceive their work environment differently than do non-key communicators (Albrecht, 1979).

Key communicators (linkers) also experience more stress than do group members (Albrecht, Irey, & Mundy, 1982), probably because of the quantity of incoming and outgoing information they must process and disseminate. And while communicating regularly with a group of people from throughout the organization appears to buffer stress (Albrecht, et al., 1982), regular communication limited to one's work unit does not (Ray, 1983a). In addition, what people perceive as stressful in their job appears to differ depending on those with whom they interact (Ray, 1983b).

The above is just a sample of some of the findings of research that has examined communication networks in organizations. The identification of informal communication networks provides a picture of how information flows within an organization and how organization members control and coordinate their activities as they attempt to meet the goals of the organization.

ORGANIZATIONAL CULTURES

Just as we defined a social culture by its shared beliefs, attitudes, and values, organizational culture implies shared assumptions about how organizational activities are performed and understood as well as shared beliefs about and interpretations of organizational life. Certainly not all members have shared interpretations aobut the organization's culture. However, some argue that the more shared assumptions, the stronger the organization's culture. Deal and Kennedy (1982) pointed out that strong organizational cultures "create meaning for people" and in turn become likely predictors of good organizational performance. Siehl and Martin (1982) claimed that strong cultures also generate commitment to the organization, assist members in "sense making," provide a means of control, and result in such dividends as productivity and profits.

In studying organizational cultures, researchers have found it helpful to differentiate between implicit and explicit forms of communication. **Explicit** forms of cultural communication include statistical information and other written documents produced by the organization. **Implicit** forms of communication include such things as stories, rituals, nonverbal cues, language, etc. Martin (1982) suggested that the form in which cultural information is disseminated makes a difference in how the content is received and how interpretations of events are made. Stories and other more indirect forms of communication which implicitly transmit cultural information are considered more effective because they are remembered longer and appear more believable than more explicit forms of communication.

Marguilies (1969) also differentiated between observable and inferable organizational culture. The **observable culture** is composed of the actual tasks performed, resulting interactions, the organization's structure, and the actions of organizational members. Such things as sign-in procedures, the way guests are greeted, the kind of work done, and the networks developed to communicate information all are part of an organization's observable culture. For example, IBM's security-minded sign-in procedures, their work in high technology, the pleasantness employees project, and the white-shirted salesman image reveals information about the IBM culture, i.e., what that organization considers important, appropriate, etc.

The **inferable culture** is composed of values, attitudes, and norms among members which are imbedded in written and oral communication as well as in the rituals and informal behavior of organizational members. For example, an organization that offers training and development programs for its members leads us to infer that the organization values education and feels attention to people is important for its success. Thus, we infer the values, attitudes, and norms of an organization based on what we see in the observable culture.

Despite the forms in which the cultural information is transmitted and despite the degree to which cultural interpretations are shared, **communication is the vehicle through which cultures are created and maintained.** Members come to know appropriate and desirable behavior by interacting with other organizational members and by reaching some agreement about the organization's culture.

COMMUNICATION SKILLS IN ORGANIZATIONS

Because of the focus of past studies on superior-subordinate communication or managerial communication, much of what we know about organizational communication involves managers. As suggested earlier, supervisors are considered to have a great impact on the degree of satisfaction with communication which his/her subordinates experience. Also we mentioned earlier those communicative characteristics important for managers which included openness, trustworthiness, sensitivity, and responsiveness. Among these factors, trust and openness are considered to be the most important characteristics of good superior-subordinate relationships.

However, more recent research focuses on the skills and abilities necessary for processing organizational communication. Sypher and Sypher (1983) found that employees' job level was positively related to communication abilities. They found that perspective-taking ability, persuasive ability, self-monitoring, and listening — those abilities which were discussed as keys to competent interpersonal communication in Chapter 6 — were among the skills that separate the higher and lower levels of employees in an organization. Sypher and Zorn (1986) also found that communication abilities were strong predictors of an individual's ability to move up. That is, employees who demonstrated more developed communication abilities, especially perspective-taking and persuasive skills, were promoted significantly more often than those with less developed abilities.

The strongest relationship between organizational level and individual abilities was found for **perspective-taking** — the ability to understand another's point of view. Empathy and perspective-taking both require an understanding of another's motives, intentions, and feelings in interpersonal communicaiton situations. Even the popular press has recognized that perspective-taking ability is a key characteristic separating successful managers from those whose careers have been derailed (McCall & Lombard, 1983). These authors said that the "derailed" executives were those who had been expected to be successful but reached a plateau, were fired, or were forced to retire early. The most often cited reason for derailment was insensitivity to others, i.e., a lack of perspective-taking ability. Other reasons included the lack of persuasive skills, arrogance, and failure to change or adapt.

Persuasive ability also is an important skill for organizational members, especially those interested in moving up in the hierarchy. **Persuasive ability** allows one to influence or change the attitude and/or behavior of others. This ability includes such things as developing persuasive arguments and targeting those arguments to a specific person. Several studies have indicated that persuasive abilities are strongly related to perspective-taking abilities in that the ability to persuade someone is based on the ability to understand the psychological characteristics and subjective perceptions of the other person(s). This understanding helps members develop persuasive messages that are adapted to the listener, and as we discussed in Chapter 6, adaptability or flexibility is a requirement of a competent communicator. In organizational studies, the more persuasive employees are found in higher levels of the organization and they have been promoted more often than those persons who are less persuasive (Sypher & Zorn, 1986).

Self-monitoring is another of those abilities that predicts success in organizations. Snyder (1974) described the high self-monitoring individual as one who pays attention to social cues (such as dress, language, behavior, etc.) and then adapts his or her behavior appropriately. The low self-monitorer, on the other hand, fails to monitor such cues and consequently is less likely to behave in ways that are appropriate or acceptable. In the organizational context, a high self-monitorer is a person who notices that there is a norm for workers to come early and stay late, even though the employee handbook may state that office hours are 9:00 to 5:00. The high self-monitorer is also one who is aware of appropriate language and when to use it, appropriate attire and when to wear it, and appropriate working behavior and when it is expected. The low self-monitorer, on the other hand, because s/he is inattentive, uninterested, or unperceptive, is not aware of situational norms and thus most often fails to act in appropriate ways. In many organizations, the high self-monitorer gets promoted more often (or possibly even joins the organization at higher levels) than a low self-monitoring peer (Sypher, Sypher & Leichty, 1983).

Listening is also considered an important communication skill for organizational members. Bostrom and Waldhart (1980) defined **listening** as attention, understanding and remembering of information. Listening is necessary for developing member-leader relationships, understanding work instructions, and coordinating activities. Sypher and Bostrom (1983) found that better listeners were found in higher levels in the organization — the more one's job becomes managing others, the more important listening becomes.

Recent studies also have shown that communication skills are related to worker attractiveness. **Worker attractiveness** depends on how dependable, competent, and desirable a coworker is to an individual in addition to how effectively the coworker is able to communicate (Sypher, 1981). Workers who were considered good at understanding how others think and feel were perceived as the more attractive coworkers. Regardless of the formal work relationship between the individuals, positive perceptions of communication abilities strongly correlated with worker attractiveness. In fact, communication skills may even influence our choice of coworkers since they appear to be related to perceptions of satisfaction and attractiveness.

The relationship between job level and various communication skills points to the importance of communication both in terms of being hired at higher levels and moving to higher levels once in the organization. As Bradley and Baird (1983) pointed out: "Good communication skills do not guarantee success, of course, but poor communication skills almost certainly guarantee failure" (p. xi). They further remind us that the success of any program or policy is a function of the communication skills of the people working within the program. Peters and Waterman (1982), authors of the best selling book, In Search of Excellence, also concluded that despite all we know about running efficient and effective organizations, the one fact remains that getting along with people is probably the most important criteria for an excellent company. And, getting along with other people is for the most part a function of effective communication skills.

SUMMARY

The purpose of this chapter was to present an overview of organizational communication. Communication in this context refers to the messages exchanged between persons involved in goal-related activities. Topics for discussion included the directions in which information flows, communication climate, superior-subordinate relationships, communication networks, organizational cultures, and communication skills important for organizational success. In organizations, communication functions to coordinate work-related activities and to aid in understanding expectations, attitudes, procedures, and policies related to the organization's functioning.

KEY TERMS

mechanistic approach
humanistic approach
systems approach
cultural approach
upward communication
downward communication
horizontal communication
formal communication
informal communication
grapevine communication
information overload
information underload
production network
innovation network
maintenance network
node
group member
liaison
bridge
isolate
explicit communication
implicit communication
observable culture
inferable culture
self-monitoring
worker attractiveness

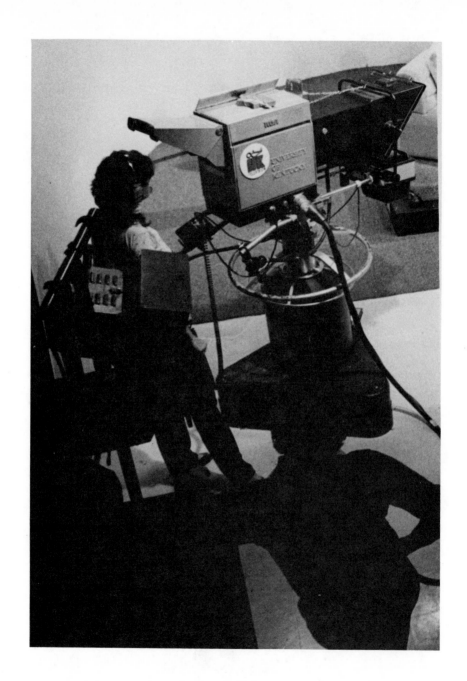

CHAPTER 9

CHAPTER 9

MASS COMMUNICATION CONTEXTS: COMPONENTS AND PROCESSES

Mass communication represents still another communication context. The contexts we have examined so far — interpersonal, small group, and organizational — dealt with communication between you and other clearly identifiable individuals. Here we will explore your interaction not with individuals but with an industry.

As with any industry, mass communication has several distinguishing characteristics. Mass communication plays a variety of roles in our society and in our personal lives as well. Like interpersonal, small group, and organizational communication, mass communication is subject to societal and cultural controls or restraints. Unlike the other contexts, though, mass communication can also be subject to a variety of legal controls. In this chapter and the next one we will look closely at mass communication in order to help you better understand and become a more astute consumer of mass communication messages.

Lest you feel tempted to set aside the ideas of earlier chapters as irrelevant to mass communication, remember that many of the principles discussed earlier affect how mass communicated messages are sent and received. Just as in the other contexts, in mass communication the professionals who prepare messages are influenced by: their own attention, perception, and attitudes; the principles of interpersonal and small group communication situations in which they gather information for messages and make decisions about messages; and the principles of organizational communication, which are no different for the mass communication industry in which they work than for any other industry.

WHAT IS MASS COMMUNICATION?

Three major characteristics of mass communication make this context different from other communication contexts — profit motive, audience factors, and technological interface. Each of these will be discussed separately in this section.

PROFIT MOTIVE

First, it should be clear that mass communication is a business. While other forms of communication may often facilitate making money, generating income is one of the principle reasons for communicating in mass communication contexts. In a free enterprise system such as ours in the United States, this income leads to profits for the owners. Even when the owner of a mass communication system is operated by a government (such as England's BBC or some of our public broadcasting stations), it requires money from that government (and ultimately the public) to operate and to pay salaries of those who work in the system. While there may be other goals or purposes, the overriding goal in mass communication contexts is the profit motive (DeFleur & Dennis, 1985).

AUDIENCE FACTORS

In most of the other communication contexts, messages are sent to a relatively small number of people who are generally known to each other. Often these people have a great deal in common which, in turn, affects how effectively they can communicate with each other. In mass communication, though, messages are directed to audiences far larger than in any other context. The people in this audience are generally **anonymous;** those sending a message cannot identify as individuals most of those who will receive it. And, partly because of the **large size,** the people in this audience will have much less in common with each other. That is, mass communication audiences tend to be **heterogeneous,** representing a wide range of social categories, interests, and attitudes.

Not only is the audience in this context large, anonymous, and heterogeneous when compared with other communication audiences, but also its members are less directly involved in the communication process. This is because mass communicators and their audiences are **physically separated** from each other in time and space (Baran, McIntyre, & Meyer, 1984). In other communication contexts, receivers switch roles with senders, back and forth, in constant interaction. Even if you were speaking to an auditorium full of people, the presence of applause, laughter, booing or other direct responses helps you to adjust the message while it is being sent. This kind of direct, instant feedback and interaction does not currently exist in mass communication. While an audience member can write a letter to the editor of a newspaper or angrily turn off a TV set (thereby, if joined by enough other people, reducing a program's rating), generally **responses in the mass communication context are limited, somewhat indirect, and nearly always delayed.**

TECHNOLOGICAL INTERFACE

Feedback is typically less direct in mass communication contexts because a **technological interface** is required to reach those large, anonymous, and heterogeneous audiences. That is, mass communicated messages reach their audiences through the intervention of electronic, print, or other mechanical means. When you write a letter to a friend or call your mother on the telephone, you are using a technological interface in the communication process. But, the organization of this linkage is one-to-one, so you are not engaged in mass communication. However, the newspaper printing press or the radio signal provides a one-to-many technological link. This one-to-many design is highly efficient and permits a message to reach large audiences at low cost which, in turn, permits the generation of profits. It also imposes a limit on feedback. As we move toward the end of the century, technology promises to make one-to-many-to-one designs economically feasible and thus would permit more immediate feedback to mass communicated messages (though even so the range of responses may remain somewhat limited).

As we look at mass communication contexts we find we can cluster them according to the kind of technological interface involved — print (newspapers, magazines, books), electronic (radio, television), and other (movies, sound or video recordings). As technology has changed over the decades, we've observed an interesting relationship among the various mass communication contexts. While each represents a business which is competitive with other mass media, there also exists an interrelationship that we can best describe as a **symbiotic relationship.** That is, each medium both affects and is affected by the others. Just as in biological symbiosis, in media symbiosis we see the media adjusting to and influencing the others. For example, as television became popular, we found that newspapers adjusted by focusing on more in-depth analyses of issues as their "specialty" and that radio shifted to formats which appealed to specific audiences (such as top 40, Christian music, news, etc.) rather than each medium trying to gain the entire audience. Or, consider the number of times you see ads for movies appear on your television screen, or the very fact that a whole new kind of magazine (TV Guide) was developed to be used in conjunction with the television medium.

THE MASS COMMUNICATION PROCESS

Several mass communication scholars have developed models to help visualize the mass communication process. These models further highlight both the differences and similarities between mass communication contexts and other contexts for communication. The key components in all these models include: communicators, messages, gatekeepers, mass media, regulators, filters, audience and effects. In addition, mass communication models typically include interference or noise which occurs in the transmission of messages and amplification (Baran, McIntyre, & Meyer, 1984; DeFleur & Ball-Rokeach, 1982; Hiebert, Ungurait, & Bohn, 1985). (See Figure 9.1.) We will discuss each of these components of the mass communication process below.

COMMUNICATORS

Mass communicators are seldom one person. Usually, mass communicators are complex organizations in which members of the organization perform specialized tasks (Hiebert, Ungurait, & Bohn, 1985). Thus, while it may appear that ABC's "World News Tonight" is presented by one person, Peter Jennings, in fact, the production of just one evening's broadcast is the result of the combined efforts of a number of people. Reporters, technicians, producers, directors, secretaries, salespersons, accountants, and a whole host of other individuals are involved in the creation and production of the network news.

This is not to say that one individual may not be quite influential in the development and transmission of a particular message. For example, the General Manager of a local television station may exercise considerable control over local programming content. If the General Manager is an avid gourmet cook, s/he may decide to have the station produce a daily program spotlighting the best chefs in

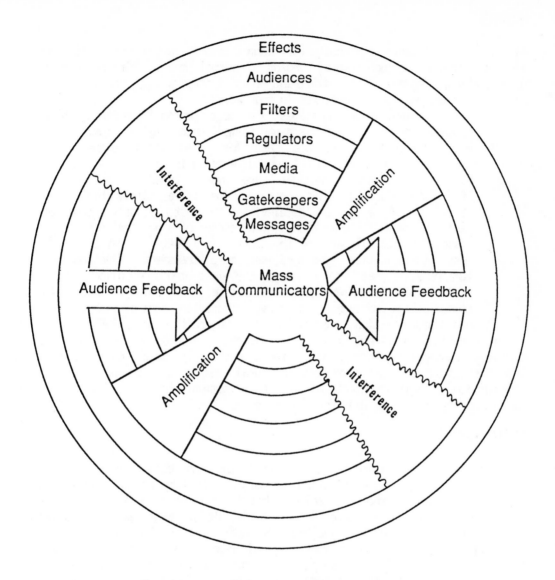

Figure 9.1. The Mass Communication Process
Adapted from Hiebert, Ungurait, & Bohn, Mass Media IV, New York: Longman, 1985.

the area. However, the General Manager must rely on others in the organization, such as writers, film editors, graphic specialists, camera operators, and sales representatives to put the show together, find sponsors, and promote the program.

Mass communicators, then, can be seen as professional communicators who originate and disseminate information. While the purposes and goals of the various mass communicators may vary, in the United States, as we previously noted, the overriding goal is to make a profit.

MESSAGES

As in other communication contexts, communicators in the mass media formulate various messages through verbal and/or nonverbal means. The **content** of mass communication, however, is different from interpersonal, small group, and organizational communication contexts in four ways:

1) mass communication messages are **less personal** in that these messages are transmitted via a one-to-many technoligical link.

2) Mass communication messages are **less specialized** because they are designed to appeal to a large, diverse audience.

3) Mass communication messages are **more rapid** as they are transmitted across distance and time in a fairly high-speed fashion. While radio and television are most obviously capable of rapid messages transmission, even copies of a new textbook can be disseminated to all parts of the country in a matter of days.

4) Mass communication messages are **more transient,** fleeting, or temporary. That is, although the mass media may allow for the preservation of messages over time, as with films, mass communication messages are more subject to fads of fashion than other communication contexts (Hiebert, Ungurait, & Bohn, 1985).

In addition, different media use different symbols and therefore transmit different messages. For example, radio must rely solely on aural messages, whereas television can use both aural and visual channels in message transmission. The content of the mass communicator's message, then, is constrained by the medium used for that message.

GATEKEEPERS

Individuals who fulfill gatekeeper roles in the mass media exert a great deal of power over the mass communication process. **Gatekeepers** are members of the media organizations who are able to directly influence the flow of information from the media to the audience (Baran, et al., 1984). Examples of gatekeepers in mass communication contexts include newspaper editors, the broadcast-standards departments of television networks, local radio station managers, and film directors. The people in these positions have the power to evaluate, censor, and edit the message to be transmitted. Gatekeepers may delete or stop a message, add to a message, or modify the emphasis of a message.

For example, the various editors in newspaper organizations serve critical roles as gatekeepers in influencing what information is printed and how that information is presented. Whatever balance or bias a newspaper has is largely dependent on the editors. By choosing one reporter over another to cover a story, the editor often expects to get a story with one slant as opposed to another because the editor understands the differences in the backgrounds of the two reporters. What the editor deletes, adds, or modifies will change the impact of the story the reporter submitted. By choosing to run one story and not another or by giving more space to one article than another, the editor controls the information which flows to the readers. Thus, the editor's work is like a gate which controls the amount and direction of information flow.

Gatekeepers are members of mass communication organizations who act as censors and editors in evaluating media content. While mass communicators formulate and create messages, gatekeepers serve to evaluate those messages. "The key distinction (between mass communicators and gatekeepers) is that gatekeepers do not originate content; they alter it" (Hiebert, Ungurait, & Bohn, 1985, p. 136). Individuals in gatekeeping positions can exercise considerable influence over the information which flows to mass media audiences.

MASS MEDIA

Usually when we think of mass communication contexts we equate mass communication with mass media. However, as we have already seen, the mass communication process involves more than the media. Further, the electronic and mechanical equipment used in the transmission of messages are just a part of the mass media.

The mass media, including books, magazines, newspapers, films, radio, television, and sound recordings, are complex organizations in our society which use electronic and mechanical means for the dissemination of messages. This textbook in and of itself is one of the mass media, but is a product of a mass media institution. When we use the term mass media we are referring to the organizations which have been formed to create, produce and distribute messages using a one-to-many technological link.

There are three basic areas of concern in a mass communication organization: business, creativity and production. The **business** concerns include the management of the organization's personnel and other resources, the marketing and distribution of the medium's creative product, and in many media the selling of advertising space or time. The **creative** concern focuses on the content of the medium, including the writing, editing, directing, and/or performing aspects. The **production** concern deals with operating the medium's technology, including the equipment and personnel needed to print, film, record, or broadcast mass communication messages.

REGULATORS

Like gatekeepers, regulators influence the mass communicator's message. Unlike gatekeepers, however, **regulators** operate outside media institutions to evaluate, restrict, and modify the content and structure of the media. Because regulators are members of the media institution, the modifications or changes they may seek are often at odds with the goals of the media organization. Because a critical difference between mass communication contexts and other communication contexts is the regulation of mass communication both-through legal and extra-legal means, we will examine this component of the mass communication process in greater detail. We will discuss extra-legal pressure which is exerted on the mass media industry, including audience economics, industry self-regulation and consumer groups, and legal pressures, which involve constitutional issues, government regulations, and civil laws.

Extra-legal Pressures

Most often, control of mass media content is **extra legal,** that is, regulation takes place without any force of law. It often occurs as a result of economic considerations and/or ethical concerns within the media organizations. However, these extra-legal pressures may also be exerted by external sources. When the possible consequences of an abuse of media power are great, controls become more formal and develop legal standing.

Audience economics. Mass communication industries and their audiences act in a kind of economic synergism which generally establishes the boundaries for acceptable content. Newspapers, magazines, radio, and television must all appeal to sufficiently large audiences for advertising dollars to be attracted; books, and movie tickets must sell in sufficient quantity to make those enterprises profitable.

In other words, for any particular topical interest, political orientation, aesthetic need, and/or moral standard to be reflected in the content of mass communication, those tastes must be shared by a large enough number of people who have sufficient income to be an economically attractive audience.

There are many implications about media content which stem from the use of **audience economics** as a measure of success. You have undoubtedly noticed how often the popularity of a film or commercial television program will spawn dozens of imitators trying to attract the same audience. Large audiences are so important in television that even when advertisers have been willing to support a low-rated program (because it delivered the quality of audience the advertiser wanted), networks have cancelled the program to avoid damaging ratings of other nearby programs.

Industry self-regulation. Practically every mass communication industry (and even professional specializations within a particular industry) has found it practical or desirable to establish a form of **self-regulation.** Such regulation generally takes the form of a code of ethics or a standard code. These codes define, sometimes in rather specific terms, the acceptable and unacceptable standards for professional behavior and/or content. Development of such codes has generally been motivated less by idealism, however, than by a desire to blunt efforts at legal regulation. Codes are considered extra-legal in character because compliance with them is voluntary and violations can only be penalized by rebuke or expulsion from the organization which administers the code, not by legal penalties or action.

Motion pictures came under fire in the late 1920s until the industry formed a self-policing unit which became known as the Hays Office (after its head, Will Hays). The motion picture production code created by that office set extremely strict limits on movie content. The code contained long lists of forbidden words (such as "mistress") and forbidden scenes (such as a man and woman in the same bed, even if they purportedly were married). Indeed, the code was so restrictive that, as public tastes exceeded it, the code fell into disuse. When the industry was later accused of excessive sex and violence, it adopted the present system of content ratings (G, PG, PG13, R, and X).

In the area of news content, professional associations of journalists and news organizations have similarly acted to define acceptable journalistic practices. Many newspapers have strict codes of ethics that employees are expected to uphold. Some of the ethical standards in these codes attempt to assure maximum objectivity by restricting reporters, for example, from accepting anything of value from a possible news source. Other standards attempt to assert rights to which journalists feel they are entitled, such as the right to keep the identity of a source secret.

Consumer groups. In addition, there are some more formal sources of extra-legal pressure from the receivers rather than the senders of mass messages. Anyone who is adamant enough about anything—including mass media content — can form an organizaiton to work for change. The history of mass communication in the United States has experienced its share of these formally organized special-interest **consumer groups.** In general, these groups lobby with one or more of the media to try to extract some change in content standards. They wield as weapons the potential economic impact of boycotts and the possibility (or threat) of increased government control.

During the same mid- to late-1960's time period, a large number of public pressure groups sprang up to protest sexual and violent content in the media, particularly on television. Congressional hearings, the Pastore Hearings, were held. These brought about the concept of "family viewing time" in the programming of the three networks. A few years later, however, the concept faded away. Many groups concerned about sex and violence in media content still exist, such as the Moral Majority. Currently, public sentiment appears to have swung away from these concerns.

There is continued concern about the possible impact of television on children. Much of this concern has been voiced through groups such as parent-teacher organizations. One group which represents concerns for children is Action for Children's Television (ACT). For more than a decade, ACT has worked with some success to change the nature of television content aimed at kids.

Other consumer groups have spoken up for various population segments over the years in an effort to change media treatment of one group or another. Blacks, Italians, women, and other groups have all been represented by organizations seeking a change in their media image. Occupational groups have similarly protested (though with less success) the way that plumbers or truck drivers have been portrayed on television. Even big business has felt maligned by the media and organized The Media Institute as a pressure group which hopes to improve the image of business people presented in the mass media.

Legal pressures

Since the first amendment to the U.S. Constitution guarantees "freedom of the press" and "freedom of speech," you might wonder how there could be much legal pressure influencing mass communication. In fact, there are constitutional issues which regularly are heard by the Supreme Court, a maze of regulatory law (particularly for broadcasting and advertising), and civil law issues as well.

Constitutional issues. Every Constitutional guarantee carries with it the potential for conflict with other guarantees and the need to interpret precisely what the guarantee means in particular circumstances. The courts have struggled for years to resolve the inherent conflict between the **First Amendment** (free press) and the **Sixth Amendment** (fair trial). Can the press, in exercising its right to cover and report on a public trial infringe on the rights of a defendant to the fairest possible trial? The debate usually focuses on the right of reporters and camera people to have access to a trial in progress. But, the issue can be more far-reaching: Is it possible to empanel a completely unbiased jury to try a defendant whose arrest has received substantial media coverage? Can justice be served if reporters are allowed to withhold material evidence, such as the names of information sources?

Perhaps no area of Constitutional interpretation has raised more controversy than the mass communication of material which might be obscene. The courts have long held that the right to free speech does not include the right to obscene speech. But, despite decades of court debate and despite continuing efforts by governments at all levels to pass laws regulating obscenity, there still exists no clear single interpretation or standard for deciding what is obscene. Playboy Magazine or an X-rated film might be considered "obscene" by some people but considered "art" by others. Conflicts between individual rights and efforts to legislate morality have been going on for a long time and will probably continue to exist in the forseeable future. As the interpretation or definition of obscenity changes with the winds of debate, the mass media must be prepared to adopt altered constraints on content.

These are only a few of the Constitutional questions which figure in the world of mass communication. Since they represent a conflict in rights, there are few clear "rules" which result. Since they involve interpretation made by politically appointed judges, the "rules" which might emerge are constantly subject to revision. In any case, the weight of constitutional case law can have substantial implications for mass media content.

Government regulations. Somewhat clearer in their implications for mass communication are Acts of Congress and the regulatory agencies that often grow from them. "Ownership rights" for creative content of books, articles, screenplays, music, and films have a lot to do with mass communication. But who grants these rights in the first place? Congress does so through the **Copyright Act.** This intricate piece of legislation has been rewritten in recent years to try to accommodate changes in communication technology; but its purpose has always been to secure for creative people the right to a reasonable profit from the products of their creativity.

Perhaps the most important Act of Congress to mass communication is the **Communications Act of 1934.** Following in the mold of earlier legislation, this act established regulatory control over broadcasting and common carrier (telephone, cable, etc.) communication.

You might wonder how this exercise of government control can be reconciled with the First Amendment guarantees. Part of the justification for the Communications Act was to allow the government to set standards so that all users of these communication technologies would be technically compatible and thereby provide the fullest service to the public. In addition, they claimed since broadcasters would be trespassing on public property (the air) for private gain, they should be scrutinized by the public's representatives. Furthermore, given that the number of broadcasting frequencies available is finite, the government should assure the best use of this scarce resource by selectively licensing people to use it. By contrast, it was presumed that a printing press is available to as many people who might wish to publish a newspaper, so no federal regulation was needed for the print media.

From the vantage point of fifty years after the adoption of the Act, these justifications appear to raise serious practical questions. As to the claim about the limited spectrum, today the cost of access to a printing press is as prohibitively high as the cost of access to a television transmitter. There now are several radio and television stations on the air for every single newspaper published. Furthermore, as to the use of the public air, there are many who point out that newspapers, which have generally received the greatest protection from the First Amendment, are approaching the day when they may be delivered by some electronic means over broadcasting, cablecasting, or satellite facilities. Will these newspapers then be subject to government regulation through the Communications Act? The answer is not yet known.

Regardless of these questions, the Communications Act exists with the fundamental purpose to guarantee that those who engage in broadcasting and common carrier communication will act in the "public interest, necessity, and convenience." To enforce this guarantee and otherwise to carry out the provisions of the Act, the Act created the regulatory agency of the **Federal Communication Commission (FCC).** As a politically appointed body, the FCC has been accused of changing the definition of "public interest" every time a new Commissioner takes his or her seat.

The Communications Act both directly and indirectly influences broadcast media content. The Act clearly states that nothing in it should "be construed as abridging freedom of speech." But, it also prohibits a regulated communication facility from carrying "obscene or indecent language, intent, or meaning." And, Congress included a provision to the Act, section 315, the so-called **Equal Time Provision** which requires broadcasters who provide air time to any candidate for political office, to provide equal time at equal prices to all candidates for the same office. This last provision has been an important factor in shaping the manner in which broadcasting handles political content. Despite the Act's assertion that "free speech" is not to be abridged, in fact these and other provisions do influence content.

Perhaps more important to the content of the broadcast media than the Act itself has been the interpretation of the intent of the Act by the FCC. A major policy established by the FCC is the **Fairness Doctrine.** Under this policy, broadcasters are required to provide comparable time to all sides in a controversy if any one side is aired. This policy clearly bears some resemblance to the notion of Equal Time. Both the Equal Time provision and the Fairness Doctrine try to assure that a licensed broadcasting station will present more than one position on matters of political or public interest if the station presents any position at all. "Equal Time" deals only with candidates for public office and is a provision of the Act itself, so it can be changed only by Congress. The Fairness Doctrine is a policy of the FCC which deals with controversial issues and ideas and which can be changed only by the Commission.

To enforce the provisions of the Communications Act and the policies of the FCC, the FCC holds the power to license a station, to deny renewal of the license, or even to suspend the license. No station can operate without a license. Licenses must be renewed periodically. From the beginning this period was designated as three years; however, with many other changes due to deregulation, this period may change. To receive a renewed license, stations must prove that they are operating in the "public interest," usually by showing compliance with FCC policies. Although the networks are not subject to the authority of the FCC, since each station affiliated with a network must be licensed, the networks are indirectly influenced by the FCC.

While these acts and policies carry the force of law, not all the power is on the government's side. The broadcasting industry operates one of the most powerful lobbying organizations in the nation's capital — the National Association of Broadcasters (NAB). The NAB has been extremely effective in fighting certain regulations as well as in gaining regulatory action which restrains competitive industries. Much of the effectiveness of these lobbying efforts can be traced to the fact that members of Congress realize the importance of good relations with broadcasters during re-election campaigns.

In fact, political entanglements affect the whole area of broadcast regulation. Recently a trend toward substantial de-regulation of radio in all areas except technical standards has developed partly due to the recognition that radio is now a far less scarce medium than are newspapers. There have also been attempts to rewrite the Communications Act to take into account the wide array of new technologies available now and in the forseeable future. The conflicting demands of the many vested interests, however, have so far prevented politicians in Congress from drafting a new Act which would have any serious chance of adoption.

In addition to the Communications Act and policies of the FCC, there are a few other federal regulatory agencies whose actions affect the content of mass communication. These are agencies which control the marketing of goods in our society. To the extent that this marketing can involve advertising, the actions of these agencies can influence the economic foundations of the major mass media.

One such agency which serves to regulate media advertising is the **Federal Trade Commission (FTC)** which has jurisdiction over all consumer products.

While it has several areas of responsibility, the FTC has been particularly active in recent years as a **consumer advocate** and as a regulator of advertising. It has adopted many policies and regulations to promote "truth and fairness" in advertising. Of course, truth is a somewhat difficult standard. On the one hand, the commission permits so-called "puffery," which is a statement of inflated opinion ("our product is the best") where no test of truth is possible. On the other hand, a statement which is literally truthful may not be permitted if the overall impression created by the statement is false.

Charges that an advertisement is false or misleading can result in a cease-and-desist order, directing the offending ad or commercial to be withdrawn from use. The FTC may also order that new advertising be created to "correct" the wrongs of an offending ad. Such "corrective" advertising was required, for example, when the FTC found that Listerine falsely claimed it could "kill cold germs." An advertiser may even be fined. Charges brought against an advertiser, though, come most often from a competitor rather than from a consumer. Consequently, when the de-regulation spirit hit Washington a few years ago, advertisers were among the most vocal groups supporting continued regulation of advertising content by the FTC. [An advertiser who does not wish to take a competitor before a federal regulatory agency may choose to file a complaint with the National Advertising Division of the Council of Better Business Bureaus, an industry self-regulating group which reviews such charges and makes recommendations which are similar to those of the FTC but which do not have the force of the law.]

Through the actions of agencies such as the FCC and FTC, government greatly influences the content of advertisements. The government also influences what products will be available to be advertised and may even act to remove an advertisement from a medium (along with the income the ads generate). For example, when the Surgeon General decided that the evidence supported a probable health hazard from smoking, the government required health warnings on all cigarette packages and in all cigarette advertising. In an unprecedented action, the broadcasting industry and the Federal government reached an agreement which banned all cigarette advertising from radio and television. At the time of the action, these advertisements comprised about 7% of all broadcast advertising revenues.

Civil law. The third channel through which legal pressure can influence the content of the mass media is **civil law.** In one form, the law, usually a state or local law defines a "tort" or a "wrong." A person who feels he or she has been "wronged" under the law, brings civil suit to accuse another party of committing the wrong and to obtain financial compensation for damages caused by the wrong. Where a "wrong" has been extremely blatant or malicious, the person who is suing may ask for additional money to be awarded to punish the offender.

Two kinds of torts that often form the basis of suits against a medium of mass communication (or an individual responsible for some mass communicated content) are libel and invasion of privacy. Since the mass media are vulnerable to large financial losses (often hundreds of thousands of dollars) when sued for libel of invasion of privacy, they have a strong incentive to avoid content which might provide grounds for such a suit. Libel and invasion of privacy laws grow out of centuries of English common law. That is, the definition of libel or invasion of privacy set forth in these laws is based on tradition and precedent. Since each state (and in some cases local governments) may have its own law, the definitions of these "wrongs" vary from place to place. It is the responsiblity of mass communicators to have a clear understanding of the law applicable to their community.

The basic elements of these two torts are fairly similar. **Libel** is generally anything that is published which might hold a person up to ridicule and scorn or in some way defame the person's character or reputation. If, for example, a newspaper column describes you as a crook, you might sue the paper for libel because a crook is not a reputable thing to be. However, there are several defenses which can be used by the newspaper to prevent your winning the suit. If the column or article were written in such a way that it didn't use your name or in any way identify you so that no one other than you knew that it was you being called a crook, then in most states there would be no libel. If you had in fact recently been convicted of, say, embezzlement, then the column is true — you are indeed a "crook." Or, if you are a public figure, such as the mayor, the newspaper may avoid penalties by claiming that "crook" was not intended literally but rather as fair comment and criticism of your public service. Even if you were a private citizen who had never been arrested and whose name were printed in the column, the newspaper may be able to defend itself successfully against libel charges if it can convince the court that the charge was published without malice intended. That is, it did not intend to hurt you or that it made an innocent mistake in which you were confused with someone else. Absence of malice as a defense is available under some (but not all) libel laws.

You may wonder about the concept of **slander** which is also public defamation of person. Generally, the difference is that libel is written or published defamation, while slander is spoken defamation. Since radio and television are aural media, one would think that slander laws would apply to them. The courts, however, have either side-stepped the issue or have taken the position that the wide dissemination of the defamation by radio or television constitutes "publication." As a result questions of slander are more likely to be limited to the town square rather than to be connected with mass communication.

Invasion of privacy is an even more complex area of torts. In general, these laws hold that, so long as you are not part of a bona fide news event or other public event, you have a right to privacy. That is, you have a right to believe that your actions will not be made known beyond your immediate surroundings. Thus, if a photo were taken of you surreptitiously as you sunbathed on your private balcony, you could sue a local paper which published it as cheesecake or beefcake based on your right to privacy. Or, if your name were used without your permission in an advertisement you could sue for invasion of privacy. These are only two of many possible examples of the way mass media content is limited by an individual's right to privacy. As in the case of libel, public figures have more limited privacy rights than do average citizens. But, even the most celebrated or infamous person has some privacy rights upon which the media cannot trespass with impunity.

Finally, there are instances of local laws which regulate specific aspects of mass communication. In some communities, for example, there are ordinances which prevent the publication in newspapers of the names of rape victims or of juvenile offenders. Many communities today have so-called **Sunshine Laws** which specifically grant to the public and the mass media access rights to government documents and the meetings of government bodies. Many Sunshine Laws are not as broad as this simple summary statement makes them sound. Some people in the mass media assert that these rights to access are inherent in the First Amendment and that a Sunshine Law, in fact, restricts access by defining the right more narrowly. Nonetheless, they have come into widespread use in recent years.

There is one Sunshine Law which exists at the Federal level. The **Freedom of Information Act of 1967** specified that any member of the public, including the mass media, has the right of access to virtually any records of the Federal government — except classified documents, personnel records, citizen tax records, corporate trade secrets, and similar "sensitive" material. Most interest in Sunshine Laws and their relationship to mass media content, however, occurs on the state and local level.

Regulation of the mass media takes many forms. There are extra-legal pressures from self-regulation and from special interest groups which influence mass communication content. There are also legal pressures: constitutional issues; regulations of the media by federal, state and local laws as well as by policies of agencies such as the Federal Trade Commission, and the Federal Communication Commission; and civil law. In addition to these regulatory pressures, there are other aspects called filters which affect the content in mass communication contexts.

FILTERS

As we learned in Chapter Two, all individuals do not process sensory information in the same way, and this holds true for mass communication contexts as well. In our model of the mass communicatioon process, **filters** are those frames of reference, schemas, or construct systems which audience members employ in interpreting mass media messages. There are three types of filters which influence the way in which receivers will make sense of a mass communication message: codification, psychological, and cultural filters (Hiebert, Ungerait, & Bohn, 1985).

Codification filters are those frames of references we have developed to respond to verbal and nonverbal codes. These filters are concerned with the meanings we have for verbal symbols, or language, and for nonverbal symbols. If we have not learned the language being used in a mass media message, or are unfamiliar with the meaning of a particular nonverbal symbol, then we will encounter difficulties in interpreting the message. In Chapter 3, we saw how different cultures or groups assign different meanings to particular nonverbal codes. For mass communicators who are usually trying to appeal to a large and diverse audience, the different codification filters audience members use to interpret nonverbal codes in media messages can lead to mass communicators failing to achieve their objectives.

Mass communicators, then, must be sensitive to their audiences' codification filters. For example, as more and more people have become "computer literate" and familiar with the terms and jargon associated with computers, the media have increased their use of computer jargon. This can be seen not only in advertisements for personal computers, but also in movies, television programs, newspaper comics, and popular fiction. However, if audience members have not developed the codificaiton filters necessary to process these verbal codes, messages using a "computerese" vocabulary will make little sense to the receivers.

While codification filters are concerned specifically with the meanings we associate with particular linguistic and nonlinguistic codes, **psychological filters** refer more generally to personality factors which influence how audience members will respond to mass media messages. For example, in Chapter Two we discussed four personality factors which affect how people process information: augmenters, who react to stimuli intensely; reducers, who decrease the intensity of stimuli; dogmatic persons, who have strong and rigid beliefs and opinions; and open-minded persons, who are willing to consider all sides of an issue. These personality factors are psychological filters which will affect how individuals react to a media message. How would a dogmatic person respond to a television advertisement for a political candidate s/he opposes? How would an open-minded person respond in the same situation? How would an augmenter's and a reducer's reactions differ while watching a particularly graphic horror film?

Finally, **cultural filters** are those frames of reference which have developed through audience members' experiences as a part of one or more cultures. In Chapter Four, we discussed how a culture provides its members with shared beliefs, attitudes and values, a language and accepted ways to use that language, and a set of rules for behaving and communicating in different situations. Our cultural background has a tremendous impact on how we will "filter" mass media messages. Cultural differences provide one explanation as to why a television show produced in Great Britain, such as "Benny Hill" is extremely popular in that country, while appealing to a much narrower segment of the American public.

Codification, psychological, and cultural filters are an important component of the mass communication process in that these filters influence how audience members will respond to media messages. It is to a closer examination of the mass media audience that we will now turn.

AUDIENCES

What sort of man (or woman) reads <u>Playboy</u>? Who watches, "Big Time Wrestling" every Saturday afternoon? Have college students become soap opera addicts? Why has "Star Trek" developed such a loyal following of "Trekkies"? Who are these people that attend the midnight showings of movies such as "Eraserhead," "Attack of the Killer Tomatoes," and "Rocky Horror Picture Show," so often that they recite the film and entire dialogue? Mass communication researchers ask these and other questions in their attempt to understand the heart of the mass communication process, media audiences.

Audiences are also of primary concern to mass communicators, particularly advertisers, because communicators want to design messages which will best appeal to their audiences. Thus, advertisers and media organizations spend a considerable amount of time, money, and effort in analyzing their audiences.

The terms **public** and **audience** are not identical. The public refers to the total population who are available to participate in the mass communication process. Members of the public have the potential to be part of an audience, but must actively participate in mass communication to be considered audience members. Audience members interact with the media in some way, such as watching television, buying a record album, reading a comic book, going to a drive-in movie, or writing a letter to the editor of a local newspaper. Audiences are therefore not simply passive sponges soaking up media messages, but are an active component of the mass communication process. We will examine media audiences in mass detail in Chapter 10.

EFFECTS

The effects of the mass media on society and on individuals have received much attention from mass communication researchers. In Chapter 10, we will discuss the influence of the mass media at the societal and individual levels, as we further analyze mass media audiences. As we will see, the mass media have a pervasive and profound impact on our daily lives and on our society as a whole.

INTERFERENCE

Like interpersonal, small group, and organizational communication contexts, communication in mass media contexts is complex and subject to a number of influences. One problem with using models to depict a complex process is that models can lead us to think that something is much simpler than it actually is. To help remind us that the mass communication process is anything but linear, smooth, or trouble-free, we recognize the presence of **interference** or noise in mass communication contexts. Interference is any distraction in the transmission of a message from the mass communicator to the audience. Interference can result from weak signals, environmental distractions, and information overload (Hiebert, Ungurait, & Bohn, 1985).

Weak signals are technical problems which result in messages either not reaching the audience or reaching them in an incomplete form. Blurred newspaper print, "snow" in your television's picture, and a warped record album which distorts the sound, are examples of weak signals which interfere in mass media message transmission.

Numerous stimuli in our environment compete for our attention. As we saw in Chapter 2, we cannot process all the information which impinges on our senses, so we selectively attend to particular stimuli. Interference in the mass communication process can result from **distractions in the environment** as various messages compete for our attention. For example, watching television in a bar usually isn't difficult, but listening is because of patron's conversations. The social activity in the bar is an environmental distraction which interferes with the transmission of the broadcaster's message to members of audience at the bar.

Audiences may also experience **information overload** which hinders message reception. Like information overload which employees encounter in organizational contexts (Chapter 8), mass media audiences can be bombarded with too much information from mass communicators. In mass communication contexts, information overload results mainly from a continuous stream of messages which allows little or no time for audience members to comprehend the meaning of the messages.

Interference, like filters, affects the mass communicator's message. However, filters involve internal audience responses over which the communicator has little or no control. Weak signals, environmental distractions, and information overload are conditions which mass communicators can seek to correct or compensate them. However, it is through amplification that the media attempt to combat interference in the mass communication process.

AMPLIFICATION

There are several ways in which mass communicators are able to amplify their messages. Recall that in Chapter 2, we listed color, contrast, intensity, movement, and change as external characteristics of stimuli which facilitate the attention process (Bakan, 1966). In seeking to amplify media messages to bring them to audience members' attention, mass communicators attempt to enhance the external characteristics of their messages by using strong signals, repetition, and redundancy.

Increasing the strength of the medium's signal is one way mass communicators can counteract interference in message transmission. Using higher quality paper for newspapers, magazines, and books can avoid the problem of blurred print, increased television transmitter power can alleviate poor reception, and improved technology, such as compact discs, have greatly enhanced the quality of sound recordings.

Repetition and redundancy can also be used in the amplification of messages. Advertisers use repetition and redundancy to increase consumer recognition of product names and services of the clients they represent. Of course, too much repetition can lead to habituation. However, communicating a message in a variety of ways, i.e., using redundancy, can provide the contrast and change necessary to facilitate audience attention. For example, advertisement campaigns for a particular product typically follow a similar theme, as with Chevrolet's series of "Heartbeat of America" commercials.

SUMMARY

Mass communication contexts were differentiated in this chapter from other communication contexts in that mass communication is motivated by a desire to generate income, the audience is large, anonymous, diverse, and physically separated from the mass communicators, and the media employ a one-to-many technological link in transmitting messages. Components in the mass communication process include communicators, messages, gatekeepers, media, regulators, filters, audience, effects, interference, and amplification. Discussion of each of these components highlighted the complexity of the mass communication process. The following chapter will further explore mass communication contexts, focusing on the role of mass communication in our society, uses of the media at the societal and individual levels, and the effects of mass communication on society and media audiences.

KEY TERMS

profit motive
technological interface
mass communicators
gatekeepers
mass media
   business concerns
   creative concerns
   production concerns
regulators
extra-legal pressures
   audience economics
   industry self-regulation
   consumer groups
legal pressures
   constitutional issues
   Copyright Act
   Communications Act of 1934
   Federal Communication Commission
   Equal Time Provision
   Fairness Doctrine
   Federal Trade Commission
   libel
   invasion of privacy
   Sunshine Laws
   Freedom of Information Act of 1967

Filters
   codification
   psychological
   cultural
effects
interference
amplification

CHAPTER 10

CHAPTER 10

MASS COMMUNICATION CONTEXTS:
USES AND EFFECTS

Now that we've looked at the components and concepts involved in the mass communication process, we'll look at how society and individuals use mass communication and what some of the effects of mass communication are on both society and individuals.

SOCIETAL USES OF MASS COMMUNICATION

All societies tend to use mass communication in many of the same ways. Of course there will be differences between societies in the kinds of specific content or particular treatment of material. In this section we will describe some of the major uses that societies have for mass communication. We focus our discussion on the United States and societies with similar cultural philosophies, such as Great Britain, but as we do so, you might ask yourself what different uses might be found in another culture, such as China or the Soviet Union.

Many people have tried to list the uses to which society puts mass communication (Lasswell; Lazarsfeld & Merton in Schramm & Roberts, 1971; Wright, 1975). The most basic list includes four: entertainment, cultural transmission, surveillance, and correlation. More elaborate lists usually make special cases for different aspects of these four uses of mass communication or to emphasize a use which might encompass more than one of these four. However we consider the ways society uses mass communication, we also realize there is a flip side to examine as well. For each of these societal uses, we can see how the various mass media will then assume the responsibility to fill these needs and as such the mass media then function to achieve each of these four needs.

ENTERTAINMENT

Societies work better if the basic needs of the members of society are met. Amusement and diversion seem to be universal human needs, found in tribal societies as well as in modern industrial nations. Think about the movies made during the 1930s which you have seen on television. You will recall that many emphasized fantasy — romantic comedies and musicals in which few people worked and many lived in ultra-modern art-deco surroundings, for example. At a time when the realities outside the walls of the cinema were grim indeed, with depression and wide-spread unemployment, these light-hearted and stylized films provided important diversion from reality for the millions who found the money to go to the movies.

Mass communication provides a wide variety of entertainment material to a large number of people and is able to do so in an economically efficient way.

And, from your own viewpoint as an individual, your use of the different mass media for entertainment should come as no surprise.

CULTURAL TRANSMISSION

In order to sustain their existence across time, societies or cultures need to establish wide-spread agreement on a number of basic values. These values indicate the range of behavior that is acceptable and under what circumstances it is acceptable. Moral and ethical values as well as artistic and aesthetic values are important to societies. Recall again those movies from the 1930's. Many of those fantasy films, as well as more dramatic ones, had a plot in which people rose above great odds to achieve happiness or success. Such films reinforced the work-ethic and/or cultural value for self-determination which was of special importance for societal recovery in that bleak era.

Mass communication provides an efficient way to gain social consensus about values, to reinforce values so members of society will not forget, and to educate new members of the society (both young and older) about these values. There is no set format for transmitting this cultural information — we can find such information in situation comedies, adventure films, drama documentaries, or even in the news. And, only rarely are these values stated explicitly. Most of the information about values is only inferred from behavior that is seen and condoned by the comedy, drama, etc.

SURVEILLANCE

A society requires a great deal of information about events which are both internal and external to it. This information can be gathered in many different ways. In some social environments there are stringent rules about what information can be given to whom. Generally in the United States we've come to believe that each of us is "entitled" to have access to as much information as we can process whether this is from watching morning news to catch us up on what happened overnight or even from reading the <u>National Enquirer.</u> But no matter what the social environment, mass communication is a major force in the gathering of information (surveillance) for the general public of that environment. And, **surveillance** is the term we give to making information about events available to you and other members of the society in general.

CORRELATION

Each society must respond to larger events in the world around it in order to give meaning to those events. This social response means that the members of the society will be expected to act more or less together. For example, in Soviet Communist society, mass communication is considered an instrument for implementing the "right" social action. In other societies (often called a social responsibility environment), the mass media have an obligation to help its citizens to distinguish between good ideas and poor ones. These are both examples

171

of mass communication being used to correlate the social response to events or to interpret the meaning for members of that society.

Newspaper editorials which argue for a certain position in international relations or TV commentators who analyze a presidential address also provide examples of this **correlation** function. They help explain the meaning of the events going on around us to provide a framework for us to understand them. Think of films from World War II which emphasized the need for correlated societal action and for everyone to act together to contribute to the war effort. We have used movies to illustrate several societal uses of mass communication, but none of these uses are restricted either to a particular medium or to a particular kind of content. Furthermore, any medium can serve more than one of these functions simultaneously, i.e., it may entertain and provide value reinforcement and correlation.

OTHER MASS COMMUNICATION USES

As noted at the beginning of this section, many more specific social uses of mass communication have been identified — often by combining two or more of the four general uses given above or by looking at particular kinds of media content.

For example, mass communication can **contribute to social stability and cohesion.** When mass communication organizes public opinion and brings consensus on social action (correlation), members of that society are inclined to be bound closer together. When mass communication reinforces values (cultural transmission), members of society may feel a clearer sense of group identity.

Society not only uses mass communication to facilitate social cohesion and stability, but also to **facilitate social change.** Particularly in a democracy, the mass media often reflect the tensions of the society, such as conflicts over social values and moral dilemmas. By exposing controversy and differences of opinion, mass communication gives new ideas an opportunity to flourish. Many people feel that without the attention given by the media to the civil rights struggle of the 1960's, much of the progress which has been made in that arena would never have taken place.

One area in which a society uses mass communication is to **serve the political system.** Certainly social cohesion and social change can involve political goals, so they represent general ways in which mass communication can serve the political system. Beyond this, mass communication is expected to inform voters before they go to the polls, which is another service to the political system. The importance of mass communication to election campaigns raises potential for great enlightenment or great abuse.

Politicians often test public response to a potentially unpopular political idea by "leaking" it to the press without their names attached, in effect sending up a "trial balloon" which might also be considered a service to the political system. Or, a political leader may say something to the nation through the mass media (for example, in an interview or a Presidential press conference) that is really intended to get a message indirectly to leaders of another country. Mass communication in this case may allow something to be said which could not ordinarily be said through normal diplomatic channels. In fact, much social and political "news" originates as press conferences, trial balloons, or other events that only happen because the media are available to report the event; these are called "pseudo events" or "media events." This is different from news that originates in events, such as natural disasters or battles, which would occur whether or not the media were there to observe.

In a supposedly classless society such as ours, mass communication helps give us a sense of social order by telling us who is important. Those people whom the mass media single out for attention acquire the aura of social importance. That is, the society uses mass communication to **confer status** on these individuals and thus provide a sense of social order. Status can be conferred on individuals from Presidents to soap opera stars, on organizations, or even on ideas. However, when status is conferred on an idea, that idea is put on the "agenda" of issues which deserve consideration by the society. As such, this "agenda-setting" function points out what issues people should be thinking about (but not necessarily which view to hold).

There are other societal uses for mass communication, but we will limit ourselves to just one more — a very important one to American society and others like it. Mass communication can also **serve the economic system.** Of course, the economic system is not separate from the political system, so being better informed on economic problems is expected to help voters make political decisions with positive economic consequences. More important, however, is the use of mass communication to stimulate economic activity through either paid advertising or "free" advertising (publicity). Like most people, you probably find certain advertisements annoying, but advertising through the mass media has proved to be the single most effective way to let large numbers of buyers know about goods and services which are available from sellers. The more goods which are sold, the more which must be produced; the more which must be produced, the more employment that is available to people, and the greater the opportunity for each of us to achieve a higher standard of living.

Most societies (including the Soviet Union) have discovered this fundamental use of mass communication (to a greater or lesser degree) as a marketing tool.

Up to this point, this chapter has dealt with societal uses of mass communication. What we have said has focused on the sender in the communication process — the politician who uses the media to send up a trial balloon, the mass marketer who sends messages to stimulate sales, the general socio-political system which expects mass communicated messages to reach the public and thereby mobilize public opinion. But, we must also remember that receivers are not just a society or mass public. The receivers also are individuals. And, individuals have their own uses for mass communication. Sometimes these parallel society's uses, sometimes they are different from society's uses, and sometimes they even contradict society's uses. The next portion of this chapter looks at how the individual uses mass communication.

INDIVIDUAL USES OF MASS COMMUNICATION

Mass communication plays an extremely important part in the lives of most Americans. Aside from working and sleeping, the average American devotes more time to this mass media consumption than to any other behavior. This is particularly true of television viewing, which demands so much of our time that many have labeled it a national addiction. Almost all homes in the United States have at least one television set, and more than half have more than one set. According to Nielsen ratings the average household has a television set turned on over six hours a day.

Radio, the other major electronic medium also commands much of our individual attention. The average audience member listens to radio over two hours a day. Our radio listening is often a secondary activity, one we do while primarily engaged in working, eating, playing, studying, or driving a car. Nonetheless, we use its wide variety of programming for many purposes in many settings. The invention of the transistor and recent developments in microminiaturization have made it possible for radio to become a truly "portable friend" (Dominick, 1974).

While most of us devote the majority of our media time to the broadcast media, the print media (newspapers, magazines, books) also consume a substantial share. The average person spends about thirty minutes a day reading a newspaper. Any trip to the magazine rack will give you an idea of the incredible variety of magazines vying for our attention, and most of us average 15-30 minutes of magazine-reading a day. While books are read with less regularity than newspapers or magazines, we easily can spend hours curled up with a good book. According to a 1977 poll, 55 per cent of American adults had read at least one book in the last six months.

Finally, despite the ever-creasing popularity of television, we also see many movies. In fact, movie audiences have been increasing in recent years, lured in part by box office sensations such as "Star Wars" and "E.T."

While media consumption affects a significant portion of our total behavior, it is important to realize where the time comes from. That is, the time devoted to the media has not been obtained by magically adding five or more hours to the day. Instead our mass media consumption acts as **replacement** for, **displacement** of, or **accompaniment** to our behavior. We may turn down an invitation to play tennis to watch the "Super Bowl" (replacement), put off going shopping until the rerun of M*A*S*H "goes off" (displacement), or keep one eye on the network evening news while eating dinner or carrying on a conversation with the family (accompaniment). It is not surprising then to begin to understand why parents and teachers (and even society as a whole) might be concerned about how children's mass media consumption affects their knowledge and learning, physical health, and also their values.

Why have the mass media become so deeply woven into the fabric of our lives? Many critics have described the content of television entertainment programs, most movies, and popular celebrity and gossip magazines as "trivial." More serious fare, such as television news programs and documentaries, has been labeled "uninforming." Newspapers have been portrayed by some as an anachronism in an

174

increasingly video-oriented society. What, then, is so attractive about the mass media that we spend so much of two precious resources — time and money — to obtain them? We need to understand what motivates our mass media consumption if we hope to understand fully the extensive role played by the media in modern society.

The most significant attempt to date to explain why people so heavily consume the mass media is called the **uses and gratifications approach.** Prior to the 1970s most mass media research presumed that our media behavior was determined by external forces (e.g., work schedule). However, uses and gratifications researchers assume that our media consumption is motivated by our individual (internal) needs. Rather than viewing the media audience as passive, these researchers contend that audience members actively seek out certain media and media content to gratify their social and psychological needs (Blumler & Katz, 1974).

A great variety of motivations for media use have been identified, including entertainment, surveillance, escape, interpersonal utility, parasocial interaction, social learning arousal, ritualization, and others. These uses are not necessarily mutually exclusive, so there may be situations in which a particular individual may appear to make use of one or more simultaneously. The key here is not to identify numbers, but to become aware that each of us actively uses the media (consciously as well as unconsciously) to satisfy our individual need(s) at that time. We will now examine these common uses of the media.

ENTERTAINMENT

Stephenson (1967) in his "play theory" of mass communication contended that most media content is intended to entertain rather than inform. Whether or not this is true, the seeking of pleasurable experience or enjoyment certainly represents one of the major motivations individuals have for attending to movies, situation comedies, television dramas, sports content, etc. Even "informational" or "serious" content, such as television news, is perceived by many individuals to be entertaining or pleasurable.

SURVEILLANCE

The media "survey" the environment for us, providing information relevant to a host of needs and problems through a vast international network of news organizations and correspondents. In a very real sense they act as "extensions of our senses" (McLuhan, 1964) to bring us "news" about political issues, economic developments, world affairs, natural disasters, or the local school board. Surveillance functions are also served by content as diverse as weather information, classified ads, science programs, or the society page. When we have a fundamental "need to know" about our increasingly complex environment, we turn to the media for relevant information in abundance.

ESCAPE

Attention to media content provides a welcome respite from the problems, cares, and worries of life. By "tuning in" a favorite sitcom, we can "tune out" a threatening world. Although entertainment content (e.g., television drama, movies, sports programs, etc.) is most frequently associated with this need for escape, virtually any content (including such serious fare as news and documentaries) which distracts us from our personal problems can serve to fill our need to escape.

INTERPERSONAL UTILITY

The media give us much to talk about with others. Our conversations are often filled with references to news read in the morning paper, an episode of Dallas, a World Series game seen on TV, a magazine article on fishing, the most recent "radar report" on the weather, etc. In a study of over 800 naturally occurring student conversations on the campus of Wayne State University, Greenberg (1975) found that about half of the conversations contained some reference to the media or media content. Moreover, the media were mentioned in 76 per cent of "political" discussions. We thus utilize media content in a very social interpersonal way.

PARASOCIAL INTERACTION

As early as 1956 Horton and Wohl suggested that people often form relationships with media personalities in a manner somewhat similar to the way they form relationships with people with whom they have direct social contact. This is particularly true of the audio-visual media (television and movies) where lifelike images and sounds facilitate such **parasocial interaction.** Soap-opera characters, movie actors, television news personalities, and game show hosts are all objects of such media attachments. Those with fewer opportunities for real social contact (both the very young and very old) are more apt to engage in parasocial interaction (Rosengren & Windahl, 1972). In other words, those who are deprived socially often will use the mass media for substitute companionship.

SOCIAL LEARNING

Both fictional and non-fictional content of the mass media contain rich portrayals of people in many different roles interacting in various social settings. People learn a variety of things from such content, including behaviors associated with different roles and social classes, rules for interacting with people in different roles, and ways to solve their own interpersonal problems (Davison, Boylan, & Yu, 1982). It should not be surprising that such social learning is also a motive for exposure to the media. For example, a study of radio soap operas in the 1940's showed that 41 per cent of listeners used the programs as sources of social advice, including how to get along with other people and principles of childrearing (Herzog, 1944).   Similarly,   a study of British school children demonstrated that many watched television to learn "how I'm supposed to act" and because "it shows how other people deal with the same problems I have" (Greenberg, 1974).   Such investigations show that we use the media as a social teacher — to accelerate the process of learning about our own society and a vast and complex social world.

AROUSAL

Our basic need for stimulation and arousal was discussed in Chapter 2. It is not surprising, then, to find that people turn to the media as a major source to fill their need for stimulation (Greenberg, 1974). Excitement is the stock in trade of action-adverture programs, televised sports, and many movies and novels. We can participate vicariously with little personal risk in such thrill-packed activities as sky-diving, mountain-climbing, auto-racing, military combat, John Wayne brawls, and slam-dunks. Life often is a hum-drum affair for us but the media can serve up many kinds of spice for those with a taste for "armchair action."

RITUALIZATION

Reality is very chaotic.   As intelligent beings, humans constantly strive to create a sense of order amid this chaos. Indeed, this is one of the reasons that people come together to form societies.   The sense of order provided by the society is usually not enough for most people, though, so individuals and small groups often create formal or informal **rituals** which serve in part to enhance the sense of order. For many young people, going out on a date is synonymous with Saturday night.   Having a date may be more important than the date itself for some, for it helps them locate themselves in time ("it is Saturday"), feel a sense of continuity across time ("people always go out on Saturday"), and feel a sense of common experience with others ("everyone in my group does this").

Since rituals are so important to people, one of the ways we use mass communication is to add a sense of order to our lives. We may turn on the evening news some nights not so much to be informed (or for any of the other reasons mentioned so far) but merely to reassure ourselves that it is six o'clock and we've made it through another day. To many people Sunday wouldn't be Sunday if an over-sized newspaper didn't arrive at their door; if that newspaper failed to arrive, these people might even feel vaguely disoriented because a ritual has been disrupted.

The nostalgic appeal of some media content may represent yet another example of ritualization involving mass communication. For most people, there are certain movies or television programs from the past that evoke strong, pleasant feelings and they are viewed repeatedly not so much for their content (which, as part of the ritual, is often virtually memorized) but specifically to evoke those feelings.   These feelings often represent a ritual re-living of periods in the person's life that were (or at least seem to be) happier, better, more care-free, or which have been in some other way romanticized by the individual. Because generations and social sub-groups usually have common media experiences, sometimes such ritual nostalgic appeal of a particular piece of media content reaches cult proportions.

Finally, mass communication sometimes may be only a part of a larger ritual. For example, studies have suggested that because they provide a socially acceptable way for young people to be alone together in dark isolation without close adult supervision, movies are instrumental to mating rituals in this society — no matter what film is playing!

OTHER USES

In addition to these major motives for attending to the mass media, other gratifications have been identified: value reinforcement, to pass the time, and vote guidance. And, the sheer complexity of human needs strongly suggests that other media gratifications will be discovered in the future (Rosengren, Wenner, & Palmgreen, 1985).

Rapid developments in media technology can expand the range of human needs which may be satisfied through media consumption. For example, a study by Shaver (1983) showed that variety and flexibility of programming were the most frequently mentioned gratifications sought from cable television by subscribers. These motives had not surfaced in studies of traditional network television. Apparently the availability on cable of a greatly expanded menu of programming offered twenty-four hours a day enabled viewers to satisfy the need for a variety of experiences. At the same time this format allows viewers much greater freedom to watch desired programming at a time of their own choosing. The department store clerk who works evenings need no longer be deprived of early evening television network news if s/he can turn on the Cable News Network whenever the work day is done. Weather buffs have instant access to twenty-four hour weather information on The Weather Channel. The movie fan who missed the 5:00 p.m. showing of "Star Wars" on HBO because s/he was jogging can catch it later at 10:00 p.m. or even 3:00 a.m.

The need to control and regulate our own environment is a basic one, and the flexibility of a modern multi-channel cable system serves this and other media-related needs much more efficiently along with the recent technology of the video cassette recorder than the system of three networks.

IMMEDIATE REWARD VS. DELAYED REWARD

It might be apparent that some of the uses we've been discussing would fulfill some needs relatively quickly, while others might involve more long-term fulfillment. Schramm (1949) called this duality **immediate reward** and **delayed reward.** While Schramm spoke only in terms of news content, the idea seems appropriate for all media content. By immediate reward we mean that the content provides almost instant gratification of some need(s), while delayed reward content is information that might be useful at some future time. When we use the media for entertainment, escape, or arousal, it is easy to see that our primary interest is in immediate rewards. When the media are sources of social learning, the reward is likely to be delayed. And, since a single piece of content can serve more than one use, it is possible for content to satisfy both immediate and delayed needs.

This notion of when the reward is received should not be dismissed too lightly. It has sweeping implications for mass communication content and even for the society as a whole. Some social critics have worried that in a fast-paced, high-tech society such as ours, there is a dangerous over-emphasis on immediate gratification of all needs which leads people to seek simplistic solutions for complex problems. For example, when a situation comedy (immediate reward) runs on one station and a documentary (delayed reward) runs on another, relatively few viewers choose the documentary. This not only encourages the production of more comedies and fewer documentaries, but it may help create demand for simplistic solutions to the complex problems with which the documentary dealt.

The concept of an immediate reward can be extended to include not just content but also the availability of the media themselves. For example, we see how the modern cable television delivery systems allows a person a great deal of flexibility in getting almost immediate gratificaiton at almost any time of day. The availability of the medium of direct mail to sell merchandise by offering in-home shopping convenience to consumers has led to rapidly growing success for the advertisers in recent years. In addition, systems of selling which provide for direct consumer response (which will be discussed in Chapter 11) promise to be enormously successful because of the appeal of an immediate reward.

THE MULTI-USE NATURE OF THE MEDIA

For the sake of simplicity we have discussed various media gratifications separately. However, they are often sought simultaneously. We may watch television news for information about politics and world affairs, while at the same time desiring to pass this information on to others, to be entertained, and/or to interact parasocially with anchorpersons and correspondents. In fact, in most cases, media exposure is a multi-use phenomenon. Rarely can a single motive adequately explain why we seek a particular medium and its content. Rather, our fascination with the mass media stems from the multiple attractions they have to offer.

This is not to say that gratifications are distributed equally across different media and media content. Television, for example, is usually perceived to be more entertaining than either newspapers or radio. Television news programs are perceived to be more informative about politics than sitcoms or game shows.

In addition to content, however, the primary gratifications which we seek from a particular medium are also influenced by situational factors. If we have just had an extremely rough day, we may flop down in an easy chair and turn on the evening news seeking escape and relaxation more than information. Or, if we are feeling rejected by our friends, we may open the pages of Gone With The Wind seeking parasocial relationships with Rhett and Scarlet in a fantasy world far removed from our own threatening social environment.

THE MEDIA VS. OTHER SOURCES OF GRATIFICATIONS

The media, of course, are not the only means available for gratifying our individual needs. In a study conducted in Israel only a few needs (e.g., political, surveillance, understanding) were perceived to be best satisfied by the media (Katz, Gurevitch, & Haas, 1973). Most needs — even entertainment ones — were felt to be more adequately served by interpersonal sources or by various non-media activities. These researchers concluded that "even media-related needs must be viewed in the larger context of human needs of which they form a small segment, and against the variety of means by which these needs can be and are, satisfied" (p. 176).

Still, Katz and his colleagues noted that "the surprising thing is to realize the extent and range of the media's encroachment on the 'older' ways of satisfying social and psychological needs" (p. 180). The noted social psychologist, William J. McGuire (1974), voiced a similar sentiment about the large amount of time people devoted to media use: "Perhaps the satisfactions that mass communication can offer to the person are better than the alternatives offered in the real life of quiet desperation which many members of the public endure" (p. 169). Thus, while the media may not be perfect providers of what we seek in life, we have found them to be efficient and convenient providers for us, and thus both useful and gratifying.

EFFECTS OF MASS COMMUNICATION

If society could always be sure that more information leads to better social action by its citizens; if you could always be sure that when you turn on the television set for entertainment, you would be entertained (and only entertained); if we could always be sure that the "right" values are being transmitted and that people are receiving them in the right ways; if all these things were true, then the uses of mass communication and the outcomes (the effects) of those uses would be the same. Not only would such a situation be ideal, but it would greatly simplify the study of mass communication because we could end this chapter right here.

Of course, nothing is so simple and idealistic. The uses we have described up to now are only a starting point. We must consider how uses interact with effects. Each time you use mass communication, it might not be only for the use you intended; it might affect you and society in multiple ways. There are at least three dimensions which can describe the relationship between uses and effects — awareness, functionality, and intention.

AWARENESS

How we will be affected by using mass communication may depend in part on the degree to which we are aware of our own motivations in using it. **Manifest motives** are those of which you are consciously aware of; **latent motives** are subconscious reasons for using mass communication. For example, you might turn on the radio every morning for the manifest purpose of learning the news. Without being aware of it, you might at the same time want the radio on so you could avoid conversation with your roommate or spouse. If this latent motivation accompanies the manifest reason for turning on the radio, obviously the overall effect of using the radio in the morning is different than it would be if your only motive were to get the news.

FUNCTIONALITY

Ordinarily, we expect the outcomes of our actions to be beneficial, in which case the actions have been **functional.** Sometimes, the outcomes are harmful, so the actions must be described as being **dysfunctional.** When you use mass communication, this use can be either beneficial or harmful to you. And, since at any one time you might use the same media content for more than one reason, the effect of one experience might be both functional and dysfunctional for you in different ways. You might, for example, watch television every night for entertainment and to escape from studying, and the television viewing could be functional in both regards in the short run. But, when the escape from study damages your grades and your chances for academic success in the long run, the use of television has been dysfunctional for you.

Mass communication use can be functional or dysfunctional for society as a whole as well as for you as an individual. Society hopes that making a great deal of information available to you and the other members of the society will lead to positive social action. If it does so, then the use of mass communication to make this information available has been functional. But when people have a lot of information available, they may feel that the knowing about it is sufficient and that they do not then also have to act on that knowledge. If this happens the use of mass communication has been dysfunctional for society because the result is just the opposite of the hoped-for benefit of social action. This potential effect is often called **narcotization,** because mass communication has acted as a narcotic to dull action, rather than to stimulate social action. [Of course, in societies which want to minimize social action, narcotization could be socially functional rather than dysfunctional.] Such a narcotizing effect does not always occur, however. For example, research shows that exposure to political affairs information is actually associated with greater political participation.

Finally, you should realize that mass communication use can simultaneously be functional for you as an individual and dysfunctional for society, or vice versa. Your motive for watching the news, for example, might be to become narcotized; if you are successful, the experience has been functional for you, though it will probably be dysfunctional for society. To take a more extreme example, if you wish to commit a crime, you might use information in the mass media to learn how to commit the crime and that would be functional for your purposes, but clearly dysfunctional from the viewpoint of society. Both of these examples, of course, represent pathological motivations for using mass communication, but it would be naive to assume that mass communication audiences contained no pathological individuals. Indeed, this kind of duality between personally functional and socially dysfunctional effects of mass communication is at the root of many of our current concerns about the impact of mass communication on our lives.

INTENTION

Intention can be closely related to functionality. That is, many dysfunctional effects can also be described as unintended effects. When narcotization occurs, for example, it is most often an unintended effect of a social use of mass communication. If someone commits a crime in imitation of an event reported in the newspaper, it is most likely an unintended result of the story having been printed.

The notion of **intention** goes beyond dysfunction, however. An unintended effect may not be harmful — it may be neutral or even beneficial. You could turn on TV intending to be entertained but suddenly find yourself watching a documentary containing information that you find interesting and valuable. Furthermore, people who produce messages for the mass media may intend their messages to have a different impact than they do. For example, a producer may make a horror film intending it to scare an audience, but find that the film is so bad that it (unintentionally) becomes a humorous cult classic.

SOCIAL CONSEQUENCES OF MASS COMMUNICATION EFFECTS

Many of the effects (or possible effects) of mass communicaiton on the individual and on the society have prompted a significant amount of controversy. In fact, these perceived social consequences are so numerous that we have space here to discuss only a few of the most salient concerns.

We have already mentioned the possiblity that some people may learn criminal methods from mass media. We have all witnessed how media attention to one event seems to spur a series of similar events, such as plane hijackings. When the news of Tylenol capsules containing cyanide made headlines for days, many people (journalists among them) worried that copy-cat poisonings would occur; thankfully, none did. In recent years, we have seen several criminal trials in which the defendant admitted guilt but tried to be absolved of responsibility by blaming the media for the anti-social roles models that they had provided for the criminal.

Many people also have been concerned about the sexual content of the media in general and of television in particular. These people feel that the content goes beyond acceptable standards of public morality. In addition to the issue of sexual content, concern over violent content in the media led to U.S. Senate hearings several years ago. Some of the public concern had to do with the potential for mimicry by pathological, feeble-minded, and/or anti-social individuals. And at least part of the concern stems from the recognition that children receive much of their social education through mass communication.

The impact of television on children has received enormous attention in the past 20 years — from the public, from politicians, and from social scientists. (In fairness, we should point out that television is singled out for so much attention because it is the "new kid" on the block; before it came along, movies, radio, and even comic books came in for their share of concern.) Some research, for example, has shown that aggressive content on television may increase a child's aggressive behaviors under some circumstances. Many parents worry that children might not develop "normal" social relationships if their most constant companion only speaks <u>at</u> them, not <u>with</u> them. Others worry that "educational" content may be presented with so much show-biz pizzazz that children will be less able to accept the fact that most learning is hard work. Still others are concerned that children are not mature enough to cope with sales messges in TV commercials. These are but a few of the concerns society has about the possible effects of mass communication (particularly television) on children.

Despite vast amounts of research in the field, there are very few definitive statements that can be made. One piece of research may show one effect under one set of circumstances, while another shows opposite impact under slightly different circumstances. In fairness to both children and television, it should be pointed out that parents who abdicate their own responsibility to guide a child in the use of mass communication are sometimes among the most vocal in accusing the media of its irresponsibility.

SUMMARY

We have identified four major societal uses of the media — entertainment, cultural transmission, surveillance, and correlation. Individuals within a society may choose to use the various media to gratify their own personal needs for one or more of the following: entertainment, surveillance, escape, interpersonal utility, parasocial interaction, social learning, arousal, ritualization, and others. Sometimes the media are used to satisfy immediate needs, other times to satisfy delayed or long-term needs, and still other times to do both. The general effects resulting from these expectations and uses of the mass media are influenced by three dimensions — awareness, functionality, and intention. Finally, concerns have been raised about the social consequences of the mass media, especially regarding what may be learned or imitated from various contents.

KEY TERMS

entertainment
cultural transmission
correlation
surveillance
social stability and cohesion
facilitate social change
serve the political system
serve the economic system
confer status
replacement
displacement

accompaniment
immediate reward
delayed reward
media uses
media effects
awareness
functionality
intention

CHAPTER 11

CHAPTER 11

NEW TECHNOLOGY AND CONTEXTS FOR COMMUNICATION

"It <u>has</u> been a long trip," said Milo, climbing onto the couch where the princess sat; "but we would have been here much sooner if I hadn't made so many mistakes. I'm afraid it's all my fault."

"You must never feel badly about making mistakes," explained Reason quietly, "as long as you take the trouble to learn from them. For you often learn more by being wrong for the right reason than you do by being right for the wrong reason."

"But there's so <u>much</u> to learn," he said, with a thoughtful frown.

"Yes, that's <u>true</u>," admitted Rhyme; "but it's not just learning things that's important. It's learning what to do with what you learn and learning why you learn things at all that matters."

Juster, 1961, p. 233*

As with Milo's journey, our path from the biological, psychological, symbolic, and cultural foundations of communication to interpersonal, small group, organizational, and mass communication contexts has been neither simple nor direct. The field of communication is still young, with the development of new ideas and schools of thought progressing in what may seem like a disorderly manner. At times we appear to have gone astray, heading down trails which have proved to have little usefulness, as with linear models of communication. However, we would agree with the princess Reason that we can learn from our mistakes and that we frequently gain more by being wrong for the right reasons than by being right for the wrong reasons.

If you've felt in reading this text and taking this introductory course in communication that there's so <u>much</u> to learn about the field, Milo would certainly understand. Even those who have studied communication for many years acknowledge that the complexity and pervasiveness of communication phenomena give us a rich basis for study but also a tremendous task in pursuing that area of study. But, as the princess Rhyme told Milo, it is not simply acquiring knowledge which is important. What matters is learning how to apply what we know and understanding why that knowledge is important to learn. It is all well and good to know that there are different types of listening and that active listening involves specific behavioral and mental skills. Becoming an effective listener, however, requires both understanding the various kinds of listening we engage in and applying that knowledge to improve listening skills. This text and this course as an "introduction" to the field of communication provide you with basic concepts and ideas which you can apply as you communicate with others in your everyday life.

Finally, just as Milo's journey took him into The Lands Beyond, we will venture briefly into future directions for the field of communication. In this final chapter, we will be concerned with new technology and its impact on communication. The following sections will examine the role of new technology in each of the contexts for communication we have discussed in this text. As you can see in Figure 11.1, new technologies are making their presence felt in all four contexts for communication. We will explore the influence of "new tech" on interpersonal, small group, organizational, and mass communication contexts (in the remainder of this chapter).

CONTEXT FOR COMMUNICATION	TRADITIONAL TECHNOLIGIES	NEW TECHNOLOGIES
Interpersonal	telephone, telegraph, print mail, copying machines	computer communications, electronic mail, mobile telephones, paging devices, personal video-taping
Small Group	telephone conferences print mail	audio & visual tele-conferencing, computer conferencing, electronic mail
Organizational	memos, telephone, inter-com	management information systems, office auto-mation, advanced manufac-turing technology
Mass	newspapers, books, magazines, films, radio, television	cable and pay television videotex, teletext, video or audio disk, interactive television, public information and computing networks

Figure 11.1 Changing Technologies in Communication Contexts

Adapted from: F. Williams (1986) Technology and Communication Behavior, p.19.

NEW TECHNOLOGY AND INTERPERSONAL COMMUNICATION CONTEXTS

A recent article in Newsweek related the story of two coworkers who, though both were interested in getting to know the other, were too shy to interact with each other face-to-face. Instead, they communicated through their company's electronic-mail system for months. Their first date finally came about when the male employee left a message for the female employee on her computer terminal, asking her out to lunch (Kantrowitz, Joseph, & Agrest, 1986). This is just one example of how new technology is changing our patterns of courtship, and at a broader level, how we communicate in interpersonal contexts.

In defining interpersonal communication contexts in Chapter 5, we argued that interpersonal contexts usually involve a high degree of immediacy. That is, participants are face-to-face and able to use both verbal and nonverbal channels in exchanging messages. We also noted, however, that we must avoid a rigid definition of this context, for surely the interaction cited in the above Newsweek story or even our phone calls with another person share more with interpersonal contexts than with those of mass communication which have technological interface between sender and receiver (via the computer or the telephone). The development of new technologies for communication, including computers, electronic mail, mobile telephones, paging devices, and personal videotaping have forced us to **modify our definitions of interpersonal communication** (Miller, 1978). In addition, we have begin to recognize and examine the impact of new technologies on interpersonal communication contexts.

To some, the entry of new technologies into interpersonal settings means a dehumanization of society and our relationships (Baran, McIntyre, & Meyer, 1984). Visions of people as glued to their television sets 14 hours each day or as chained to computer terminals at home and at work raise the spectre of individuals becoming incapable of interacting with one another face-to-face. While concerns about the influence of new technologies on our daily lives should not be dismissed, neither should we ignore the ways we can use new technologies in interpersonal contexts to facilitate effective communication. In fact, Cushman and Cahn (1985) argue that the future of new communication technologies "lies in the interface of persons and machine(s), that is, interpersonal communication and communications technology" (p. 160).

New communication technologies allow us to **extend our interpersonal communication contexts** (Williams, 1986). AT&T recognizes this when the company's advertisements encourage us to "Reach Out and Touch Someone" by using AT&T's long-distance service. Many interpersonal communication theories, and general wisdom suggest that interpersonal relationships are difficult if not impossible to maintain when face-to-face interaction is limited, as with couples who are geographically separated. However, Stephen (1986) found that over a two-year period, "long-distance" relationships actually had a higher survival rate than relationships in which couples were able to see each other on a daily basis. One explanation Stephen had for has this finding is that because telephone interactions restrict the range of sensory channels available for message transmission, geographically separated couples monitor their talk more carefully. That is, long-distance couples may interact less frequently, but the talk is more focused, relevant to the relationship, and less trivial. This is consistent with the suggestion by Williams (1986) that "we can compensate for the restrictions of a medium by making our language choice or message structure more personal" (p. 78).

There are numerous other ways in which new technologies have extended our contexts for interpersonal communication: families can videotape the festivities of a birthday and send a copy to grandparents who can't attend the gathering; car telephones can be used to call your date to tell that person you're stuck in a traffic jam and will be a few minutes late for dinner; messages can be left for friends on their computer accounts or terminals; paging devices can be used to contact parents, spouses, and children; and the "singles scene" can be approached through computer-dating services with videotaped profiles.

As new communication technologies, such as E-mail and mobile telephones, displace the more traditional technologies, such as the telegraph and print mail (see Figure 11.1), **individuals will need to adapt to the changes this "new tech" brings to interpersonal contexts.** How do we manage our interactions with others when using computers to transmit messages? What are the norms or rules in E-mail exchanges? How do we define the parameters of appropriateness in using paging devices? We discussed in Chapters 4 and 6 the importance of norms of interaction in the communication process. Yet, we know from our own experiences that cultural rules which define communication and how we organize our conversations have not kept pace with these new developments communication technology. This does not mean that interaction involving new communication technologies is without order. Rather, interactants have had to modify or create rules to meet situational demands. For example, in the company cited in the Newsweek story, "there are new rules of etiquette governing the genre (electronic mail). At 3Com it's called E-manners" (Kantrowitz, Joseph, & Agrest, 1986, p. 71).

New communication technologies have both influenced how we define interpersonal communication contexts and how we communicate within those contexts. Although some people fear that the introduction of new technology leads to more impersonal communication and the dehamanizing of our social relationships, others see new technology as contributing greatly to the expansion of our interpersonal communication contexts.

NEW TECHNOLOGY AND SMALL GROUP COMMUNICATION CONTEXTS

Our previous discussion of small group communication contexts focused primarily on problem-solving groups which engaged in face-to-face interaction. A law student study group, seven-member grievance committee in a local factory, communication research team, and set-design team for the television station were cited as examples of problem-solving groups. In each case, group members were able to communicate with each other face-to-face in order to make decisions and achieve the group's objectives.

Meeting face-to-face, however, is not always convenient or possible in some problem-solving groups. Suppose, for example, that each of the members of the communication research team taught at different universities located in various parts of the United States. Rather than have to meet periodically in some central location, rely on written correspondence, or even use telephone conference calls, team members can employ a variety of new communication technologies to aid in accomplishing their goals. The research team could set up a teleconference with audio and visual links, use computer conferencing, and/or use electronic mail to interact with one another. With **teleconferencing,** group members in several locations use a visual, aural, or text interconnection to exchange messages in a type of long-distance conference.

A more sophisticated form of teleconferencing, **videoconferencing** links two or more geographical locations for both audio and video transmission and thus allows participants to see and talk with each other (Williams, 1986). This can be contrasted with **computer conferences** where "participants type into and read from a computer terminal" (Hiltz, Johnson, & Turoff, 1986, p. 227). Electronic mail, which is correspondence transmitted and delivered by electronic means, can also link several individuals together via interconnected computers (Williams, 1986).

The use of new communication technologies in group work has become more accepted as a way for participants to share information. There are advantages as well as drawbacks to using mediated linkages, such as audio and visual teleconferencing, computer conferencing, and electronic mail in small group communication contexts (Williams, 1986). The primary reason for using new technologies is the saving of time and expenses involved in travel. Second, there tends to be less straying from the topic and "chit-chat" when participants are interacting through some form of teleconferencing.

However, while the use of new communication technologies in small group communication contexts can greatly aid group processes, effectiveness of group interaction is not assured by simply relying on "new tech." Williams (1986) stresses that using mediated linkages such as teleconferencing requires careful planning. It is important that participants have already become acquainted and that they have acquired the skills to use the technical equipment necessary for message transmission. Further, group members' abilities in using the medium for the teleconference can shift the balance of power in the group, leading to conflict among group members as they attempt to resolve this new issue of control. Finally, there are situations in which the use of teleconferencing is inappropriate or would not be as effective as face-to-face interaction, as with delicate political negotiations (Brilhart, 1986).

A recent study by Hiltz, Johnson, & Turoff (1986) found that although the quality of the decisions reached were found to be equally good for both communication modes, there was a higher instance of agreement in the face-to-face groups. The authors suggest that the lack of nonverbal cues in the computer conference groups can provide advantage when decisions must be made in an objective, neutral, detached manner, but a disadvantage when decisions are less clear-cut or require greater group solidarity in taking responsibility for the decision.

As in interpersonal communication contexts, new technology influences our conceptualization of small groups and is changing the ways in which members interact. Much of the study of new communicaiton technologies and small group interaction has been concerned with work groups in organizations, as we will see in the following section.

NEW TECHNOLOGY AND ORGANIZATIONAL COMMUNICATION CONTEXTS

The new communication technologies discussed within the interpersonal and small group contexts are equally applicable in organizational communication contexts. In addition, there are several other new technologies such as management information systems, the automated office (Thomas & Fryar, 1988), and advanced manufacturing technology (Sypher, Sypher, & Housel, 1987). These new technologies involve an integration of several types of technology which link organization members, organizational units, and the organization with its environment.

Management information systems (MIS) are specifically designed to aid in organizational decision-making (Daniels & Spiker, 1987). Rather than being one piece of equipment, a management information systems is "a configuration of existing or new office technologies in an integrated system" (Williams, 1986, p. 108). Further, two criteria must be met for an organization's data-processing equipment to be utilized as a management information system. "First, the system must be able to produce reports with essential information in appropriate form for use in the performance of management functions. Second, performance of routine decision making must be computerized" (Daniels & Spiker, 1987, p. 127). Williams (1986) argues that MIS not only facilitates managerial control over activity within the organization, but also enhances the ability of the organization's decision makers to exercise control over the environment and essential resources.

The **automated office** is an umbrella term for much of the new communication technology which is concerned with the clerical functions in an organization (Daniels & Spiker, 1987; Thomas & Fryar, 1988). Central to the automated office is the computer terminal, whether it is linked to a mainframe minicomputer or microcomputer. A mainframe computer is large enough to store, retrieve, and process all the information in a complex organization such as our entire university. Microcomputers (also called personal computers) are, however, becoming increasingly popular as more sophisticated ones are developed. Some organizations link a mainframe or minicomputer to their microcomputers giving employees greater flexibility in their information-processing duties (Thomas & Fryar, 1988). The computer terminals, "intelligent" typewriters, and facsimile machines of the automated office often replace the filing cabinets, conventional typewriters, and ditto machines in the traditional office (Williams, 1986).

While MIS focuses on managerial and decision-making concerns, and automated office systems are designed to assist in clerical work, **advanced manufacturing technology** (AMT) integrates automation and information technology for the production aspects of an organization. "By AMT we mean several types of technology, including computer-aided design (CAD), computer-aided manufacturing (CAM), manufacturing resource planning, etc." (Sypher, Sypher, & Honsel, 1987, p. 2-3). For example, computer-aided design refers to the use of computers in designing machinery and electronic components. The introduction of new technologies into the manufacturing component of an organization leads to substantial changes in the organizations' structure and requires much employee effort to learn new skills and even new jobs.

There has been considerable debate over the impact of new technologies on organizational structure, employee interactions, individuals' psychological well-being, and organization-environment relationships. For example, some researchers have found that organizations become more centralized with the introduction of a mainframe computer and more de-centralized when microcomputers and word processors are used (Rue, 1987). However, other researchers argue that the same technology applied in two different organizations can lead to quite different structural changes (Daniels & Spiker, 1987). Whether organizations tend toward increased centralization or decentralization or even both simultaneously at different levels in the hierarchy, with the introduction of new technologies some kind of structural change does occur.

Organization members' relationships and patterns of interaction are also influenced by the adoption of new communicatioon technologies in the workplace. We already saw a case in which electronic mail facilitated the development of an interpersonal relationship between two coworkers. Supervisor-subordinate relationships, so crucial to employee job satisfaction as we discussed in Chapter 8, are also influenced by new communication technologies in organizations. Cushman and Cahn (1985) argue that because we are a post-industrial society which has entered the Information Age, the very nature of work, and therefore the supervisor-subordinate relationship, has changed. Since less work must be done in a central location, as with the factories of the Industrial Age, employees have more options in choosing where and when they work. "The traditional centralized industrial model, which is characterized as a highly rigid, top-down, hierarchical communication system popular in assembly line style factories, is being replaced by a new decentralized telecommunications model which is described as highly flexible, lateral, diagonal, bottom-up, interdisciplinary network where people serve one another and share information in more equal and informal management styles" (Cushman & Cahn, 1985, p. 160). Rice (1987) agrees that "new management approaches are needed" to cope with the implications for boss-employee relationships in this Information Age (p. 124).

Sypher, Sypher, & Housel (1987) recently examined the effects of the implementation of advanced manufacturing technology on a 6,000-employee plant. These researchers found that the introduction of new technology resulted in: job relocation and change; physical changes at the plant, such as the redesign of work stations; employee stress due to uncertainty about organizational changes; and possible conflicts in management-employee relations. They also noted three positive outcomes for employees: learning new skills; prestige associated with knowing how to use sophisticated technological equipment; and being part of changes considered to be on the "cutting edge" of the industry.

Finally, the effectiveness of introducing new technology in organizational contexts rests with the degree to which an organization commits itself to facilitating employee participation in all phases of the innovation process. Sypher, Sypher, & Housel (1987) stress the important "role that communication plays in ensuring that major technological changes are socially responsible. Employee participation and communicating accurate and timely information about major technological innovations and their impacts appear crucial for successful implementation" (p. 16–17).

NEW TECHNOLOGY AND MASS COMMUNICATION CONTEXTS

In the past mass media have advanced singly, serially and over extended periods of time. However, the industrial revolution changed all this. The material advancement of the world made information a much sought-after and perishable commodity. There was need for the fast movement of innovation to allow the wheels of industrial progress to churn efficiently. Developments in electronics contributed to periods of growth in communication technology. Since World War II we find outselves in the midst of a bonanza of communication technology, including communication satellites and computers which allow for newer formats, production, and/or dissemination of information for virtually all of the mass media. This technology makes information available at the switch of a button. Clearly we are living in an Information Age.

It has become nearly impossible to stay abreast of the many and frequent changes in mass communication technology, some of which are highly dramatic. Since 1983 Channels publishes each year a Field Guide to the Electronic Media to help readers keep up with some of the current changes as well as to make them aware of the immensity and complexity of the "electronic revolution."

We all are familiar with the term "satellites" but may not fully understand what the present satellites are capable of doing. With direct broadcast satellites, it is possible to directly transmit educational programs to very remote areas, transmit computer data world-wide, and even provide extremely localized meteorological forecasts. It is also possible to form satellite networks to provide programming to people separated geographically but without a broadcast station. Cable television systems hook up with satellite signals to offer the possibilities of programming such as HBO, MTV, ESPN, etc. In addition they provide access to the electronic media by local individuals and groups. Based on current technology, we can also envision in the very near future voting from your home and access to library facilities for information or for checking out books.

Fiber optics have revolutionized our concept of telephoning to the extent that we currently are able to transmit many more messages simultaneously than is possible with traditional steel or copper phone lines. Industry is now working on how to use this technology and we can only imagine the possibilities in potential changes in technology which will result.

The new technology even affects our own television sets. Many of you have, or have access to, video games which give you the opportunity to play and even master games in your home rather than have to go out to some arcade. You may have a video cassette recorder which allows you to tape a program on one channel while you watch another or to tape a program while you are in some other location for playing back at your own convenience. Television sets can become monitors for personal computers which provide capability for electronic banking, access to world-wide data bases, electronic mail, and on-line interaction with mainframe computers.   And the technology of the optical disc allows for the storage of vast amounts of visual information, a veritable electronic encyclopedia.

Two technologies — teletext and videotext — are especially important to consider here for the likely impact they will have on us in the very near future. **Teletext** is a one-way information retrieval system which utilizes the vertical blanking interval on your television set (the heavy black bar that bobs up or down to provide the vertical hold for the TV picture). It functions as a kind of specialized magazine in that it can be pre-programmed with weather reports, sports scores, stock prices, and perhaps even lists of job openings or goods and products available from particular stores or industries (up to 100 pages worth) which the user can "call up" by using a special decoder. At the present, however, few of these decoders are available to unscramble signals.

Videotex, on the other hand, is a two-way interactive system which allows users to directly contact a central computer via telephone line or two-way cable and to receive selected information on their television set.   With this interactive capability, the user him/herself has access to much more information and is not dependent on "packaged" information.

Currently much of the experimentation in the United States with both teletext and videotex is funded privately by newspaper and broadcast industries. Newspapers seem especially interested in the possibilities of using videotex technology as a new way of delivering classified ads and of utilizing the powerful information base of their news collection and dissemination information capacities.   Broadcasters, cable companies, and publishing companies have been especially interested in getting teletext into households via television sets. CBS, AT&T, and others are urging that teletext and cable-view data systems be made fully compatible so that both can be used with the same television set.   ABC and NBC networks are involved in teletext ventures but face potential competition from cable television and from local affiliates who may be unwilling to carry network teletext signals because they prefer to keep that business for themselves.

These technological changes seem to create as many problems/questions as they resolve.   How long will newspapers as we know them continue? Will teletext (which comes from print media origins) be counted as a print medium (thus not subject to FCC regulations) or as a broadcast medium? Will teletext become the information tool of the poorer segment of society once decoding capabilities become a standard part of the television set? Will videotex become the tool only of the wealthier people who can afford the rising costs of telephone hookup, a terminal, and subscription fee?   How do these technologies affect our right to privacy as well as our "right" to information? Is federal regulation needed for all of the mass communication media?   These are only some of the questions raised by the technology presently available to us.   We will consider these and other implications which result from the technological changes, but we must keep in mind that even while we consider these concerns, changes in technology continue.

CONTRIBUTIONS OF NEW COMMUNICATION TECHNOLOGY TO MASS CONTEXTS

More than twenty years ago Marshall McLuhan (1964) envisioned broadcast media and technology as leading to what he termed the "global village" in which the world, rather than individual tribes in an area, would once again be dependent on oral means of communication rather than on the print media and the resultant dependency on linear, word-by-word processing of information and ideas. While this concept of significant change resulting from technology has not yet been fully realized, it is apparent that technology has resulted in much change in our individual and social lives. Williams, Phillips, and Lum (1985) identified five especially significant implications from technological changes.

Making distance all but irrelevant

The amazing development of space telecommunication has made us aware that distance between individuals and nations has shrunk. From the first launch of the Telestar satellite more than two decades ago to the present sophisticated satellites lodged in geostationary orbit, the utility of satellites in terms of world-wide linkage through earth receiving stations cannot be overstated. The satellites enable industrialized nations to increase their broadcast programming beyond the present capabilities of congested terrestrial broadcast frequencies. At the same time these capabilities enable less developed countries to leap forward to use the technology without having to develop the telecommunication infrastructure first (Hanell, 1983).

Freeing television from the restrictions of broadcast schedules

The commercial television networks presently have fixed schedules for their programming. With the advent of technology such as video cassette recorders, however, audiences can record their favorite programs and play them back at a more convenient time. At present we do know that people who own recorders seldom fully utilize all of what they record. Nonetheless, changes in the present concept of programming are certain to result.

Providing for non-linear access to information

Ever since the first electronic computer was developed by UNIVAC in 1942, storage, retrieval, and dissemination of information have rested at the finger tips of human beings. The process of miniaturization resulted in the rapid altering of the commercial landscape in the United States and other Western nations. As small, yet powerful, home computers become easily affordable, the emergence of a telecity where information and ideas move more than things and people is becoming a reality (Pelton, 1983).

Offering unlimited availability of two-way voice or text communications

Since Alexander Graham Bell invented the telephone in 1876, the changes in technology accommodating two-way voice transmission have been tremendous. Presently, mobile telephones have made effective strides in voice transmission. Impressive developments with satellite interfacing allow for the teleconferencing we've previously discussed. The technology interface also allows for computer conferencing in which computers at different geographical locations are linked for an interactive transmission of text communication. Instant transfer of textual information, by-passing printing and transportation requirements, is quickly becoming a day-to-day activity especially with the development of videotex which we have discussed above.

Transmitting many simultaneous messages

We have become a "wired society" with the de-regulation of communication industries. The development of co-axial cable has led to a tremendous spread in cable television penetration. It is estimated that by 1990 half of the United States will be wired for cable. Cable, which initially began to serve those rural areas unable to receive traditional TV signals, now has the capability of transmitting simultaneous messages (program content) more clearly than ever. In addition, a two-way cable capability can enable you to send signals from your house back to the station or message source. This makes possible some services like interactive instruction, shopping via television, and banking.

The widely heralded Information Age brought about by the revolution in communication technology even causes some persons to make enthusiastic claims. Naisbitt (1982) ended his best-selling Megatrends about ten new directions transforming our lives with, "My God, what a fantastic time to be alive!" We have been caught up with the fervor, the power of hope, the "praise stage" of the acclaimed Information Age. And, in some ways we cannot help but to be swept along in this tide of triumph because it appears that the importance of communication in our lives is finally being acknowledged for its basic and primary role in human affairs.

Perhaps Masuda (1981) summed it up best when he discussed the Japanese national plan for the information society as that which "brings about a general flourishing state of human intellectual creativity, instead of affluent material consumption where . . . people may draw future designs on an invisible canvas and pursue individual lives worth living" (p. 3).

While there certainly are many positive implications resulting from technological changes, numerous problems have also developed. We will now consider some of these problems and then some possible ways to resolve them.

NATIONAL CONCERNS WITH NEW TECHNOLOGY

As more and more newspapers experiment with the delivery of the written word via cable, questions about legal issues arise for citizens of the United States. Does this publishing come under the jurisdiction of Congress and the FCC as broadcast media are? Or, will it be protected under the First Amendment as newspapers are? Or, since technologies have blurred the previous distinctions between print and broadcast media, must totally new regulations (if any) be created? We cannot answer these questions here, but we would like you to keep these broad issues in mind as we consider two age-old problems — privacy and copyright — which have been exacerbated by technological change.

PRIVACY

Privacy, like other rights, is not unconditional. It may at times be abridged or overruled, for example, in a criminal case to protect law and order. However, new communication technologies now pose added threats to our right to privacy. In the last two decades of the nineteenth century three technologies which provided much convenience to the world — the telephone, the camera, and the voice recording — also have made it easier to invade another's privacy. As we experience more new technology, especially with computers, we find that it is often a combination of technologies that presents the most problems.

The **1968 Omnibus Crime Act** worked to protect privacy by severely restricting the use of electronic surveillance unless federal authorization was provided. Even then the use of electronic surveillance was restricted: bedrooms could not be "bugged" nor could conversation between a lawyer and client. However, there is now concern about the interception of messages interchanged by computers over telephone lines. Does the 1968 law cover such situations? Most experts agree that it does not apply because Congress defined "intercept" as the "aural acquisition of information." Vast amounts of textual information being interchanged by computers for government and corporate use as well as by individuals, then, does not seem to fit this definition of "aural" acquistion. As the telephone lines translate more and more conversations into digital codes, even signals that carry traditional telephone conversations may be unprotected.

Avid computer buffs using small machines to ride the telephone lines and break into government and corporation computers appear to pose more of a security problem than one of privacy. However, business use of small computers does raise questions about privacy, especially since computerized records can be searched anonymously (as long as one has the password).

The greatest danger to the privacy of individual citizens, though, may come from the convergence of records made possible by the sharing of computer records. In 1983 President Reagan gave up a plan to require the U.S. Census Bureau to share data with several other agencies. That same year the governor and legislature of the State of New York passed the **Personnel Privacy Protection Law** which would: 1) give individuals the right to correct records they believed to be inaccurate; 2) establish guidelines for the release of information about individuals; and 3) require a review by a Committee on Open Government before an agency could match its records with those of another agency. At the time this legislation was considered, the State of New York maintained almost 2,000 separate systems of records, each containing between one million and ten million records and that state agencies regularly disclosed 43 per cent of their information to other state agencies or to individuals. Such vast record systems and the computer's ability to match these systems rapidly point up the potential threat to individual privacy.

Copyright

Copyright laws attempt to encourage individuals to be creative and productive and thus enhance society by protecting their rights to their innovations. The framers of the U.S. Constitution gave Congress the power to: "Promote the progress of science and useful arts, by securing for limited times to authors and inventors the exclusive right to their respective writings and discoveries" (Art. I, Sec. 8, Par. 8). The first American copyright law was passed in 1790. There were major revisions in 1831, 1870, and 1909, but little was changed until January 1, 1978, when the Copyright Act of 1976 took effect (Boorstin, 1981).

Largely these revisions resulted from changes in technology and they focus on answering three general questions: 1) What works are suitable for copyright protection? 2) What constitutes "fair use"? and 3) Who should pay and how should payments be made? Although the basic premise of copyright law is simple, how it is interpreted and enforced makes the issue a very complex one.

Through the twentieth century it has been generally agreed that materials which can be copyrighted fall into seven types: literary works, musical works (including words), dramatic works (including music), pantomime and choreographic works, pictorial, graphic, and sculptural works, motion pictures, and sound recordings (Johnston, 1982). The aspect of a literary production that is copyrightable is "literary style" which refers to the order or words, phrases, sentences, paragraphs, and distinctive aspects of style. The facts, themes, and ideas cannot be copyrighted. Courts, however, have had difficulty drawing the line between literary style and ideas.

In 1980 Congress amended the 1976 Copyright Act to extend protection to owners of computer programs even though the data base exists only electronically. In 1981 a Federal District Court in California ruled that a computer program held on a computer chip could be copyrighted (Neudstadt, Skall, & Hammer, 1981).

The laws are vague on another important aspect of copyright law — what constitutes "fair use." New ways of distributing information have made it easier to copy works protected by copyright, whether they are printed or recorded on discs, audio tape, film, or videotape. Protecting the authors while allowing reasonable use of their works has become a problem of major proportions because the technology for copying works is available to more and more people.

The problem of "fair use" of the use of copy machine often arises regarding classroom material. Despite several court cases and settlements, however, the definition of "fair use" is still not very clear. Professors may copy items for use in research or teaching, but must meet requirements of "brevity," "spontaneity" and "cumulative effect" (terms which are also vague) or else they must seek official written permission from the copyright holder. One of the few specifics that came from a New York University agreement is that professors are not required to seek permission to copy 10 per cent or less of a prose work or 250 words of a poem (Palmer, 1983).

As the popularity of sound- and video-recording equipment has grown, the question of "fair use" also was raised. In a 1984 decision the U.S. Supreme Court ruled that individuals do not violate the copyright laws when they videotape television programs for their own use. The court concluded that most people do not build up home libraries of films but really use the recorder for "time shifting," to view something at a more convenient time, and this, does not damage the film companies or the broadcasters. This problem is not settled, however. The court reached the decision by a 5-4 vote only after a long delay and a re-hearing of the arguments, which indicate much uncertainty in the court (Greenhouse, 1984). Troublesome it is, and it will become more so as new technology and high financial stakes continue to confuse the issues.

Obviously the question of "fair use" is directly related to the question of who pays for use and how payments should be made. Remember that the key concept of the copyright law is to encourage individuals to be creative and to protect their right to their innovations, including receiving credit (financial or otherwise) for them. Songwriter Sammy Cahn summed up the problems of copyright in a time of changing technology when he said in 1984, "You'd be surprised how many people have asked me to autograph a Xerox of the sheet music for one of my songs" (Palmer, 1984). Mr. Cahn's remark showed the creator's frustration with an admiring public which, by using a cheap copying process, avoids paying the copyright fees which are the author's source of income.

Before the days of sound recording it was relatively easy for songwriters to collect fees due them for the performance of their works. The American Society of Composer, Authors, and Publishers (ASCAP) cleared songs for broadcast and collected and distributed the fees. Off-the-air sound recording has cut into sales of records, however, and in 1984 the songwriters were asking for an amendment which would require a fee from the makers and sellers of high quality audio tape which would be distributed to composers.

Information has become a valuable property and protecting it is a concern of giant corporations as well as individual authors. It will become increasingly significant in the immediate future as specialists estimate that the communication industry will grow at twice the rate of the general economy during the nineteen-eighties and will reach an annual rate of $109 billion in 1990 (Slack, 1984). The social implications are as critical as the economic factors. Copyright laws help to determine who gets what kind of information and at what price. If information is kept cheap and available to everyone, opportunities are opened to those with few resources. If information is tightly held by only a few groups and organizations and is priced beyond the reach of the poor, then opportunities for most people are severely limited. Information policies and democracy are closely entwined.

INTERNATIONAL CONCERNS WITH NEW TECHNOLOGY

While the concerns of the United States as a single nation focused primarily on regulatory issues, the concerns which face the whole world are on the economic and social implications of the new technology. In this section we will look at two major issues — non-communication and electronic colonialism — which have world-wide implications based on the distribution of information, both what is distributed or communicated and the technologies used to do so.

NON-COMMUNICATION

Marien (1982) claimed that in this so-called Information Age there was a "multitude of instances where communication ought to occur but does not" (p. 62). These instances constitute his definition of **non-communication.** He identified four categories of non-communication:

1. **failed communication** — a message of importance not sent (information withheld, a book not published) or a message not received (lost in the mail, a purchased book that isn't ready,);
2. **flawed communication** — a wrong message sent as a result of unintentional error or intentional lying or distortion (government explanations of events, citizen income tax returns);
3. **miscommunication** — a message received but not understood or believed or one which results in unintended effect(s).
4. **junk communication** — a message received and understood, but not of importance (such as with much of the advertising we read, see or hear) which detracts from time that could be spent with more important communication.

Obviously non-communication does not occur simply because of new technology. It should be clear that a number of other factors including language, censorship, and governmental secrecy also will affect the likelihood of problems in communication of the kind Marien defines as non-communication.

Language usage certainly would seem to be responsible for some of the instances of non-communication. When the language used by one nation must be translated into the language of another, failed communication, flawed communication, miscommunication, or even junk communication all become likely possibilities. We've already discussed how language affects our communication and information-processing both as an individual receiver and sender of messages. Problems of non-communication are likely even when the communicators use the same language; however, when the language must be translated, non-communication becomes a much greater probability. And, when not only the verbal cues but also the nonverbal cues need to be interpreted, we can begin to understand how and why non-communication frequently occurs.

Non-communication is also affected by political or ideological differences, especially due to censorship or governmental secrecy. If information is stopped at or before it reaches the border, the consequences for international communication are obvious. Withholding of information and supplying false or misleading information have often been noted as characteristic of Iron Curtain countries; but Western governments also are prone to do so, particularly in crisis situations. As most of us are aware, the two major Russian newspapers, Izvestia and Pravda, are so closely controlled by the government and the party that they are recognized both inside and outside the country as representing the official view of events. The same is true of China's official People's Daily which is noted for its dull "good news" (even omitting most news of natural disasters) and its publication of what the government wishes their citizens to know.

Censorship and governmental secrecy are among the most common ways in which governments try to control information. More subtle but still effective is limitation on the activities and access of reporters to events. One such instance occurred when media personnel were excluded from covering the American invasion of Grenada in 1983. Another instance is that of the Burmese government which barred Western journalists from the country. Journalists may travel to Burma only as tourists; they write their stories only after leaving the country (AP log). And, in Iran since the Ayatollah Khomeini came to power in 1979, foreign correspondents cannot travel outside Teheran without special permission nor interview Iranian citizens except in the presence of a representative of the ministry of national guidance.

As we consider these factors of language, censorship, and governmental secrecy, we can see how the new technology works along with these factors to increase the likelihood of non-communication whenever two or more nations attempt to communicate with each other. For many years the governments of Britain, the United States, Russia, Canada and many other countries relied on short-wave broadcasting technology to get messages through to citizens of other countries. And, as audio- and viedo- technologies developed, it also became more possible to get informaiton against the desires of the government of a country out to others. In 1983 during a period of government censorship in the Philippines following the assassination of Benigno Aquino, Jr., a videotape cassette was smuggled into Manila with the false title of "Playboy Lovers." The Filipino who smuggled the tape had erased most of the original tape and replaced it with a taped copy of a Japanese documentary of the assassination and of information from two American and two Japanese networks about the event. It even included a section in which the action of the actual assassination was frozen at climactic points which contradicted the official Philippine government view of the event that Aquino was shot by a lone gunman rather than by a government security officer.

As miniaturization of much of the equipment we now know continues and as new technology develops capabilities we may now not even be able to fathom, we can certainly appreciate how the new technology can be used to block communication as well as to improve it. We can even begin to see why Marien (1982) was so concerned about what he believed was the dangerously widespread phenomenon of non-communication.

ELECTRONIC COLONIALISM

In addition to the problem with non-communication, we need to consider how the new technology has affected the distribution or dissemination of information economically and culturally. Information has become a commodity — to be packaged, traded, and sold. Whoever controls information and the flow of information assumes a great deal of power. As a result, what we see developing is a division of the world into "information haves" and "information have-nots" which functions similarly to the concept of economic haves and have-nots.

The leaders of nearly three quarters of the world's population, generally developing nations in the Southern part of the hemisphere, believe that they are not being treated fairly in the distribution of information and information technology. They see developing a new form of colonialism — **electronic colonialism** — in which the developing nations (information have nots) see information being used to destroy their economic base as well as their cultural heritage just as colonial powers did in the past through their military, administrative, and language structures (McPhail, 1981).

Developing nations were excluded from much of the early decision-making processes and were only marginally involved in the creative stages when the processes of generating the forms and contents of new communication systems. In other words, they were left out of crucial matters which could affect them. For them it was a "trickle down" theory of information distribution. With information the key commodity and with access to information dependent on technological development, it is not hard to see that the developing nations would be very anxious that they would fall further behind in both information and power. These nations often lack the technical skills, the infrastructure, and/or the economic stability to make the transition from an agrarian economy to an industrial one, let alone to plunge ahead into an advanced stage information-based society.

There is concern over whether there will be any "parking spaces" left in the geostationary orbit above the Earth where satellites are positioned when the developing nations actually acquire the money and technical capability to launch their own satellites. Developing nations are anxious to have their own satellites because not to have them means a continued dependency on other nations. To many of those countries, this adds up to nothing more than control by others of message and data channels as well as the messages and data transmitted through the channels.

In addition to economic factors developing nations are also concerned about their "cultural dependency" on the developed nations. Western commercials, entertainment, and ways of reporting and distributing the news appear to rob these nations of their own views and news of the world about them. Newer and less powerful nations maintain that their stories, their national developmental goals and objectives, their plights and sorrows, successes and failures are strained through a media "formula" in which only the sensational, the violent, the unusual emerge — in the form of reports of terrorism, natural disasters, military coups or take-overs, and human encounters of the worst kind. Developing nations claim that not only do developed nations not understand them but worse, because of their own dependencies on the developed nations to report their stories, their own people do not understand themselves or their cultural heritage.

These concerns have led to the development of what is most often called the **New World Information Order** (NWIO), although it also goes by other names and attributes. NWIO deals with allegations by the developing nations of a serious imbalance in the flow of news, information, entertainment, and communication technology around the world. In 1978 the United Nations Educational, Scientific, and Cultural Organization (UNESCO) approved a new Declaration on the Mass Media that gave added prominence to the conception of "free and balanced flow" of information. It was an effort by the developing nations to stress the desirability of reversing the technological and message flow imbalance without snatching away the freedom within which the imbalance arose in the first place. UNESCO also commissioned a study of NWIO, the MacBride Report, which has since been published in book form under the title, Many Voices, One World (1980). This report clearly noted that "the confrontation about 'free flow' and freedom of information has come to be a key issue in the international debate on communication" (UNESCO, 1980, p. 142). The commission found that imbalances in information flow did, in fact, exist (as the developing nations had alleged) and it urged that "utmost importance" be given to eliminating that imbalance.

In large part, however, discussion/debate has been conducted only with elitists — government, business, and the media themselves. Published accounts appear in government documents, trade and professional journals, and an emerging body of literature in scholarly publications. Much of the severe criticism about the flow of information has been directed at the United States because it has tremendous technical and economic capabilities to produce, distribute, and consume information. Yet, the general American public knows little or nothing about the issue.

Have the U.S. media been silent because, as Schiller (1982) claimed, the debate about information policies has direct consequences for the future of the media and represents a conflict-of-interest for them? What will be the impact of the U.S. withdrawal from UNESCO where much of the debate has taken place? Answers to such questions of public interest and involvement do not come easily, as is often the case with complex, international issues. But the question of information and, thus, distribution of knowledge cannot be viewed as "business as usual." Perhaps it's time that information be considered too important to be left only to decisions made by media, business, and government.

SUMMARY

In this concluding chapter, we have been concerned with the influence of new technology on interpersonal, small group, organizational, and mass communication contexts. Although some scholars and researchers fear that new technology impacts negatively on communication processes, causing our interactions with others to be more impersonal and leading to a dehumanizing of our world, we side with those who are more optimistic about the present and future role of new technology across communication contexts.

At the interpersonal level, new communication technologies such as electronic mail and mobile telephones require us to re-think our definition of the interpersonal communication context and recognize the capabilities of new technologies for extending these contexts. In addition, we observed that these new modes of communication have necessitated modifying or creating norms of interaction to guide and assess our social exchanges. Teleconferencing with audio and visual links, computer conferencing, and electronic mail are new communication technologies which can dramatically change the ways small groups work. New technologies have also had a tremendous impact on the workplace — changing how organizations are structured, the ways in which employees communicate with one another, and how organization members do their jobs. The key to effective integration of new technologies in organizational processes, the key is encouraging employee participation and keeping all organization members informed about upcoming changes. New communication technologies of cable television, videotex, teletext, videotape, interactive television, and public information, and computing networks have also influenced mass communication contexts. The rapid progress of new technology in mass media capabilities has greatly contributed to our individual and social lives, while at the same time has led to raise questions both at the national level, especially with issues of right to privacy and of copyright, and at the international level, with concern over non-communication and electronic colonialism.

At the outset of this text, we stressed the complexity of the communication process and its centrality to our everyday lives. This final chapter has underscored both the dynamic and intricate nature of communication and the importance of studying communication to better understand ourselves, others, and our social world. And now we invite you to venture into the Lands Beyond and explore the implications of new communication technologies for the future.

KEY TERMS

teleconferencing
videoconferencing
electronic mail
computer conferences
management information systems
automated office
advanced manufacturing technology
teletext
videotex
1968 Omnibus Crime Act
Personnel Privacy Protection Law
right of privacy
copyright laws
electronic colonialism
non-communication
New World Information Order

REFERENCES

Adler, R., Rosenfeld, L., & Towne, N. (1986). Interplay: The process of interpersonal communication, 3rd Ed. New York: Holt, Rinehart and Winston.

Albrecht, T. L. (1979). The role of communication in perceptions of organizational climate. In D. Nimmo (Ed.), Communication Yearbook 3. New Brunswick, NJ: Transaction Books.

Albrecht, T. L., Irey, K., & Mundy, A. (1982). Integration in communication networks as a mediator of stress: The case of a protective services agency. Social Work, 17, 229–235.

Altman, I., & Taylor, D. (1973). Social penetration: The development of interpersonal relationships. Chicago: Holt, Rinehart, & Winston.

Andersen, P. A. (1985). Nonverbal immediacy in interpersonal communication. In W. Siegman & S. Feldstein (Eds.), Multichannel integrations of nonverbal behavior (pp. 1–36). Hillsdale, NJ: Lawrence Erlbaum Associates.

Asch, S. (1956). Studies of independence and conformity: I. A minority of one against a unanimous majority. Psychological Monographs, 70, 1–70.

Baird, J. E., Jr., & Weinberg, S. B. (1981). Group communication: The essence of synergy, 2nd ed. Dubuque, IA: Wm. C. Brown.

Bakan, P. (1966). Attention: An enduring problem in psychology. Princeton, NJ: D. Van Nostrand Co., Inc.

Bales, R. F., & Strodtbeck, F. L. (1951). Phases in group problem-solving. Journal of Abnormal and Social Psychology, 46, 485–495.

Baran, S., McIntyre, J., & Meyer, T. (1984). Self, symbols, & society: An introduction to mass communication. Reading, MA: Addison–Wesley.

Bavelas, A. (1950). Communication patterns in task-oriented groups. Journal of the Acoustical Society of America, 22, 725–730.

Benne, K. D., & Sheats, P. (1948). Functional role of group members. Journal of Social Issues, 4, 41–49.

Bennis, W. G., & Shepard, H. A. (1956). A theory of group development. Human Relations, 415–437.

Berkowitz, N., & Bennis, W. (1961). Interaction patterns in formal service-oriented organizations. Administrative Science Quarterly, 6, 25–50.

Berlo, D. K. (1960). The process of communication. New York: Holt, Rinehart, & Winston.

Berger, C. (1979). Interpersonal interaction and self-awareness. Paper presented at International Conference on Social Psychology and Language, Bristol, England.

Berlyne, D. E. (1960). Attention. In conflict, arousal and curiosity. New York: McGraw-Hill.

Blumler, J. G., & Katz, E. (Eds.) (1974). The uses of mass communication: Current perspectives on gratifications research. Beverly Hills, CA: Sage.

Boorstin, N. (1981). Copyright law. Rochester, NY: The Lawyers Co-operative Publishing Co.

Boring, E. G. (1930). A new ambiguous figure. American Journal of Psychology, 42, 444–445.

Bostrom, R. N., & Waldhart, E. S. (1980). Components in listening behavior: The role of short-term memory. Human Communication Research, 6, 211–227.

Bowers, J. W., & Bradac, J. J. (1982). Issues in communication theory: A methatheoretical analysis. In M. Burgoon (Ed.), Communication Yearbook 5. New Brunswick, NJ: Transaction Books.

Bradley, P. H., & Baird, J. E. Jr. (1983). Communication for business and the professions, 2nd ed. Dubuque, IA: Wm. C. Brown Co.

Brilhart, J. K. (1986). Effective group discussion, 5th Ed. Dubuque, IA: Wm. C. Brown.

Bruner, J. S., & Goodman, C. C. (1947). Value and needs as organizing factors in perception. Journal of Abnormal and Social Psychology, 42, 33–44.

Buerkel–Rothfuss, N. (1985). Communication: Competencies and contexts. New York: Random House.

Burgoon, J. (1985). Nonverbal symbols. In M. Knapp & G. Miller (Eds.), Handbook of Interpersonal Communication (pp. 344–390). Beverly Hills, CA: Sage.

Burgoon, J., & Saine, T. (1978). The unspoken dialogue: An introduction to nonverbal communication. Boston: Houghton–Mifflin.

Christ, W. G. (1985). The construct of arousal in communication research. Human Communication Research, 11, 575–592.

Cooley, C. H. (1902). Human nature and the social order. New York: Scribner.

Coulthard, M. (1977). An introduction to discourse analysis. London: Longman.

Cox, A. (1982). The Cox report on the American corporation. New York: Delacorte Press.

Cushman, D., & Cahn, D. (1985). Communication in interpersonal relationships. Albany, NY: State University of New York Press.

Daniels, T. D., & Spiker, B. K. (1987). Perspectives on organizational communication. Dubuque, IA: Wm. C. Brown.

Davis, K. (1973). Care and cultivation of the corporate grapevine. Dun's Review, 102, 46.

Davison, W. P., Boylan, J., & Yu, F. T. C. (1982). Mass media: Systems and effects. New York: Holt, Rinehart, & Winston.

Deal, T. & Kennedy, A. (1982). Corporate cultures: The rites and rituals of corporate life. Reading, MA: Addison–Wesley.

DeFleur, M., & Ball–Rokeach, S. (1982). Theories of Mass Communication, 4th Ed. New York: Longman.

DeFleur, M., & Dennis, E. (1985). Understanding mass communication, 2nd ed. Boston: Houghton Mifflin.

Dominick, J. R. (1974). Gratifications of television viewing and their correlates for british children. In J. G. Blumler and E. Katz (Eds.), The uses of mass communications: Cureent perspectives on gratifications research. Beverly Hills, CA: Sage.

Donohew, L. (1981). Arousal and affective responses to writing styles. Journal of Applied Communication Research, 9, (2), 109-119.

Donohew, L., & Palmgreen, P. (1971). An investigation of 'mechanisms' of information selection. Journalism Quarterly, 48 (4), 627-39, 666.

Donohew, L., Palmgreen, P., & Duncan, J. (1980). An activation model of information exposure. Communication Monographs, 47, 295-303.

Donohew, L., Nair, M., & Finn, H. S. (1984). Automaticity, Arousal, and Information Exposure. In R. Bostrom (Ed.), Communication Yearbook 8. Beverly Hills, CA: Sage.

Duck, S. W. (1982). A topography of relationship disengagement and dissolution. In S. W. Duck (Ed.), Personal relationships 4: Dissolving Personal relationships. New York: Academic.

Farace, R., Monge, P., & Russell, H. (1977). Communicating and Organizing. Reading, MA: Addison-Wesley.

Festinger, L., Schachter, S., & Back, K. Social pressures in informal groups. New York: Harper & Row.

Finn, H. S. (1982). An information theory approach to reader enjoyment of print journalism. Ph.D. dissertation, Stanford University.

Fisher, B. A. (1970). Decision emergency: Phases in group decision making. Speech Monographs, 37, 53-66.

Fisher, B. A. (1980). Small Group Decision Making, 2nd Ed. New York: McGraw Hill.

Fiske, S. T., & Taylor, S. E. (1984). Social cognition. Reading, MA: Addison-Wesley.

Garner, A. (1980). Conversationally speaking. New York: McGraw-Hill.

Gibb, J. R. (1961). Defensive communication, Journal of Communication, 11, 141–148.

Gilchrist, J., Shaw, M., & Walker, L. (1954). Some effects of unequal distribution of information in a wheel group structure. Journal of Abnormal and Social Psychology, 49, 554–556.

Goffman, E. (1959). The presentation of self in everyday life. New York: Doubleday.

Goldhaber, G., Yates, M., Porter, D., & Lesniak, R. (1978). Organizational communication: 1978 state of the art. Human Communication Research, 5, 76–96.

Granovetter, M. S. (1973). The strength of weak ties. American Journal of Sociology, 78, 1360–1380.

Greenberg, B. S. (1974). Gratifications of television viewing and their correlates for british children. In J. G. Blumler and E. Katz (Eds.), The uses of mass communications: Current perspectives on gratifications research. Beverly Hills, CA: Sage.

Greenberg, S. R. (1975). Conversations as units of analysis in the study of personal influence. Journalism Quarterly, 52, 125–131.

Greenhouse, L. (1984). Television taping at home is upheld by Supreme Court. New York Times, Jan. 18, pp. 1, 42.

Halberstadt, A. (1985). Race, socioeconomic status, and nonverbal behavior. In W. Siegman & S. Feldstein (Eds.), Multichannel integrations of nonverbal behavior (pp. 227–266). Hillsdale, NJ: Lawrence Erlbaum Associates.

Hall, E. T. (1959). The silent language. Garden City, NY: Doubleday.

Hall, E. T. (1966). The hidden dimension. Garden City, NY: Doubleday.

Hall, J. (1985). Male and female nonverbal behavior. In W. Siegman & S. Feldstein (Eds.), Multichannel integrations of nonverbal behavior, Hillsdale, NJ: Lawrence Erlbaum Associates, 195–225.

Hanell, S. (1983). Telecommunication Satellite: Reality and Promise. In I. B. Singh (Ed.), Telecommunications in the year 2000: National and international perspectives. Norwood, NJ: Ablex Publishing Corp.

Hersey, P., & Blanchard, K. H. (1972). Management of Organizational Behavior. Englewood Cliffs, NJ: Prentice-Hall.

Herzog, H. (1944). What do we really know about daytime serial listeners. In P. Lazarsfeld and F. Stanton (Eds.), Radio Research, 1942-1943. New York: Dull, Sloan & Pearce.

Hewitt, J. P., & Stokes, R. (1975). Disclaimers. American Sociological Review, 40, 1-11.

Hiebert, R., Ungurait, D., & Bohn, T. (1985). Mass Media IV: An Introduction to Modern Communication. New York: Longman.

Hiltz, S., Johnson, K., & Turoff, M. (1986). Experiments in group decision making: Communication process and outcome in face-to-face versus computerized conferences. Human Communication Research, 13, 225-252.

House, R. J. (1971). A path-goal theory of leadership effectiveness, Administrative Science Quarterly, 3, 16, 321-338.

Huseman, R. C., Logue, C. M., & Freshley, D. L. (Eds.) (1974). Readings in interpersonal and organizational communication, 2nd ed. Boston, MA: Holbrook Press, Inc.

Hymes, D. (1972). Models of the interaction of language and social life. In J. Gumperz & D. Hymes (Eds.), Directions in sociolinguistics: The ethnography of communication, (pp. 35-71). New York: Holt, Rinehart & Winston.

Jablin, F. (1980). Organizational communication theory and research: An overview of communication climate and network research. In D. Nimmo (Ed.), Communication Yearbook 4. New Brunswick, NJ: Transaction/International Communication Association.

Jablin, F. (1979). Superior-subordinate communication: The state of the art. Psychological Bulletin, 86, 1201-1222.

Janis, I. L. (1972). Victims of groupthink. Boston: Houghton Mifflin.

Kantrowitz, B., Joseph, N., & Agrest, S. (1986). A new way of talking: E-mail affects everything from disputes to dating. Newsweek, March 17, 71.

Katz, E., Gurevitch, M., & Hass, H. (1973). On the use of the mass media for important things. American Sociological Review, 38, 164–181.

Katz, D., & Kahn, R. (1978). The social psychology of organizations. 2nd ed. New York: Wiley & Sons.

Kelley, H. H. (1950). The warm–cold variable in first impressions of persons, Journal of Personality, 18, 431–439.

Kennedy, G. P. (1983). Pricing the 'have nots' out of the information market. In Emery & Smythe, (Eds.), Readings in mass communication. Dubuque, IA: Wm. C. Brown.

Knapp, M. (1978). Nonverbal communication in human interaction, 2nd ed. New York: Holt, Rinehart, & Winston.

Knapp, M. (1984). Interpersonal communication and human relationships. Boston: Allyn & Bacon.

Laberge, D., & Samuels, S. (1980). Toward a theory of automatic information processing in reading. Cognitive Psychology, 6, 293–323.

Langer, E. (1980). Rethinking the role of thought in social interaciton. In H. Harvey, W. Ickes & R. Kidd (Eds.), New Directions in attribution research, Vol. 2. Hillsdale, NJ: Lawrence Erlbaum.

Lasswell, H. D. (1971). The structure and function of communication in society. In W. Schramm and D. F. Roberts (Eds.), The process and effects of mass communication. Urbana, IL: University of Illinois Press.

Lazarsfeld, P. F., & Merton, R. K. (1971). Mass communication, popular taste, and organized social action. In W. Schramm and D. F. Roberts (Eds.), The process and effects of mass communication. Urbana: IL: University of Illinois Press.

Leavitt, H. J. (1951). Some effects of certain communication patterns on group performance. Journal of Abnormal and Social Psychology, 46, 38–50.

Lester. D. (1974). A physiological basis for personality traits. Springfield, IL: Charles C. Thomas.

Likert, R. (1967). The human organization. New York: McGraw-Hill.

Malandro, L. & Barker, L. (1983). Nonverbal communication. Reading, MA: Addison-Wesley.

Marguilies, N. (1969). Organizational culture and psychological growth. Journal of Applied Behavioral Sciences, 5, 491-503.

Marien, M. (1982). Non-communication and the future. In Didsbury (Ed.), Communication and the future. Bethesda, MD: World Future Society.

Martin, J. (1982). Stories and scripts in organizational settings. In A. Hastorf & A. Isen (Eds.), Cognitive social psychology. New York: Elsevier North Holland, Inc.

Masuda, Y . (1981). The information society as post-industrial society. Bethesda, MD: The World Future Society.

McCall, G. J. (1982). Becoming unrelated: The management of bond dissolution. In S. Duck & R. Gilmour (Eds.), Personal relationships, volume 2: Development of personal relationships, (pp. 211-231). New York: Academic Press.

McCall, G. J., & Simmons, J. L. (1978). Identities and interactions, Rev. ed. New York: The Free Press.

McCall, M., & Lombard, S. (1983). What makes a top executive? Psychology Today, 47, 118-119.

McGuire, W. J. (1974). Psychological motives and communication gratifications. In J. G. Blumler and E. Katz (Eds.), The uses of mass communications: Current perspectives on gratifications research. Beverly Hills, CA: Sage.

McLaughlin, M. L. (1984). Conversation: How talk is organized. Beverly Hills, CA: Sage.

McLuhan, M. (1964). Understanding media: The extensions of man. New York: McGraw-Hill.

McPhail, T. L. (1981). Electronic colonialism. Beverly Hills, CA: Sage.

Miller, G. R. (1962). On defining communication — another stab. Journal of Communication, 16, 92.

Miller, G. R. (1978). The current status of theory and research in interpersonal communication. Human Communication Research, 14, 164–178.

Mintzberg, H. (1973). The nature of managerial work. New York: Harper & Row.

Naisbitt, J. (1982). Megatrends. New York: Warner Books.

Neustadt, R. M., Skall, G. O., & Hammer, M. (1981). The regulation of electronic publishing. Federal Communication Law Journal, 33 (3), 331–418.

Newcomb, T. (1960). The acquaintance proces. New York: Holt, Rinehart, & Winston.

O'Keefe, B. J. (1984). The evolution of impressions in small working groups: Effects of construct differentiation. In H. E. Sypher & J. L. Applegate (Eds.), Communicaiton by children and adults. Beverly Hills, CA: Sage.

Palmer, R. (1984). Songwriters express copyright law concern, New York, Times, Jan. 16, p. 16.

Palmer, S. E. (1983). Publishers withdraw lawsuit. Chronicle of Higher Education, 26 (8), 1, 22.

Palmgreen, P. (1971). A daydream model of communication. Journalism Monographs, 20.

Pearson, J. C. (1985). Gender and Communication. Dubuque, IA: Wm. C. Brown.

Pelton, J. N. (1983). Telecommunications and Life in the Year 2000. in I. B. Singh (Ed.), Telecommunication in the Year 2000: National and international perspectives, Norwood, N J: Ablex Publishing Corporation.

Peters, J. & Waterman, R. (1982). In search of excellence. New York: Harper & Row.

Ploman, E. W. (1982). International law governing communications and information. Westport, CN: Greenwood Press.

Premack, D., & Premack, A. (1983). The mind of an ape. New York: Norton.

Putnam, L. (1982). Paradigms for organizational communication research: An overview and synthesis. Western Journal of Speech Communication, 46, 192–206.

Rardin, R. (1982). Correcting common discussion leader mistakes, Training and Development Journal, 36, 14–15.

Ray, E. B. (1983a). Job burnout from a communication perspective. In R. N. Bostrom (Ed.), Communication Yearbook 7. Beverly Hills: Sage.

Ray, E. B. (1983b). Identifying job stress in a human service organization. Journal of Applied Communication Research, 11(2).

Redding, N. C. (1972). Communication within the organization: An interpretive review of theory and research. New York: Industrial Communication Council and Purdue University.

Rice, R. E. (1987). Reinvention. In F. Williams, Technology and Communication Behavior, Belmont, CA: Wadsworth, 122–125.

Richards, W. D. (1975). A manual for network analysis: Using the NEGOPY network analysis program. Stanford, CA: Institute for Communication Research, Stanford University.

Roberts, K., & O'Reilly, C. (1974). Measuring organizational communication, Journal of Applied Psychology, 59, 324–326.

Roloff, M. E. (1980). Self-awareness and the persuasion process: Do we really know what we are doing? In M. E. Roloff and G. R. Miller (Eds.), Persuasion: New Directions in theory and research. Beverly Hills, CA: Sage.

Roloff, M. E. (1981). Interpersonal communication: The social exchange approach. Beverly Hills, CA: Sage.

Rosengren, K. E., Wenner, L., & Palmgreen, P. (Eds.) (1985). Media gratifications research: Current perspectives. Beverly Hills, CA: Sage.

Rosengren, K. R., & Windahl, S. (1972). Mass media consumption as a functional alternative. In D. McQuail (Ed.), Sociology of mass communications. Harmondsworth: Penguin.

Scheidel, T. M., & Crowell, L. (1979). Discussing and deciding: A desk book for leaders and members). New York: Macmillan.

Schmeck, H. M. Jr. (1982). Study of brain's receptors reveals secrets of emotions. Lexington Herald-Leader, September 19.

Schramm, W. (1949). The nature of news. Journalism Quarterly, 26, 293-306.

Schramm, W., & Roberts, D. F. (Eds.) (1971). The process and effects of mass communication. Urbana, IL: University of Illinois Press.

Scott, M., & Lyman, S. (1968). Accounts. American Sociological Review, 33, 46-62.

Shaver, J. L. (1983). The uses of cable television. Unpublished master's thesis, University of Kentucky, Lexington.

Shaw, M. E. (1976). Group dynamics: The psychology of small group behavior. New York: McGraw-Hall.

Shepard, C. R. (1964). Small groups: Some sociological perspectives. San Francisco: Chandler.

Sherif, M. (1936). The psychology of social norms. New York: Harper & Row.

Siehl, C., & Martin, J. (1982). Learning organizational culture. Unpublished paper, Graduate School of Business, Stanford University.

Slack, J. (1984). Surveying the impacts of communication technologies. In B. Dervin & M. Voigt (Eds.), Progress in communication sciences. Norwood, N J: Ablex.

Snyder, M. (1974). The self-monitoring of expressive behavior. Journal of Personality and Social Psychology, 30, 526-537.

Stech, E., & Ratliffe, S. (1976). Working in groups: A communication manual for leaders and participants in task-oriented groups. Skokie, IL: National Textbook Company.

Stephen, T. (1986). Communication and interdependence in geographically separated relationships. Human Communication Research, 13, 191-210.

Stephenson, W. (1967). The play theory of mass communication. Chicago: University of Chicago Press.

Sypher, B. D. (1981). A multi-method approach to employee communication abilities, communication satisfaction, and job satisfaction. Unpublished doctoral dissertation, University of Michigan, Ann Arbor.

Sypher, B. D., & Bostrom, R. N. (1983). Listening abilities and level in the organizaiton. Unpublished paper, Department of Communication, University of Kentucky.

Sypher, B. D., & Sypher, H. E. (1983). Perceptions of communicaiton ability: Self-monitoring in an organizational setting. Personality and Social Psychology Bulletin, 9, 297–304.

Sypher, B. D., & Sypher, H. E. (1984). Seeing ourselves as others see us: Convergence and divergence in assessments of communication behavior. Communication Research, 11, 97–115.

Sypher, H. E., Sypher, B. D., & Housel, T. J. (1987). Communicating information about technological change: A case study. Paper presented at the joint meeting of the Central States and Southern States Speech Communication Associations, St. Louis, MO., April.

Sypher, B. D., Sypher, H. E., & Leichty, G. B. (1983). Cognitive differentiation, self-monitoring and individual success in organizatioons. Paper presented at the Fifth Annual Congress on Personal Construct Psychology, Boston, MA.

Sypher, B. D., & Zorn, T. E. (1986). Communication related abilities and upward mobility: A longitudinal investigation. Human Communication Research, 12, 420–431.

Sypher, H. E. (1980). Illusory correlation in communication research. Human Communication Research, 7, 83–87.

Tagiuri, R. (1969). Person Perception. In G. Lindzey & E. Aronson (Eds.), The handbook of social psychology, 2nd ed., Vol. 3. Reading, MA: Addison-Wesley.

Taylor, F. (1923). The principles of scientific management. New York: Harper & Row.

Taylor, J. A., & Eagle, L. J. (1980). Communication networks and organizational structure. In S. Ferguson & S. D. Ferguson (Eds.), Intercom: Readings in organizational communication, Rochelle Park, NJ: Hayden Book Co.

Thomas, D., & Fryar, M. (1988). Business communication today, 2nd ed, Lincolnwood, IL: National Textbook Company.

Tuckman, B. W. (1965). Developmental sequence in small groups. Psychological Bulletin, 63, 380–399.

Vernon, M. D. (1966). Perception, attention, and consciousness. In P. Bakan (Ed.), Attention: An enduring problem in psychology, (pp. 37–57). Princeton: D. Van Nostrand.

Watson, O. M., & Graves, T. D. (1966). Quantitative research in proxemic behavior. American Anthropologist, 68, 971–985.

Watzlawick, P., Beavin, J., & Jackson, D. (1967). Pragmatics of human communication. New York: Norton.

Weick, K. (1979). The social psychology or organizing, 2nd ed. Reading, MA.

Weinstein, E., & Deutschberger, P. (1963). Some dimensions of altercasting. Sociometry, 26, 454–466.

Whorf, B. (1956). Language, thought and reality. J. B. Carroll (Ed.). Cambridge, MA: M.I.T. Press.

Wiio, O., Goldhaber, G., & Yates, M. (1980). Organizational research: Time for reflection. In D. Nimmo (Ed.), Communication Yearbook 4. New Brunswick, NJ: Transaction Books.

Williams, F. (1986). Technology and Communication Behavior. Belmont, CA: Wadsworth.

Williams, F., Phillips, A., & Lum, P. (1985). Gratifications Associated with New Communication Technologies. In K. E. Rosengren, L. A. Wenner, & P. Palmgreen (Eds.), Media gratifications research: Current perspectives, Beverly Hills, CA: Sage.

Wright, C. R. (1975). Mass communication: A sociological perspective. New York: Random House.

Zuckerman, M. (1979). Sensation seeking: Beyond the optimal level of arousal. Hillsdale, NJ: Lawrence Erlbaum.

Zuckerman, M., & Driver, R. (1985). Telling lies: Verbal and nonverbal correlates of deception. In W. Siegman & S. Feldstein (Eds.), Multichannel integrations of nonverbal behavior, (pp. 129-147). Hillsdale, NJ: Lawrence Erlbaum Associates.

APPENDIX: CAREERS IN COMMUNICATION

COMMUNICATION-RELATED CAREERS IN ORGANIZATIONS

The future for individuals with degress in communication appears bright. No longer are business school graduates (especially MBA's) cornering the market on all of the openings in American business and industries. Perhaps even more important is the service sector in the job market. Boyatzis (1982) reported that in the next few years more than two thirds of all employed persons will be working in some kind of service organization. The demand for effective communication increases as the organizational goals focus more and more on people-related concerns.

Business and service industries are just two of the potential career paths for communication majors. Political, religious, legal, and social organizations are also looking for persons with a broad understanding of communication and the ability to use their knowledge to communicate effectively. Some of the types and areas of jobs for which communication majors may be trained will be described further.

Personnel/Human Resources/Employee Relations

According to the Careerism Newsletter (1982), we are likely to see a 60 per cent increase in the number of interviewers needed because of the new high tech jobs. Many employers are hiring younger, more recent graduates with effective interpersonal communication skills to recruit for these positions.

Employee relations is another area in which communication graduates find employment. Recent reports show more emphasis on opinion surveys and in-house publications. Careerism Newsletter (1983) reported there will be more jobs for writers because of his interest in keeping employees better informed about new technology, related organizational changes, and other activities in the organization.

Currently non-profit organizations are experiencing a need for members with good writing as well as good interpersonal communication skills. With the increasing competition for financial resources to keep spouse- and child- abuse centers open, family-planning agencies functioning, and social services provided, effective communication skills become increasingly important.

Over half of the jobs organizations in the mid-south geographic area set aside for student interns are for writing in company publications such as newsletters, brochures, press releases, employee handbooks, etc. Videotapes are also used more and more frequently among organization's communication managers for training, morale boosting, and educational purposes. Persons who can write for and/or produce this type of organizational communication will find jobs from which to choose.

Other human resources jobs predicted for the immediate future include meeting-planners and exhibit-managers. Careerism Newsletter (1982) reported an increase in jobs for persons who can help large corporations plan meetings, possibly using teleconferencing and videoconferencing. Studies show that hotels and even cruise ships are beginning to hire persons who can organize meetings. Exhibition managers are also expected to increase in demand. As more and more trade shows are organized to promote and sell organizations' goods and services, the variety of communication skills needed increases. Local Chambers of Commerce and Travel and Convention Bureaus also are expected to compete more aggressively for the tourist dollar and to use exhibits and trade shows as a communication tool for their organizations.

Public Relations

Public Relations (P.R.) specialists need both strong oral and written communication skills. In managing an organization's internal and external image, the success of public relations practioners depends heavily on effective communicaiton. P.R. jobs include writing for newsletters and other organizational publications, fund-raising, marketing and sales, group meetings, and/or making public presentations. In a survey of University of Kentucky communication majors who had graduated recently, almost half said they were employed in some public relations capacity.

Political Communication

Both voluntary and paid positions are always available with political campaigns including positions in fund-raising, campaign management, dealing with the media, speech-writing, and lobbying.

Management/Administration

In a recent survey, business employers rated the factors they considered important for hiring and promotion decisions. At the top of the list was oral communication skills. Almost 70 per cent of those surveyed said that oral communication skills were very important and almost 40 per cent thought written communication skills were very important. These two factors also were rated as the strongest factors related to promotion once on the job. Even such business-oriented publications as Business Week and Fortune are telling their readers that to be a successful manager, they will need good communications skills.

Communication Consulting

A growing number of organizations are finding that communication contributes to the organization's effectiveness. As a result, managers are seeking expert help in determining the communication needs of employees and in developing and implementing communication programs. Some of these jobs are beginning to appear in educational and employee-relations departments while other jobs are available on a contract basis from the organization.

Persons with an understanding of effective organizational communication and an expertise in research or training are likely to find interesting careers as consultants for organizations willing and able to pay for these services. However, graduate and technical training are often required for persons choosing careers in communication consulting.

New Technology

In 1982, Careerism Newsletter reported that one million computer or data terminals joined the four million already in use. Projections show a 25 per cent increase expected for the next 10 years. This new technology alone is likely to account for a large number of communication-related jobs. Careers in sales, research, operations, education, and management will be available for persons with a high tech background. Such operations as telemarketing, wordprocessing, electronic mail, teleconferencing, videotexts and video tapes all increase the demand for persons trained in communication.

Training and Education

With the advent of the Information Age and the resulting new technological advances, jobs for technical educators abound. Persons with good communication skills are especially suited to these kinds of positions. Another educational career arises in the health care areas as a result of the current focus on the prevention of and education about health problems.

Re-training employees is also considered a major growth area for the 1980's and 1990's. As a result, colleges and business will be providing more opportunities for placement- and career- counselors and specialists. Jobs are also increasing for employee training in the areas of listening, conflict management, group decision-making, and effective public speaking. One manufacturer of data processing equipment has launched a national advertising campaign to promote the idea that good listening is a key to successful performance. All the new technologies provide educational types of employment for communication graduates. Training business persons or educators in the use of teleconferencing, video production, and computer use is now a demand in the job market.

Sales and Marketing

Since selling products or services involves persuasion, the importance of good communication skills is obvious. Companies are realizing the importance of effective communication skills and consequently are beginning to hire communication majors for sales management positions.

Marketing is closely related to advertising. The person hired in marketing usually attempts to determine how and to whom a product can be sold. These positions are reserved for persons with both research and communication abilities. The sales or marketing person is often involved in personal contacts, group meetings to plan and/or present marketing or sales strategies, responding to customer complaints, and identifying consumer needs. Almost all of these activities involve effective communication at the individual, group, organizational and/or mass level.

CAREERS IN MASS COMMUNICATION

Newspaper Careers

The newspaper industry still employs more people than any other mass communication industry. About 400,000 people work for newspapers today — in editorial jobs, in advertising sales, in management, in research, in promotion, in the printing trades, and so forth. While growth of employment is slower here than in some other mass communication industries, it has been relatively steady. Over the past 25 years, the number of jobs in the newspaper industry has increased about 25%.

Magazine Careers

Despite the large number of magazines published, the industry is comparatively small as an employer, due in part to the reliance on free-lance writers, photographers, and artists and in part to the fact that many small magazines are essentially family-operated and/or edited by volunteers. The industry employs about 80,000 people mostly as editors or in management (advertising sales, circulation). Employment declined during the 1970's but has begun to show new growth in the early 1980's. The overall growth rate for employment, however, remains low — only about 5% growth compared with 25 years ago.

Book publishing careers

Although a small industry, book publishing has generally enjoyed steady growth as an area of employment. Again, as with magazines, the salaried jobs available within the industry are not in the creative area of authorship, but rather in editorial capacities and business capacities (production management, marketing, distribution fulfillment, and so forth). Today, about 60,000 people are employed in the book publishing industry. Growth in the employment between 1958 and 1970 was about 55%. Employment stabilized during the early seventies but has begun to move up again. Overall, growth for the past 25 years remains at 40%, making it the fastest growing employment area among the print media.

Careers in radio

Radio has experienced steady growth, both in the number of stations and the number of employees, over the past 25 years. Today, about 100,000 people are employed in radio, up 105% over the 25 year period. Nearly 90% of the jobs are at the local station level rather than at networks. Unlike the figures we've given for many media, these employment statistics do include many of the creative personnel in radio — the disc jockeys, the continuity writers, news personnel, etc. Employment by independent suppliers of syndicated programming material, however, is not included here.

Careers in television

Despite the pervasiveness of the television medium, it employs fewer people than almost any other. There are about 75,000 people working directly in the television industry (excluding creative personnel associated with independent production companies). About 20% of industry employment is with the national networks, while 80% of employment is in local stations (including public television stations). Growth rate for employment over the past 25 years has been 90%. Cable television and related "news media" segments of the television industry offer additional growing opportunities for employment.

Film industry careers

Due to the diversity of the industry today, it is difficult to get a good grasp on employment. Many people are involved in tangential and part-time ways. Nonetheless, the best estimate is that there are about 220,000 people currently employed in the film industry (many of whom obviously also support the television industry). During the 1960's before the heavy involvement in television, employment declined somewhat, but has been rising since the early seventies. The 25 year growth rate for the industry is about 5%. It should be noted that the majority of the people (about 65%) who are considered employed in the film industry are in the exhibition phase, that is, they are people who staff the local theatres. Only about a third of the people employed are involved in the other two components, production and distribution. Furthermore, the majority of production workers are technicians (camera operators, sound technicians, lighting specialists, prop people, and so forth), rather than performers, writers, or directors. According to Union figures, about 60,000 people are available to work as actors, directors, writers, and in technical crafts; but at any given time, less than 20% are employed.

Careers in the recording industry

Although we didn't have the space to discuss the structure and operations of the recording industry, it clearly represents a medium of mass communication and one with which you're probably very familiar. With the rise of high fidelity sound reproduction and the growth of independent producing companies, both during the late fifties and early sixties, the recording industry experienced a strong employment growth. Over the past 25 years, the growth rate has been about 170%. Still, the industry employs relatively few people. Recent figures show about 20,000 people working in production, manufacturing, distribution, and promotion.

This number does not include those working in retail sales; nor does it count performing artists who, as in some of the other media, are essentially free-lance workers, rather than salaried employees.

The development of markets for video recordings will undoubtedly spur new growth and increased employment opportunities in this industry. At this writing, however, these developments are too recent to allow any trends to be identified.

INDEX TO KEY TERMS

(Page listed contains definition of term)